D0358150

Black and Blue

How Racism, Drugs and Cancer Almost Destroyed Me

Paul Canoville

headline

First published in 2008
by HEADLINE PUBLISHING GROUP

1

Cataloguing in Publication Data is available from the British Library

ISBN 978 0 7553 1645 8

Typeset in Palatino by AvonDataset, Bidford-on-Avon, Warwickshire

Printed and bound in Great Britain
by Mackays of Chatham plc, Chatham, Kent
Statistics compiled by Jack Rollin

Headline's policy is to use papers that are natural, renewable and
recyclable products and made from wood grown in sustainable forests.
The logging and manufacturing processes are expected to conform to
the environmental regulations of the country of origin.

HEADLINE PUBLISHING GROUP
A division of Hachette Livre UK Ltd
338 Euston Road
London NW1 3BH

www.headline.co.uk
www.hodderheadline.com

Dedications

Mum – although the road has been very rocky, I couldn't have walked it without you.

June – sister, friend, counsellor, as well as a shoulder to cry on. Has and always will be a rock.

Dad – for just being you.

Arthur 'Dishy' Pettifer, Annette Brooks, Joyce Benjamin, Auntie Roselyn, Tye Canoville.

Auntie Stephanie and daughters – always, always believed in me. Love and respect you so much.

Maria Samuels – mother of my son. Always been there through thick and thin. Thanks 'Meme'.

Sonia Watson – for helping me give myself a chance when I fell ill a second time. Thanks, baby.

Countess, Jasmine, Lesley, for standing by me.

A special message to my children, Natalie, Derry, Dwayne, Lorreen, Jermell, Pierre, Udine, Nickel, Paris, Caysey, and my grandchildren – the loves of my life. I know I have been distant but you've never been far from my heart. If I was to do it all over again, I'd still have you all. Love you big time!!

Contents

	Acknowledgements	vi
	Homecoming	1
1	God Bless The Children	11
2	Saying You Love Someone Takes Nothing	21
3	'You're Not Welcome'	39
4	Playing At Being Pelé	46
5	From 'Lamplight' to 'Mr Loverman'	55
6	The First Time	63
7	Cricket And The Missed Chance	73
8	A Child Is Born	87
9	Finding My Feet	100
10	Chelsea? Gwaan!	115
11	'We Don't Want The Nigger!'	121
12	The Wider World	133
13	Bench-warming Blues	141
14	The Golden Age At Chelsea	172

15 A Legend Is Born At Hillsborough   190
16 The Writing On The Wall   207
17 Rupture   233
18 Hard Times   250
19 The Crack Creeps In   262
20 From Bad To Worse   269
21 Lifeline From An Old Friend   281
22 The Tragedy of Tye   286
23 Checking In Before I Checked Out   291
24 Tryin' To Make Me Go To Rehab   299
25 Island In The Sun   316
26 Paradise Postponed   322
27 Back On The Street   333
28 Getting To Grips With Myself   341
29 The Curse Returns   353
30 Facing My Demons   366
31 Back In The Chelsea Family   373
    Vital Statistics   393

Acknowledgements

I'd like to thank: the staff at Milton House, Phoenix House, Bexhill, Donna at Hungerford North; the doctors and nurses at Royal Free and Guy's hospitals; the staff and management at Camden Transport for putting up with me; Peter Daniel, Wendy Buddin, Suzi Raymond for giving me the chance to get involved in the Chelsea FC workshops; the children and teachers at St Matthews School for giving me another chance in life.

Love and respect to my friends: John Sandiford, Michael Gilkes, Joycelyn, Bella Daniels, Boffer and Shandy, Sonya Davis and daughter Leya, Helen (Seventh Day Adventist – bless you), Frank Healy (could be the next Five Bellies!), Maureen Da Silva who was so encouraging, and Simon Chandler ('Wright Choice') who was so patient, plus Pro Cut and Mystic for keeping me looking sharp. Hi to Marsha – you done good! Also Graham Wilkins, a special friend in my life – thanks mate; and the Chelsea Old Boys for making me feel welcomed back (I don't know about that after this!); Keith Jones and Keith Dublin – keep looking out for each other's backs. My gratitude to Rick Glanvill for his help on this project, Cat Ledger, my agent, and David Wilson and Wendy McCance at Headline.

Biggest thanks go to the Man above who's been watching over me and given me so many chances in my life. I sometimes took Him for granted when I thought He didn't care. Then in the darkest hour I'd feel He was there telling me: 'You can do it.' Thank you Lord!

And finally, for those I truly hurt and took advantage of – I was so wrong and selfish. I truly am ashamed and sorry.

Homecoming

I don't know what I felt when that confirmation phone call came through – a mixture of hope and expectation mingled with a deep, dull ache of remembrance for an old, familiar pain. The caller said I was definitely booked to return to Stamford Bridge and that they were going to introduce me to the crowd at half-time. I hadn't been back since 1987. Some of the people in the stands would be the same ones – older and hopefully wiser – who had given me such horrific abuse when I played there, just for being a black man in blue. Now it was time to face them again, and to see how much water had passed under the Bridge. On the morning of the game I had an even longer shower than usual. I let the water flow over my face for ages, thinking, trying to rinse away the doubts. On the way there I got butterflies in my stomach – the same feeling I used to get just before playing a match, especially for Chelsea.

So here I am. It's the first game of the season, 20 August 2006, and the visitors are Man City. I'm quite tired because ... well, I'm tired a lot ... but also because I haven't slept well. I've been going over this moment for days, discussing it good and hard with various people. I had no idea what lay in store. How will I be received? What if they ask me to say something?

It sounds so naïve, but I'd actually sat down and penned a little speech. I wrote something along the lines of 'I never imagined that I would take this journey actually to return to this stadium, and at last be recognised for my contribution to the club as the first black player for Chelsea, and I would like to take this opportunity to say thank you to all those fans who supported me at the time.'

Martin Luther King, eat your heart out. The speech was in my pocket when I met up with a bloke from work, Jeff, a long-time Chelsea fan, and travelled to the game.

It started to hit me when we got to Fulham Broadway tube station, the nearest one to the stadium. It used to be old-fashioned and a bit ramshackle when I used to arrive there as a young footballer. To me, coming out of the station was always a bit testy. You knew there were some people there who wished you ill. They were threatening, and happy to make themselves heard. You ran a bit of a gauntlet to the stadium, even though it was only a few hundred yards. I dreaded it, what I'd overhear them saying or shouting at me. I just kept my head down all the time. I didn't want anyone to recognise me.

The station's totally different now, lost in a huge,

modern shopping mall. 'Maybe that's a good sign,' I thought. 'Maybe other things have changed too.'

In the press box it's nice to see some familiar faces still there from my day. But I'm nervous as hell. I just keep thinking, 'What do the fans think of me now?' Half-hearted applause would be bad enough. Supposing they don't remember me? It would be understandable. My name's hardly been on everyone's lips since I left. Or worse, supposing they don't wish to remember me?

I've rarely been to a game as a spectator, and it feels so different. I get a sense of adrenalin and passion coming from the fans. All the way through the first half I'm barely watching the match, though. My mind is spinning, my heart throbbing. It will be half-time soon. Then it's the moment.

How mad is this? I've seen off cancer twice and I'm in bits about having to walk out on a piece of grass in front of an audience. God, let's just get this thing over.

At some point Jeff nudges me and points out the Chelsea subs warming up – Salomon Kalou and John Obi Mikel. It takes a moment and then I realise what he means. I look slightly to my left and confirm it – every one of Chelsea's outfield subs is black. We both know and we both smile. That's a pointer.

Chelsea are their usual selves and pretty soon it's 2–0. They're looking invincible, like reigning back-to-back champions should, and for me those two goals provide a little bit of insurance. They reduce the chance of a bad reception. And I don't know if I could take a bad reception now.

I can't believe I feel like this, but to understand why I do, you have to go back to the night of Monday, 12 April 1982.

It was supposed to be the fulfilment of my life's ambition. Since I could run all I ever wanted was to become a professional footballer. And there I was, only twenty years old, about to make my debut in the Second Division for one of the biggest clubs in London in a local derby against Crystal Palace.

It should have been one of the greatest days of my life, not a nightmare that came back again and again.

But this debut wasn't the Hollywood version. This was the snarling, nasty, eighties-Britain version. It was a miserable evening but we were winning 1–0 thanks to a goal from popular winger Clive Walker, and the last few minutes were ticking by.

Then manager John Neal leant over and told me to warm up, I was coming on. I stood up and ran along the side of the Selhurst Park pitch.

Nothing could have prepared me for what happened next. As I'm stretching and running, I hear loud individual voices through the noise: 'Sit down you black cunt!', 'You fucking wog – fuck off!' Over and over again. Lots of different people. I hardly dared look round. They were right behind me. I snatched a glimpse. They were all wearing blue shirts and scarves – Chelsea fans, my side's fans, faces screwed with pure hatred and anger, all directed at me.

Then it came. Chanting, not just by one or two people,

but what sounded like scores of people, a huge mob: 'We don't want the nigger! We don't want the nigger! La la la laaa, la la la laaa!' Again and again. So loud. My God. This ain't the way it's supposed to be. A banana landed near me as I walked back, head bowed, to take off my training top. I felt physically sick. I was absolutely terrified.

Play stopped and I was on – for the goalscoring hero, Clive Walker, of all people. So the crescendo of abuse got worse. It was as much as I could do to run about, leave alone have any effect on the game. Thankfully, the ordeal was soon over and I dashed off to the dressing room, those cruel voices chasing after me down the players' tunnel.

That was the experience of the first black man ever to play in Chelsea's first team. I made history and the fans made my life hell.

In the dressing room, dazed and confused, I sat, hunched, motionless, muttering to myself, so many thoughts racing through my head. Why all that hatred against their own player? Why did the manager have to take off their hero? A few team-mates, including Colin Pates, the skipper, good people, came over and asked if I was OK. 'How d'you think I am!' I didn't say that – didn't say anything at all – but that's what I was thinking. I felt so isolated, not for the first time in my life. It had taken me completely by surprise and I was stunned.

John Neal, the Chelsea manager and a man of experience, eventually came over to reassure me. 'Paul,' he said, 'what kind of people do you think they are? They pay their hard-earned money to watch the team home and away, and then they abuse one of the players who can help get results. That's how stupid they are. Don't pay them any heed.' His kindness would sustain me a little during the crap I was to face over the next few months. At least I knew the geezer who picked the team was on my side. I always respected him for that.

After that, the rest of the evening is a blur. I have absolutely no idea how I got home all the way to Slough. I was lost in myself with no one to turn to. I'd had a big bust-up with my family a few days earlier and none of them were there. None of my friends came to watch me either because I'd not told anyone about it. Did someone drop me off from the game? I still don't know. I remember feeling so alone. What on earth was going to happen next?

I soon learned that the Selhurst Park crowd was not a one-off. Every game the following season I heard the same abuse. I trained like it didn't affect me because I'd wanted this career all my life. To get on, I knew I'd have to deal with it, mentally equipped or not, and the best way was to keep my head down. When I was interviewed for the Chelsea newspaper, *Bridge News*, two years later, I even cited that first game as the 'best moment of my career'. I kept hold of my dream, but I can't say I wasn't shaken – it was crushing me, every single time I heard that disgusting abuse. I knew there were good people in that crowd too, though, most of them silent. I'd meet some near the gate after games. 'Don't listen to the idiots, Paul,' they'd say, and eventually I won the majority over. I still remember when my name was first sung. But mostly I remember the abuse, and how it affected me.

So here I am, all these years later. The first forty-five minutes are up and Neil Barnett, the pitchside announcer, asks me to follow him. We go through the media room under the stand, where the press conferences take place, through a door and suddenly I'm in the players' tunnel, almost unchanged since my day. I get a slight flashback of the dread I used to feel at this point, but when I see who's lined up next to me in the tunnel it vanishes. Michael Ballack has signed for Chelsea and is about to meet his new public. As a Chelsea fan, despite everything, I'm impressed.

His name is called and he walks out to an enormous ovation. 'Damn, that's just great,' I think. 'Reassuring.'

Then I hear Neil's announcement about a 'very special guest' to bring out. There. He's said it – 'Chelsea's first ever black player.'

I'm amazed by the response. Even before he says my name I hear applause and cheering. It's like some of them know how nervous I am and are making a special effort, making up for what went before. I walk up the steps and out on to the turf, and when I look around the stadium, it's a standing ovation everywhere, whistling and clapping. It's more than I dreamed of. I stroll out to the middle, but Neil wants to walk me all round the edge of the pitch, every stand. I look up everywhere, at all the faces, taking it all in.

The emotions are overwhelming. My legs are shaking.

Thank you. I want to cry. All I can do is wave, clap my hands and, over and over, just say 'damn' for how my world has suddenly changed.

You have no idea what that meant to me. Acceptance. Confirmation. Validation.

I sit back in my seat afterwards and see Chelsea play out a professional 3–0 win, and I think about what people have been telling me over the last few months. How there would be no black champions, no Drogba or Essien, today without a Canoville. Not a Hasselbaink, not a Gullit.

Eddie Newton, who came through the youth team at Chelsea in the nineties, called me the pioneer, and I suppose I am. Like other Chelsea youngsters, he would sit up in the stands wincing at what other fans called me back then, until at last I was accepted because of how I played.

That's why so many organisations – schools, the BBC, Kick It Out, Red Card, Chelsea, even the Met Police – are asking me to front their campaigns to combat racism. Mine is one of the worst examples in football because the abuse came from my own club's fans. They don't want any more Paul Canoville situations, and neither do I.

Now I feel confident that I can contribute but back in 1987 I was out of football after an injury and soon out of touch with Chelsea. I had no idea how people felt about me until very recently. I didn't think anybody cared any more.

I had my own heap of troubles to get on with, and that proved a big enough challenge. My life's been tough, and it got worse after football, a vicious cycle of drugs, rehab, cancer, hospital . . . I'm only just coming to terms with it all, looking to the future.

When I look back, a part of me would just like to forget the early days at Chelsea, but I can't do that. My experiences affected me completely, changed me, and I think about that every day. Some questions never get resolved in my head. Why did it happen to me? Why did I respond the way I did? Were there lessons I missed along the way? Why did I always make the wrong choices?

To forget is not an option.

CHAPTER 1

God Bless
The Children

There's no doubt a man is shaped by his experiences
as a child – perhaps even more so if a man's not around to
influence him. I don't have many close male friends even
now. Lots of people around, but not many stood alongside
me, riding shotgun through thick and thin. That's down to
me, the way I operate. I always stay in touch but you don't
necessarily see me for a long time.

All my life I've been surrounded by women. In the early
days, of course, it was my mum and my kid sister, June.
But from my teens I was what West Indian people call a
'gyallist', a girl chaser, a womaniser. That's brought me
great pleasure and deep heartache in equal parts down the
years. It's also brought the blessing of eleven children, all
of whom I cherish, with ten different women, not all of
whom were well treated by me, or vice versa.

I confess to that. The only close long-term relationships I've managed have been with June and my mum. Again, that's my responsibility. I am at last facing up to lots of things I've done.

It sounds stupid, but you're so busy getting on with the day-to-day in your life that you don't see the way you've lived it. You don't analyse. That's a luxury of writing a book. You learn a lot of things you didn't know at the time. When I looked back on my childhood, I came to a better understanding of why I am how I am. I'll tell you the truth. Most people look back on their early years as a time of love and comfort, but I can't do that. I can't say I had a happy childhood. In fact, I remember it as mostly bleak, joyless and alienating.

I was born on 4 March 1962 at 10 Albert Road, Southall. On the same day, US Teamster boss Jimmy Hoffa was convicted of bribing two juries, and in England two people died and a hundred were injured at the Sunderland–Manchester United Cup replay. No one noticed another child being born to a migrant family west of London.

The Southall of 1962 was a lot different from the one in which I spent my teenage years, especially in terms of racial mix. A year earlier the local Labour MP, a Mr Pargiter, reckoned 10 to 12 per cent of his constituency were immigrants from countries in the new Common-wealth, and he was warning that a few local white people had already started a 'keep 'em out' residents' association. He said the pressure on local schools and social services to cope with the influx was becoming immense. (His

Conservative rival in the 1964 election, Miss Maddin, wanted a total halt to all immigration except for 'top priority people like doctors and nurses' – lucky Mum, who came to England to be a nurse!) Southall was one of those areas just outside the capital where jobs and housing were available for newcomers from (mostly) Asia and the Caribbean. In previous generations immigrants had arrived from Ireland and other parts of the UK. (I've been told that in the twenties landlords put up signs saying 'No Welsh here' in the windows of their lodgings!) But from the sixties, as the years passed, the racial tensions became stronger and stronger, as I was to become all too aware.

June and I were brought up by my mother. My father was never around. Mum's full name is Udine Patricia Lake, but she's known to everyone as Patsy. Mum and I are very much alike. We're both stubborn, wilful, caring and determined. We can say the cruellest things to each other but if one asks the other to do something, we'll do it. To understand myself, I have to use her as the starting point, because what she went through and how she handled it made me the way I am.

Mum was born in November 1943 on tiny Saint-Martin, an island in the eastern Caribbean that's half French, half Dutch. She was named Udine after a supposed French spy and she's kept a lot of things secret ever since.

Luckily for me, she's a survivor. When she was about three months old, her cousin was looking after her and let her fall asleep on the sand. After that she developed a very bad cold, a sort of bronchitis I suppose. She was so bad the doctors on Saint-Martin couldn't do anything for her, and her dad took her by boat to the next island, Anguilla, where a Scottish doctor, Dr McDonald, gave her some medicine – they didn't have penicillin there in those days. Dr McDonald didn't give her much chance, so her dad decided to leave her there with her grandmother rather than have her die on the voyage back to Saint-Martin. In those days, if you died at sea, they buried you there, threw your body over the side.

So my mum was left with her grandmother, Sylvanie, in Anguilla. I never met her. Her husband died young and she had to raise ten children on her own (although one died), and then five grandchildren including my mum.

She was always one of those very hard workers, Sylvanie. Her husband had left her a large plot of productive land, and she cultivated fruits and vegetables like you never saw. All day long she'd work. And she was big into community. She'd organise what you call a 'jollification' for people who didn't have much. They'd work on her land and get food, plus a bit of rum, in return. It wasn't the men who were the great providers in her world, it was Sylvanie.

When food was scarce, people would come from all over the island to buy peas and corn because Sylvanie was the only one who still had any. She would sell them just enough so that she had more for others in the same boat.

Sylvanie was heavily into natural remedies and healing, so when Mum was seriously ill, she knew all the right herbs to use in her concoctions, and she fed them to Mum every hour for days, until gradually she fully recovered.

It may sound strange but because Sylvanie took a shine to Mum, she was allowed to keep her. That wasn't an unusual occurrence. Gladys, Mum's sister, was sent to live with her aunt, my granddad's sister, while Roy, Mum's brother, went to live with a great aunt. They were all in Anguilla at the same time.

It's a Caribbean thing. Mum, Gladys and Roy were three out of eleven children and their parents needed helping out. It made sense to farm the kids out to family nearby. Saint-Martin was only half an hour away, six miles across the sea, and the kids frequently travelled back there – Mum always spent the long school holidays in Saint-Martin – so they were regularly in touch with their parents, brothers and sisters. On a clear day they could almost wave to each other, especially standing on one of Saint-Martin's hills.

Mum didn't feel as though she'd been singled out, or that it was unusual. Living with her grandmother was no great hardship for her and she just accepted it. She's very fatalistic like that, and I've realised I'm exactly the same. Life is a long road with no deviations. You just keep driving and don't stop to wonder if you missed a turning.

Mum prefers Anguilla, anyway. You ask her where she's from and she'll say with pride and honour that she is an Anguillan. She believes that if she hadn't been raised there, she would have never made it to England.

Anguilla was a British colony, and there was no real language difference between there and Saint-Martin – English is spoken everywhere. One big difference between the two islands, though, was that Anguilla tended to have a much less changing population than Saint-Martin. It's ironical, considering my mum and her siblings were 'newcomers', but most Anguillans have been there a long, long time. Saint-Martin seems to be much more of a mixture of Haitians, Jamaicans, Santo Domingans, Dominicans – people arriving and staying. It makes Saint-Martin a buzzier, more cosmopolitan place than Anguilla, but with the faster pace and higher crime rate that always ride side-saddle with those sort of benefits.

If I was to say that since I've been going there Anguillans have tended to go to Saint-Martin for the shopping and the nightclubbing, while Saint-Martin folks go the other way for the peace and quiet and the beautiful beaches, you'll have a fair idea of the distinctive characters of the two islands. One is for raving, the other for chilling.

Anguilla is home as far as Mum's concerned. She used to treat Sylvanie as her mother. Sylvanie was a big figure on the island and meant everything to Mum. She still always blesses her. Sylvanie was very religious, Church of England. Mum had been baptised a Catholic, because that was her mother's persuasion, but having been brought up in an Anglican household, Mum continued in that faith when she got to England, attending a high Anglican church.

Mum had a typical Caribbean upbringing on Anguilla.

Her grandmother was very strict – speak when you're spoken to. Half the time West Indian children weren't supposed to be in the same room as adults.

The rulers of small Caribbean islands were stuck in the Victorian era. The people in power didn't care about education for black people, who were hardly expected to become leaders of men in a tiny British colony in the 1940s. Eventually, like a lot of spirited young people, Mum decided she had to move if she wanted to achieve anything. When Sylvanie developed diabetes, Mum cared for her, and after that she decided she wanted to go to England to become a nurse. She was fourteen at the time. In those days, moving to Britain and getting professional qualifications was a sign of great achievement. And nursing was one of the few avenues the Mother Country kept open for Caribbean people.

I have to hand it to Mum, she must have been a very self-confident teenager. Anguilla wasn't like the bigger islands, Barbados for example, where Britain was recruiting people after the war: 'Come and work in the Mother Country'. Organising the trip to England was largely her own doing and it took her a couple of years.

One thing Mum couldn't arrange, though, was the money. Her grandmother found $300 for the fare so she could go. It was a huge amount of money then.

I can just imagine Sylvanie sitting in a rocking chair on the veranda in the heat of a sunset, tired from the back-breaking work in her fields, Mum watching as she shouts out to every respectful passer-by who doffs his hat. She was a big personality in the local community, and she knew everyone.

It still shocks me that Mum came over pretty much on her own. Sylvanie was a very strong woman and that rubbed off on Mum. I obviously got some of my determination from her side of the family, but I can't imagine sorting out such a thing at the same age.

So sixteen-year-old Udine Patricia Lake sailed for England in early 1960 on the SS *Montserrat*. Two other people she knew from Anguilla were on board – Victor, a cousin, and someone called Inez. Victor was on his way to visit his mother in Southall in Middlesex, twenty minutes from Heathrow (London Airport as it was then). Naturally, that's where Mum was heading to stay and change her life.

When I asked her about it recently, it sank in what an expedition that journey was for someone of her age from such a small backwater. The ship stopped at several islands around the West Indies and, trapped on board, Mum felt increasingly cramped and bad tempered as the days passed and more people boarded. As a teenaged black girl from an insignificant place, Mum experienced routine rudeness from the white people on board, and even had to take stick from West Indians from the bigger islands, who look down on 'small island' people. She remembers, for example, that they had to share an iron. Mum would wait her turn like everyone else, but it was never long before someone was hassling her to hurry up. She gave as good as she received, though.

After three and a half weeks they reached the busy docks of Southampton, which must have seemed very cold and inhospitable compared to home.

I know from talking to her that before she arrived she thought England would be a lot grander than it was. She was disappointed when she saw the reality. Britain was still run-down after the war. 'All those grey houses.' That's how she describes it.

It didn't help her to settle when her big ambition was immediately squashed. You had to be at least eighteen to train as a nurse in England, and she was two years short. It must have been a huge disappointment for her, undermining her whole reason for emigrating from Anguilla.

Instead of studying for a professional qualification that would impress the folks back home, once she was installed at her aunt's, her first job was working as a packer at the Wall's meat factory in Isleworth. They had trouble getting staff, so the factory would send coaches to pick up people from Southall, and they accepted new migrants such as Mum. She was quite fortunate because an older lady took her under her wing and it was quite pleasant as an introduction to the London labour market.

Worse was to follow for Mum the following year, 1961, when her aunt left the house in Southall and went back to the Caribbean. At the same time, the Conservative Government was pushing through legislation to limit the number of arrivals from the old Empire – especially the Caribbean – looking for work. People from India and Pakistan had been arriving in large numbers in Southall since the mid-fifties, and they already far outnumbered Afro-Caribbean migrants.

After the upheaval of arriving in a new country that didn't really want 'her kind' after all, I know Mum felt suddenly quite alone and exposed when her aunt left, especially on top of the blow about the nursing. But she just had to get on with it and earn her living, otherwise she'd starve.

Mum was always looking for a better job with more acceptable hours, but trying to find one really opened her eyes to what was available to her in British society. A hotel near Heathrow Airport was looking for staff. When she applied, they told her they only had vacancies in the kitchen at that moment, but two white girls who came after her landed jobs as a chambermaid and a waitress. Typically, Mum complained. 'That's not fair,' she said. 'They've come after me . . .'

The man told her it's either kitchen or laundry. She didn't ask why, but she knew it was because he thought the white customers might not approve of her handling food and being in their bedrooms.

That's the first time she realised how bad things could be in England. Mum told the hotel owner to stuff his job and walked out, went back to Wall's, packing bacon and sausages. It was a long way from the nursing she'd set her heart on.

CHAPTER 2

Saying You Love Someone Takes Nothing

When Mum arrived at her aunt's house in Albert Road, Paul Vernon Canoville was a lodger in a downstairs room. He was from Dominica, a lush, volcanic island, very natural and unspoilt, with none of the big hotel chains you see in other parts of the Caribbean. It's still very rustic and people live close to the soil, but it's hard to make a living and put a roof over your head.

Like hundreds of others leaving 'paradise' for England – my mother included – my father was hoping to better himself. He dreamed of returning home in a few years, able to impress his family and friends with how well he'd done. Wherever they are, Caribbean people stick together, and so it was with Dad and his Dominican friends who had settled in Southall.

Vernon had one killer gift – he made Mum laugh. She

was lonely after her aunt left, and as they were living in the same house they saw a lot of each other. His sense of humour is a bit like mine – sarcy, snappy, play-acting to entertain a room. The national symbol of Dominica is a parrot and he had a gift for mimicry that I inherited.

They were married in 1961, I arrived in 1962 and June was born the following year. Mum will tell you now that she was far too young to deal with two tiny kids and make a go of the relationship; they both were.

I was a forceps delivery and the labour took two days. It would be the first of many times her difficult child kept her waiting.

My mum says that, for some reason, I never crawled. As soon as I could, I would just run, even when I wasn't really capable of it, until I fell down. I used to get bumps on my head all the time. From the time I could stand, I wanted to kick a ball. It used to drive her mad.

So did my dad! I understand he liked his drink and his cards. Mum went into labour on the Friday night and it was her cousin John who took her to hospital. I didn't arrive until the Sunday morning. Dad didn't even know until Sunday evening. That's when he emerged again to look for Mum and me.

I wasn't aware that my dad wasn't present at my birth until Mum told me recently. I think the only one of my babymothers' labours I was absent for was Sonia's with Caysey in 1995. As I have had eleven children, I've probably seen more births than quite a few nurses.

I'm always a bit nervous. You want the baby to come,

and you don't want any problems. You don't like to see your partner going through all that pain. It must be excruciating. You sit there, holding her hand, trying to soothe and encourage as the cursing comes out, and the pressure she's under becomes dramatic. You've got to be there to help her through it. Dad wasn't there and that is that.

They were incompatible from the start, really – chalk and cheese. The only thing they had in common was stubbornness. Dad was very laid back. He was happy to potter around, repair bicycles or whatever, but proper work was a different matter. It was hard for black people to get decent jobs in the 1960s anyway, but he really didn't get along with the whole work ethic. He'd been a labourer for Taylor Woodrow on the M1 but had trouble with his eyes and stopped. Of course, when work is a problem, money is too.

Mum thought it was something to do with the way he was brought up – probably spoilt by his parents – but he found it difficult to get or keep a job. He never used to like to drag himself out to work every day. I can sympathise with that! Maybe he didn't like people telling him what to do either. He never seemed to keep a job for more than a few days. Meanwhile, Mum was trying to get all the work she could.

After my sister was born in June 1963, Mum became so unhappy at having to bear everything and raise two babies virtually on her own, it made her depressed. Vernon would just disappear for three, four days at a time.

He would be hanging out in the betting shop or playing

dominoes and drinking, and squandering their rent money in the process. It used to infuriate Mum. Dad lacked any sense of responsibility towards her and us children. At the time, he was solely interested in enjoying himself. He didn't mean it maliciously. He just didn't have much commitment to raising a family. What with her temper and his ability to shut things out, they barely seemed to talk about anything. I think that contributed to the breakdown of their marriage.

These are things about him I didn't know until quite recently. They've made me reflect on my own way of doing things with relationships, and I can't say that I've avoided the pitfalls as I should have. If Mum had been more open with me, maybe I could have been more aware.

Mum hated the lack of stability then. Dad just wasn't reliable. But she is at heart a survivor, whatever the cost, so one day when she had had enough, she decided to leave him, taking us with her. I was two and June was still tiny. She found somewhere else to rent nearby on Cherry Avenue, and we moved out. We didn't see him again for twenty-one years.

The house on Cherry Avenue had separate rented rooms and we were one of four households living there. One of Dad's Dominican mates, Sheffield, lived in another room, and he looked out for us to a degree. Everyone shared a kitchen and a bathroom. Our room was very basic, with a table, a double bed and a paraffin heater over which we would boil milk for our cereal every morning.

Mum made sure we rarely strayed out of the room

because we were so young. There were lots of comings and goings, and all sorts of people came to the house. We were the only children living there, and Mum was the only woman, still barely twenty. I guess she was worried about us coming to any harm in a situation that was far from secure. Our room in Cherry Avenue was supposed to be a safe haven, but it often seemed like a prison.

Mum thought she was doing the best for us when she left Dad but, for me, the upshot was that I missed out almost entirely on having a father figure, and during my childhood I felt that a lot. I always wanted an older brother because I got into so many situations that I simply couldn't cope with on my own, especially later on. I often made the wrong choices. A while after the break-up, Mum became friendly with a Venezuelan, Henry Quijada. He was an electrician. I got on very well with him. He tried to help the family and was great with June and me.

He made a proper stereo system for Mum, record deck and everything, from scratch, just from components. And he was a good artist. He took a little postcard of a horse and copied it into a big painting. He was very talented and a nice guy.

Word soon got round. What black community there was in our locality back then was small, tight-knit, and everyone knew everyone else's business. I've only just found out what happened. I was too young to know about it at the time. Unbeknown to June and me, Dad was living round the corner and one day he came round in feisty mood because Sheffield had told him Mum was seeing someone else. According to Mum, Dad came over five times that day to pick a fight with her. She called the police but they said it was just a 'domestic' and didn't want to interfere.

Then around eleven at night, she was in the kitchen, and he came again, having another go. Sheffield, who had let him in, was holding Mum while Dad hit her. Mum is a big, strong woman, and she picked up the first thing that was handy, a milk bottle, and smashed it on Sheffield's head. He backed off and went to fetch the police. When they arrived, they immediately arrested her and slammed her in a cell.

She'd never been in trouble with the law before and it must have been a bewildering experience for her. The following morning, an officer came in and advised her to plead guilty. She'd rung the police five times and they hadn't come, then she hit someone trying to defend herself and they told her to plead guilty.

It was Henry who sorted things out. He came round and stood up to Sheffield and Vernon. He stood in the hallway and said, 'Any one of you ready, I'll take any of you on if you wanna play bad.' My dad sloped off into Sheffield's room. They didn't want the confrontation. Nothing bad happened after that in the house. But a little later Mum changed her surname from Canoville to Alexander to remove that connection permanently.

Henry was good for Mum, and for us kids but to us the relationship seemed to end suddenly. Apparently, when Henry said his company was moving to the south coast,

Mum felt she wasn't ready for that and refused to go with him. You never miss your water till the well runs dry. But that was the end of the affair. Mum was never good at explaining things like that, so we never learned the real reason why they broke up. There were no goodbyes. He just wasn't there any more, and we knew it was over.

Mum claims their affair cooled as soon as he told her they had anacondas in Venezuela. He said he wanted to go back there at some stage, and she has a serious phobia about snakes, so she just kind of started to wean herself off him. Strange as that may seem, she is very cut-and-dried like that. If there was more to it, I'll probably never know what it was.

June and I felt it bad. Henry had a positive effect on us. For me, it was nice to have a masculine influence around for a while. He was patient, calm and solid. I was feeling my way and he was a proper example to look up to.

I'm no churchgoer now but I believe in God and like to say my prayers. When I was small I was an acolyte at St George's Church round the corner on Lancaster Road in Southall. The church was high Anglo-Catholic at the time and multiracial – just right for Mum. The priest, Father Morgan, was Welsh and had been through the war. He was really nice. Every year he'd take us to the seaside and we loved it. We went to France twice. He was an excellent man. He died in 1976. For me, it was bad timing to lose such a good influence just as I was making my way in life.

In 1974, Mum took June and I out to the Caribbean for the first time to meet our grandparents on both sides –

Dad's family in Dominica, as well as her own in Saint-Martin.

Meeting them was one of my best experiences. Back in England, it felt like all we had in the world was each other. To get to know blood relatives was a thrill I will never forget. And it was remarkable really for Mum to make sure we met Vernon's folks; she didn't have to do that.

Although Dad was never mentioned and had no influence in our lives, she felt it was important that we had a bond with his side of our genes. I thought that was really big of her. She must have felt so bitter towards him. Of course, June and I both found it hard to understand why he never came to see us.

Delightful as the Dominicans were, it was slightly odd meeting Dad's parents and family. We had no common experiences with Dad to share – we were effectively strangers. It wasn't as moving as it was meeting Mum's folks. They made us feel really special and we were given lots of gifts. We also found out we were their oldest grandchildren.

In some West Indian cultures expectations are very different for boys and girls, men and women. I saw in the Caribbean that you'd sometimes have this system where boys weren't allowed to do anything. It was the girls who did all the work. Maybe Dad was just that way inclined because of his upbringing, but more likely he was young and still wanted a single life. What I realise now is that both of them found it difficult to show affection and love, and that's no recipe for a healthy relationship.

On top of that, Mum already knew what Vernon was like. She was aware that he had a son back in Dominica – our half-brother. In fact, we met him when we went there in 1974.

We were taken care of in the Caribbean, but it was nothing compared with what Mum lavished on our relatives, skint as she was, when they started to visit us in the seventies. My argument is over how Mum treated her family differently from us in those early days. When they came over she put herself out for them, even when it was struggle enough for her, on her own with two kids.

We were often strapped for cash. By this time, we'd moved to a flat of our own and Mum could just about manage to pay the rent, council tax, food and other bills, but she pulled out all the stops for them to show she could provide for them in England. Although there wasn't a lot in our place, it was always neat and tidy and Mum made sure there was plenty of food when they were around. They probably got the impression she was doing well and building up her savings, as most West Indians strived to do.

She does the same thing to this day. I watched her one time in the 2000s. Christmas was coming and what was she doing? Buying a new suite of furniture.

I asked her straight out, 'What you doing getting new sofas? Who are you trying to impress?'

'Well, you know, your aunties are coming over.'

That was all so different from how Mum was with June and me when we were young and money was tight.

Whenever we asked her for something it was always, 'No, no, no – money doesn't grow on trees.'

That's why we hated asking her. Other kids were going out on treats, days out, but not us – unless it was through the church. It wasn't always because of the money, though. It was the same whenever we were invited to other children's parties.

'Mum, can we go?'

'No.' Occasionally, we went to works Christmas parties, but never to other kids' parties.

Don't get me wrong. Mum pulled out some surprises sometimes. Like all children, I hated going shopping with her, especially to a big supermarket. Where we lived in Southall, the Spar was at the end of the road but we had to walk all the way down to Safeway and back through the park when she wanted to do a proper shop, because it was a bigger store.

Mum couldn't afford a car until much, much later, so we walked everywhere. What made it worse for me was that she had one of those wicker trolley baskets, the type old ladies used, with the long metal handle and the tartan cover. Oh my God! I swear I never walked alongside my mum. I was either in front or behind, like I wasn't with her. Naturally, it was even worse when she asked me to pull the damn thing. I was so embarrassed. I never wanted anybody to see me with it. In the shop it was a case of rushing around, grabbing things on her list, bam, bam, bam, bam – 'You got everything? Come on! Let's go!' And fingers crossed none of my school friends would see me.

Then one time, when I was about eleven or twelve, on the way home from one of these expeditions, out of the blue, she pulled the wicker basket to a halt at the local bike shop. She was winding me up now, I thought, because I knew she wasn't buying a bicycle for me, even though I'd wanted one for years.

'Try the bikes,' she said. I went along with her, even though I knew standing astride it was as far as my fun would go.

'What do you think?' She was stretching this out a bit.

'I like this one, this is nice.' It was a Raleigh – the top brand in those days – great to sit on it, my toe hardly touching the ground. I'm thinking, 'Yeah, that's terrific, but what's the point? She's never buying me something like that.'

Then all of sudden she stepped away and paid the man for the bike. It completely shocked me! I pushed it along, looking at it as if it was a magic carpet or something. I didn't even ride it. I walked with her, staring at it in shock all the way home. You couldn't have taken the smile off my face with a hot iron. I was amazed, so happy.

'Thanks, Mum.'

'Make sure you look after it.' And she meant it. I couldn't wait to get home. June had a surprise coming, too. Mum bought her a secondhand piano. She wanted June to learn, despite it being a surprisingly middle class thing, out of keeping with how skint we were, but Mum always wanted us to better ourselves. There wasn't much furniture in our lounge so there was just enough room for a stand-up piano. And the yard was just fine for a bicycle.

'Is it all right if I ride my bike?'

'Go on, half an hour.' Is that all? I could run around on it all day, but some restraints never changed. 'Yeah, Mum.'

I'd already had the occasional go on other people's bikes in snatched half hours over the years, and I swear to you, I went darting down the road, working up a speed and having my share of little accidents.

So I'd ridden bikes before but this one was different. I had a Raleigh now. I'd got five gears, and I was stress-testing each one as I belted off. So there I was, motoring along and fiddling with the gears, but when it came to stopping I didn't know any better than to yank on one of the levers. It happened to be the front wheel brake. Of course, that sent me hurtling straight over the handlebars, head first, bashing into the wall. I was in agony. I'd grazed myself and had a few bruises, but luckily nothing too visible that would let on what had happened on my maiden voyage. No way could I tell Mum. She would have scolded me for not looking after it and probably marched it straight back to the shop for all I knew. So I just came back on time, parked the bike up and said nothing.

I loved that precious bicycle and was so proud of it. I taught June to ride it, although she was younger and smaller. I'd push her along so carefully. I really didn't want her to fall over with it, partly because she was my kid sister and I cared for her, but mostly because this is a Raleigh, man! Five-gear Raleigh bikes were kicking in those days! Now it's ten, fifteen – I don't know why they bother with those extra gears. I was always fine with five.

Then it got to a stage where the Chopper bicycle was the one to have – the long black padded seat, the gear shift on the frame in front of you and the high, wide handlebars. Choppers were the new craze. In those days the technology was simple and it was easy to build or maintain your own two-wheeler. Every teenaged kid was getting out his box spanner and customising his bike by replacing the straight handlebars with moustache or cow horn-shaped ones. Passers-by used to shout, 'Get off an' milk it!'

Of course, I wanted to tart up my prized Raleigh. So I took a spanner, found the bolt that held the bars firm and loosened it. When the retaining brackets were loose enough, I eased out the standard issue straight handlebars and set them to one side. In no time, I thought, I'd have the big high-sided replacement handlebars tight and the bike would be ready to ride away. So I began threading the bars through the bracket. Something wasn't quite right, however. The new handlebars wouldn't fit, no matter how far I twisted them or loosened the bolt. I hadn't told Mum I was even messing with the bike, which was still quite new, and she couldn't possibly see it like this. She would have blown her top and it would have meant another beating, without a doubt. As things weren't going to plan, I decided simply to put back the other bars. That would be OK. But now they wouldn't go back either. Nightmare!

I was desperate for Mum not to find out what I'd done. My heart sank. I knew how this story would end. She mustn't see this bike. Just at that moment she walked in and caught me red-handed, with my bike in pieces.

'What's going on?' She was aghast, staring at the rare gift she'd trusted me with and how I'd treated it.

'Er, hi Mum, just fitting this in here.'

'What d'you mean? You fittin' what?'

'Erm, actually, I don't know how to fit it.'

'This is why I don't buy you lot nuttin'!' she screamed. 'That cost a lot of money! All you do, you ruin the thing, you break it up!'

She never bought me anything like that again. That was it. The bike stood there for months and months – nothing wrong with it, just the sorry-looking handlebars lying next to it. I couldn't repair it and, even though I asked around, no one else could fix it, either. And there was no way Mum was going to find anyone after what I'd done.

For me, that was a practical reason why I missed a man's influence around the house. Years later I became more competent messing about with bikes, but at the time it stood there as a symbol of her rare acts of kindness and my always letting her down.

Gestures like buying the bike for me or the piano for June were never rare when it came to our relatives coming over from the Caribbean or America. It was always a big 'Yes' to them and in the same breath a 'No' to us. And that's partly why, in a year or two, I started to take decisions for myself. I'd sneak out at night, gallivant on the street, because I knew the answer to any request even before I asked her.

She couldn't or wouldn't help me do what I wanted. I had to find my own way, unsupervised. Obviously, she didn't like me doing that, but I had to take the blows to find my way in life without her. For good or bad, I would learn to become self-sufficient with my pleasure-seeking.

All in all, since Southall was such a female environment to grow up in, it made me feel at ease with women on a social level, and it helped when I had different interests later in life. In the early days, I remember that on Saturday afternoons the professional wrestling on ITV's 'World Of Sport' was hugely popular. Whoever could afford a television, their house was full. Even the kids were caught up in that.

Families from miles around would be there, making themselves at home. I can picture the scene now, all gathered round the TV watching Johnny Kwango, Adrian Street, Jackie Pallo, Mick McManus and the rest faking all their slams and submissions. As soon as it finished, all the men would go off to a pub or somewhere, leaving the mums and kids together, the boys acting out the moves. Of course it was all fixed, but it was entertainment, not sport.

If you think about it now, when people came over from the Caribbean, they were so isolated from the rest of society, they had to have this sort of get-together in a house where they could feel comfortable and not harassed. It was like a multitude of people who were excluded from other places.

That was the world I tried to make my way in as a teenager. Mum always hoped her male friends would have a positive effect on me, more positive than the man who was never mentioned in our home.

Dad was the cause of a lot of hardship really. He is certainly a calmer person than she is, and may have brought some balance if they could have worked it out together. Life would have been a lot easier if he had been around, or at least, it would have been if he had been a different sort of person. Mum was really struggling in his absence, and boy did she make me pay for the sins of my father.

I'm laid back. I want something, I go and get it, but it'll take time. I'm not that desperate. She kept telling me, 'You're just like your dad.'

She wasn't like Vernon at all. When she wanted to achieve something, she'd go and get it done, no matter what. She wouldn't care about anybody else. It's not that she was unemotional, just that the only emotion she ever showed us was anger.

I'd always say I'm much more frightened of my mum than of the police. She took most of her frustration at her situation out on me, 'Lickle Vernon'.

She saw, of course, how much I loved her and June. She talks about watching me help my tiny sister down the stairs, so conscientiously, one step at a time on her behind, making sure she didn't slip an inch.

June looked up to me, and would follow me round constantly, calling 'Polly Scot Scot', her pet name for me. We have always been so close. June wasn't like me. She never got into mischief and never got the beatings that I did.

Mum's anger didn't need much provocation where I was concerned. Once when I was very young, Mum was doing June's hair and I went and got my comb, walked up and said, 'Mummy, look . . . comb?' All I wanted was some care and attention. And all she did was shout her head off at me. I must just have been a constant reminder of why life was so hard.

Maybe when Mum whacked me, it was like she was getting back at Vernon. She had no patience with me. She never gave me any cuddles or showed me any affection; but that was pretty much the same for June, too.

When I was older, she took to giving me regular beatings over the slightest thing – not doing the housework properly, saying something slightly cheeky – with whatever was handy at the time. A zip, the wire you'd hang curtains by, hairbrush, vacuum cleaner pipe – I've been beaten with all of them. My skin would welt up and when she first did it, I would naturally burst into tears.

But as I approached my teenage years, I got more defiant. One day when she beat me, the tears didn't come. It was like a scene from 'Roots' where a slave getting whipped didn't want to show it was hurting. I'd sniff, but tears wouldn't come. I just took it.

If at first I stopped crying, pretty soon I stopped caring.

People reading this may find it incredible, but Mum didn't realise that we craved and needed affection from her. It was only in the eighties, when she was studying nursing and reading about childcare as part of the course, that it hit home to her for the first time that children need constant tenderness and reassurance. In all honesty, it had never occurred to her that such things were as vital to a child as the roof over his head and the food on the table. The lack of them left us emotionally impaired. Survival had been her only consideration in the early years, and I understand that. But even when she was no longer a young mum but a mature woman, for some reason, she still chose to withhold any tenderness from us.

That lack of my mother's love affects me to this day. I crave it and armour myself against rejection. You hear me on the phone to my children and it's all 'love you, princess', 'well done'. I always tell them I love them. I never had that one single time from my mother. Saying you love someone takes nothing, does it?

In all my relationships, I have to have a lot of affection. If I can't have it, it ain't happening. But I also have a problem with getting too close to a woman; when closeness leads to opening up, I feel prickly. That's the bottling-up I took from my mother. And at the first sign of conflict, it soon starts to mess with my mind and I have to put some distance between us. That's just one thing I inherited from my father.

CHAPTER 3

'You're Not Welcome'

Of all the challenges Mum faced after her arrival, I think she found the standard of accommodation available to her in England the hardest thing to bear. On Anguilla, Sylvanie had had a big house, loads of space, a glimpse of paradise out of the window. But for pretty much my entire childhood we lived in a single room of a shared house on a terraced street in a built-up area. That one cell was our bedroom, living quarters, storage space. In the kitchen, each room was allocated one burner on top of the stove and a small amount of shelf space to store food. It was always crowded in there, with everyone wanting to cook when they got home from work.

We were stuck, living on top of each other. We didn't have money to go out like other kids did but we just took it in our stride, as kids do. It was all that we knew.

The eight or so years in Cherry Avenue set the home

routine I remember most vividly and painfully. It was extremely strict and not much fun. Even when we were older we were rarely allowed out of the room. It was almost always silent, too, very oppressive. Over the years we became very self-sufficient and self-contained. Often it was just June and me there, doing our homework or the housework. Mum would be out earning a crust whenever she could. Surviving.

In some ways, things were even harder for her. She was getting what jobs she could to make ends meet, including shift work. It wasn't like we had childcare. Sheffield looked out for us when he was around during the day. That's one thing with black families, they'd keep an eye out – but as Mum found out, that cuts both ways.

I always say if social services had acted then as they do today, we'd have been taken away from Mum. No problem.

For a while she was working nights at the airport, serving food in a canteen for airline staff. She would put us to bed in the evening at 7 p.m. and go off to work, leaving our breakfast and clothes out because we were going to have to get ready for school by ourselves. Then she'd actually physically bolt us in the room all night – young kids locked in on our own.

She did that because she was so afraid something might happen to us, and it was the best way she could think of dealing with it. Apparently, all the time she was out she was thinking, 'My God, suppose they get a bit cold and go to light the paraffin heater?' But we had to use the paraffin heater to heat our breakfast milk. She was petrified. All in all, I'd say 'Home Alone' had nothing on June and me. If anything had happened, we would have had to deal with it ourselves. The other men in the house would only look out for us so much.

Eventually, it drove me to find an escape route. What Mum didn't know is that after a while, as soon as she was out the front door, I used to climb out of bed, stand on the chair to climb through a small top window, jump out in the yard and come round through a conservatory at the back and into the kitchen.

Once I was in there I'd grab crackers and milk and take them back for a 'feast' with June. There was a ledge outside for me to climb back in.

I was like that Carling Black Label advert from the late 1980s, set to the 'Mission Impossible' theme, where a squirrel climbs, leaps and balances across various obstacles in a garden to reach some hazelnuts. At the end, as the squirrel chomps away, a watching owl says to another one, 'I bet he drinks Carling Black Label'. With me it was Jacob's crackers! But no one witnessed my night moves.

After a while Mum cottoned on to what we were doing and realised she was going too far. She still shut the door when she left, but it stayed unbolted.

Mum had to take all this responsibility on herself. I see that now. Who else was there to do it? In the sixties you didn't have a benefit system like you have today. You just had to work, and for a black woman, job opportunities were limited. It was hand to mouth.

June and I would look at other kids and think, 'I'd like a new pair of those shoes.' We're talking about the days of plimsolls. They lasted about a week for me because I played football and a hole would come straight through where your toe was. I'd just have to tape over the holes. I couldn't ask Mum for a new pair. No point. So we just had to sit and moan and sulk. We did a lot of sulking.

Throughout the sixties and seventies, times were hard at home. Sometimes we were so skint we had to have porridge in the morning and porridge at night. It was better than nothing at all, but not much. Mum always made sure she paid the rent, although the landlord was reasonable and sometimes allowed her to settle a little late.

There were other circumstances that didn't help. Two years after I was born, the local Residents' Association had called for segregated learning for 'coloured' and white pupils. They said there were 6,000 Asian people among Southall's 54,000 inhabitants. The local MP backed them. 'I want to see the coloured population here disperse,' he said. 'I want to help them find homes and jobs so that some of them can move away to other areas with their families.' At the election in 1964, one in every ten Southall voters backed an anti-immigration British National Party candidate. A few years later leaflets were going around the area saying, 'Do you want a black grandchild? If not, stop immigration now.' That's the sort of stuff my mum was reading about every week in the local paper. 'You're not welcome', basically.

In my day, as now, most children entered the education

system at the age of five. I didn't go to school until I was nearly seven. The under-pressure, Labour-controlled local authority told Mum that no spaces were available in local schools because there were so many immigrant children in the area. Southall supposedly had the second highest concentration of migrant children in the UK, with 19 per cent, after Hornsey in north London. In some local classrooms two-thirds of the pupils were immigrant kids, in others there were hardly any. Local white parents were in the papers complaining that their children weren't getting a proper education and demanding moves to schools with fewer black and Asian pupils.

I was an innocent pawn in all this politics. The ridiculous situation dragged on until at last the education authority wrote to say I could start at a school in another part of Ealing.

The only problem was that the school chosen for me at last was near the Hanger Lane roundabout where two big arterial roads meet, Western Avenue and the North Circular Road, and it meant a forty-minute, five-mile coach journey along west London roads that were always jammed in the rush hour. Thank you for your contribution to my schooling, Southall Residents' Association and Mr Pargiter, MP!

Still, I'd missed nearly two years of schooling already and Mum was desperate, so that's where I went to school. As usual, June and I were inseparable and she joined me. Every day I'd diligently walk my sister to the stop for eight o'clock and we'd both be bussed the forty minutes to north

Ealing. It was gruelling but we were told we just had to get on with it.

Then one freezing winter's day, when I was seven and June was six, we were waiting at the stop at eight o'clock as usual and the coach just didn't arrive. We were the only ones who were picked up there, so it was down to me to decide what to do.

I thought, 'God, we've missed the coach. We can't tell Mum, she'll kill us.' We were genuinely petrified of what Mum would do if we missed the coach and didn't go to school. I was mulling it over and was sure I could remember the way the coach went. So I said, 'We'll walk.'

It's quite a daunting route at that time of the morning, but I was oblivious to the narrow pavements and the rumbling traffic. Believe it or not, we set off just after eight and reached school at one o'clock in the afternoon. Everyone was worried about us. 'Where have you been?' the teachers asked. As it turned out, the coach had come ten minutes after we'd left. I was always impatient.

We hadn't eaten and we were both knackered. The school couldn't believe we'd walked for five hours, in bad weather, too. They didn't give me a note for Mum, though, or ring up to explain what had happened.

That night, June was boiling up with a fever and Mum couldn't understand it. It was only then I said, 'Oh Mum, coach didn't come today, so we walked to school.' June had caught a chill. She recovered from that but soon afterwards she developed asthma and I always blame myself, even though Mum suffers from it, too.

I was actually quite proud of myself for finding the school that day. That's when I realised that you could take me somewhere once and I'd remember how to get there. I was born with that sense of direction. Another time, shortly after we'd moved into a new flat, Mum was taken very ill. We weren't registered at a nearby surgery, so I said, 'Don't worry, I'll get your old doctor for you.'

'No you can't, it's too far,' she protested, but I was so desperate to please her. Mum wrote a letter and I found the doctor and brought him over.

I don't know whether it was the coach incident that brought about the change, but we were transferred to a local school, Beaconsfield Primary, soon afterwards. It was very multiracial and only a quarter of a mile from our house. No more coaches, not even when I went back to the senior school, Brentside High, a few years later.

When I see how confident primary age children are now, I'm amazed. I wish I could have felt like that in the classroom. But I'd started education later than everyone else and I never really caught up. I wasn't the academic type unfortunately. I learned to develop other strengths, in and out of school. PE was what I enjoyed most, and the social side – my best friend was a white kid called Clive and I went round with him.

CHAPTER 4

Playing At Being Pelé

Around 1973 Mum was earning enough money to rent a flat at 159 Cranleigh Gardens, near Lady Margaret Road, still in Southall. It was the other side of the Uxbridge Road, next to a nice park with a grassy area for football and a small children's playground. There were woods nearby with a pond, and a canal. More importantly, the flat offered privacy and our own space.

In one way, Cranleigh Gardens offered no respite though. I was friends with Clive and soon made friends with local kids, but June and I hardly ever went out to play. Even though we were older now – nine and ten – Mum would never let us out of the house until we had done some serious household chores, and there was more to do now. We'd be dusting, tidying, vacuuming up while looking longingly out the window, seeing the other kids kicking around in the street, having a whale of a time.

Meanwhile, we had to finish our work to perfection before we could venture out to play. Mum would check how well you'd done your chores, and if it wasn't up to scratch, she'd make you do it again. Even when you passed the inspection it would be strictly half an hour's leisure time and that was it.

At last we'd snatch a few moments playing with our next-door neighbours, with a football or on bikes. We'd never be allowed to invite anyone back. Mum was so private she would have blanched at the idea of anyone seeing inside her home.

Naturally enough, I had a childish take on colour and society then. We were the only black family in the street – there were only two Afro-Caribbean families in the wider neighbourhood. The kids outside enjoying themselves, they were all white. It seemed to me that all white kids were carefree, did what they wanted. Not like us, stuck inside, noses to the grindstone. I wanted to be like them. I wanted to be white.

You wouldn't believe how mixed up I was at the time. Ours was not a very 'black' household at all. My icons were all white. I loved John Wayne Westerns, the TV detective 'Columbo', I thought David Essex was a god – the music, the cheeky smile – I knew nothing of black culture because there were virtually no other Afro-Caribbean kids of my age to socialise with other than June at that time. And she was under the same influences as I was.

Mum wasn't a very traditional Caribbean cook at home,

either. She couldn't be – good West Indian foodstuffs were not widely available where we lived and too expensive to have regularly. The meals I remember having most often were classic English, huge fry-up breakfasts on a Saturday morning for instance – sausage, bacon, black pudding (I don't know if I'd take it now, but at that time it was a luxury) and the rest. Fried bakes – flattened balls of dough, typically West Indian – gave it something of a Caribbean slant. That breakfast was the one I looked forward to and Mum never let us go short in that, at least. And on Sunday it was generally a roast dinner.

Only occasionally would we have something very Caribbean, such as corned beef and rice, or some cornmeal porridge with condensed milk, vanilla, nutmeg and cinnamon. It was said to be good for your digestion and many West Indians still swear by it.

Anyway, since I was older and more able now, Mum had added cooking the family meal to my list of to-dos, and I had little idea of how to cook Caribbean food until Mum showed me. Over the years, I became quite proud of my ability to rustle up something from what we had in the cupboards. It made me passionate about food and cooking, and that holds to this day.

Funnily enough, Mum never encouraged June to cook at all. I have no idea why. It was as if she couldn't trust me outside enjoying myself and that was another thing to keep me busy.

God, that Saturday morning fry-up was nice, though. Then sometimes Mum would give us the money to go to the Saturday morning pictures. That was our big treat. It was wicked. That's one thing we really looked forward to.

As June and I got older and went round to friends' houses, saw how other kids' folks were with them, we realised we were missing something. There it was always, 'How are you, Paul?'

'Not too bad.'

'How's school?'

That's all we wanted from Mum, but she never had that common touch with us. Naturally, Mum's repressive approach had had an effect on me. Until I was around eleven, I would hardly say boo to a goose. Mum made us ultra polite, respectful to adults. People would keep saying what nice children we were and why couldn't their children be more like us. That's what other kids' parents said; we were never praised at all by our own mother.

We knew Mum would provide for and protect us, but I can't say we ever felt loved. We'd overhear her singing our praises to other adults: 'Oh, Paul's very good. He washes dishes, he Hoovers . . .' And I always have, because that's the way she brought me up! But at home, it was, 'You're no good! You don't do nuttin'! I asked you to do something, but you can't even do that . . .'

Of course, I understand now how difficult life was and that Mum probably felt by providing for us and raising us she was showing how much she loved us. But I still think she could have showed us some affection.

You couldn't talk to Mum because she was so busy, and you didn't ask her for anything because the answer was always, 'No.' So I became a secretive person. We were growing up fast and, as for every other kid, things were going on in our lives, whether at school or out playing. It could be a brilliant goal you scored in the playground, an issue you had with a teacher, or an incident in the street outside with other boys. Most kids would have shared their good news or problems with a mother, father or older brother. We only had Mum and we didn't tell her because she just didn't seem at all bothered. If we had a problem, it was always our fault, and if it was good news, she wasn't interested. It was as if her mind was so full of trying to get us by that she had no room for anything else in her head – joy or pain.

The first time I was racially abused I didn't tell her about it. I'd made friends with some white boys my age from the local estate, and I used to go and play football with them over Cranleigh Park. At junior school, football was the most important thing for me, and whenever Mum let us off her tight leash it was always a kickabout for me, for as long as possible. These local white boys and I would play the knockout game 'World Cup' against the park gate till seven or eight in the evening. I represented Brazil – as their greatest ever player Pelé, of course – and I was pretty good. I was big for my age – nine or ten – and nippy with it. I liked to take people on with the ball at my feet and use my pace. There were usually some older boys involved and they always seemed to try to kick me, but I was fast enough so that they couldn't get near me most of the time.

I suppose they had to find a way to get back at me, and

it was these bigger ones who suddenly took to calling me names, 'nigger' and 'gollywog'. I guess it was a normal, casual thing for them, but it really shocked and upset me every time they used those words. I couldn't say much in reply. Large as I was, I was a lot younger than the big kids, and I was really frightened of them.

It was just a few years since the MP Enoch Powell had stoked the flames of race hate in Southall and elsewhere by warning about white majority Britain being swamped and 'rivers of blood' being on the nation's streets. Lots of people sympathised with his views, whether in public or private, and we knew it.

There's only so much anyone can take of that sort of regular abuse, though, no matter how young or frightened. Eventually, something just snapped in me, I lost my temper and had a go at one of them for the name-calling. Well, it all kicked off after that, a big scrap. As it happened, another of their friends was passing by at the time and saw what was going on. He was about three times my size, bigger than they were, and most important, black. He came over and petrified every one of them, telling them that he'd bust their heads if he ever heard those words coming out of their mouths again. From that moment the racial abuse stopped, just like that. I was glad I'd stood up for myself, even though it took a bigger kid to bail me out. Later on I found out that he was a Chelsea supporter who used to stand regularly in the Shed. Bless him! I can imagine him recalling that park incident when he heard the abuse I got from the Chelsea fans surrounding him in the eighties. It must have hurt him almost as much as it did me to hear that.

I didn't want to get into fights, but they happened all the same. One day a few years later, I squared up to an older kid who used to pick on my best friend Clive. I told him, 'Why don't you pick on someone your own size?' I was scared because he was a big old lump, but I was physically well developed for my age and suppose I had begun to want to test my new prowess. Once I'd picked the fight, though, I realised the problem – he was so big I couldn't reach to land a proper punch on him. So I ended up having to restrain him. I got him in a headlock and held on. Of course, that just made him angrier. It was a 'Catch 22' situation and I knew if he got out of it, I was in trouble. I'd jumped in and taken on more than I could handle. My head was going, 'How the hell am I gonna get out of this?' I was tiring from the grappling, and facing a beating at any moment.

Just then his mum came over and called him in for dinner. So we called it a truce. It may have been a stalemate, but it gave me confidence that I could stand up to a bigger boy. I knew I was strong physically. I just needed to work out how to channel it.

I'd also got into the habit of nicking little bits of money round the house. Inevitably, when you were going to the park you'd want to buy an ice cream or sweets. You come across a little money, you take it. Funnily enough, despite beating me for the slightest thing, Mum didn't have a problem with that so much because she used to do exactly the same thing when she was a kid. Back home in Anguilla there was a 'wagonette' cabinet where the glasses, cups and saucers were stored. When she was told to do chores round the house, Mum would always ask to do the living room where the wagonette was.

When her grandmother had a little spare money she would leave it on a saucer beneath an upturned cup on the wagonette. Mum would dust there so that she could clean up in the pocket too. She'd spend it on cakes and sardines and stuff. Sylvanie was well aware that she was doing it but simply turned a blind eye. Neither of them looked on it as theft. It was just taking from your mum or your granny, which was better than stealing from other people.

Not everyone felt the same way about my bad habit, though. One time in Cherry Avenue, I must have dipped into Mum's boyfriend Henry's pocket and taken some change for sweets. I came home and to find my sister looking serious.

'What's going on?'

'Come inside!' Henry looked furious. 'Somebody went in my pocket and took some money.' He knew it was me. 'So who is it?'

'N-n-not me.'

'I'll ask again. I said, "Who is it?"' You only had to ask me twice. I swear Lord, I was always the same, and Mum knew that. The first time you asked me if I'd done something wrong I said a lie, but the second time you asked me, I admitted it.

'Yes, I did it.' That was it.

'You want to go on taking money, picking pockets? Strip!'

'What?'

Henry made me take all my clothes off down to my underwear. He wanted to frighten me with a short sharp shock, and he did.

'I've got this hammer and I got the nail too, now come down outside.'

He made me climb on a chair in the garden and told me he was going to nail my ears to the railings. I was wailing. June was panicking, shouting, 'Paul!'

And now Henry went, 'Where that damn nail? Where that damn nail?'

I eventually realised he was playing around with me, but I swear to you I never put my hand in *his* pocket again.

CHAPTER 5

From 'Lamplight' To 'Mr Loverman'

Mum always says I was a sweet child until I met up with a group of Dominican boys, around 1976 or 1977. It was a few years after our move to Cranleigh Gardens. They were older and far more worldly than I was, and they introduced me to things I'd never seen or done before. I came out of my shell a little and had such a good time hanging out with them, such a laugh all the time. I found I could make people laugh quite easily, especially with my little cheeky comments and impersonations. These didn't go down so well at school, but they gave me some status with the older boys. Here was the strong male influence that wasn't available at home – and the kick-start to my rebellion against childhood and my mum. I was about 14 at the time, growing quickly and becoming aware that there was a man bursting to break out of this child's skin. To me, they were the 'in crowd', but to Mum, they were just the wrong crowd. But mostly they were black and their world was one I didn't know at all. It fascinated me, especially the clothes and the music. Over the next two years I changed completely.

At home Mum would listen to Elvis Presley and the country singer Hank Williams – West Indians love him. At the weekend you'd be vacuuming round and that would be the music blaring. We didn't have ska, reggae or soul pumping out, like other Caribbean households. None of that. And I still liked blue-eyed pop singer David Essex. That was definitely something I couldn't let on to these Dominican boys, so I started pretending I knew what they were talking about when they mentioned Gregory Isaacs and Dennis Brown, the big Jamaican music stars of the day. I probably held it down, more or less. Then when I heard those artists for the first time, well, this was music, man. Real reggae. These boys wore Ferrari pants, Hush Puppies, designer jumpers, and walked with the Jamaican rude boy 'limp'. It was the style. I had to learn to put on a limp, quick.

'What's that walk you put on?'

'What?'

'Nothing.'

I copied everything they did, just to be in among the boys. I rebelled completely and started to go to late night dances. I was taking sides. I was fifteen when I went to my first proper party. I had to ask Mum if it was all right.

'What did you say?'

'Er . . . is it all right to go to my friend's birthday party?'

'What!!?'

It was the first time I'd even asked to go to a party – you can see why I hadn't bothered before with a reaction so extreme. Eventually, she said I could go if I made sure I was back at twelve. What I didn't know was that the party only really starts at twelve.

'And furthermore,' she added, 'take your sister with you.'

'But Mu-um!'

What I didn't tell her was that this was not your typical birthday party with cake and maybe a shandy or two. This was actually a blues dance, a huge West Indian house party with a massive sound system, DJs and decks, loads of cans of Red Stripe lager, the whiff of marijuana and a crowd intent on enjoying themselves all night long. Sometimes, these parties even had pinball and pool tables! Mum would never have let us go if she'd known that.

So I'm with my sister. I'm in there. Music's just starting to kick off. The reggae's in there. Bob Marley I knew, but not In Crowd or Louisa Mark ('Keep It Like It Is'). Barry Biggs' 'Wide Awake In A Dream' just about summed up how I felt in what was a whole new world to me, this dance. I did not have a clue what to do, how to behave. I was wide-eyed watching couples doing the 'wind and grind' – rubbing against each other intimately in the dance, and having a ball. I couldn't see anybody I knew, but they felt like my people. I was standing there, nodding my head, hearing new music, taking in new experiences.

After that I soon picked up the thread. Before long I

started meeting girls and I thought, 'This is all right.' Suddenly, from being a boy barely allowed out I had stumbled upon a whole new scene of people and side of my background I knew nothing about – from 'Lamplight' to 'Mr Loverman' in a matter of months. If Mum had still had me shackled up, I'd have known nothing about it. But I was out there now, man, and I liked the look of everything I saw. The genie was out of the bottle.

I started to go to more and more events like that blues dance, with or without Mum's agreement. The dances I most regularly went to in the late seventies were organised by Mellotone and especially Fatman Sound. Fatman had one of the biggest reggae sound systems of the day. These were exciting times for music, and those with the best sound systems had massive followings. They would play in halls all over London and the UK. These were intense and atmospheric events. The room would ricochet with tinny treble and throb with trouser-shaking bass from huge stacks of Fatman's homemade speaker boxes. The room would be rammed with a crowd blowing whistles or letting off horns in response to the tracks they liked best, or a clever rhyme from a 'toaster' (a rapper in hip-hop parlance), or a nice turn of voice from a singer. Vocalists used a microphone over the top of an instrumental track or 'version'.

The room would often be almost entirely dark save for a little light hovering over the single record deck for the selector, and the mark of a good crew was how they added their own sound effects and used the echo chamber to the most hypnotic effect. Sometimes Fatman would compete with a rival sound crew in what was called a 'soundclash', and there would be an extra buzz in the air with the supporters, or posse, of the two sounds. Fatman rarely lost back then, and they still play big venues all over the world to this day.

For someone who had been chained to the home and felt deprived of fun, this was like an explosion of the senses. Like a typical convert, once I stumbled across Caribbean youth culture, I threw myself into it with enthusiasm. One time I decided I wanted to be a Rastafarian like the fellas I saw skanking away at the dances, throwing their long dreadlocks around in the air, smoking huge joints of pungent-smelling weed. I had to respect how they were. 'Jah! Rastafari!' they seemed to have something about them – coolness, rebellion, status.

I listened intently to righteous reggae artists Burning Spear and Culture. They were kicking it. So I set about growing the matted ropes of hair that were the Rastas' most obvious feature, and with June's help – not that she knew about Rastafari, but she was a girl and knew about hair – I hoped they would grow quickly. Back then, when you were fifteen, you got a few plaits on your head and thought you'd got locks. I got serious.

'June, I ain't having no pork. I'm not joking,' I insisted. 'I'm turning Rasta.'

Proper Rastafarians, I knew, ate only natural 'Ital' food, and definitely no pig meat. I was as steadfast as the most righteous Dread for two weeks at least. Then the lure of

Mum's Saturday morning fry-ups grew too much and bacon was very much back on the menu. The trainee Rasta copped out.

What the hell did I know about 'Jah'? I'd been listening to Elvis and Hank a few months earlier. It was still kind of embarrassing when the Dominican boys were playing reggae music and I didn't recognise any of the singers. I'd been listening to Radio One and had to pretend, 'Yeah! This guy's wicked, you know!' I had no idea who he was but I got away with it. I was always a good improviser.

Once I started to venture out I found my own route to all sorts of things. I had my first marijuana spliff when I was fifteen. Did that joint knock me out or what! I couldn't believe the effect it had on me. It was like a cloud closed in on my mind. My eyes watered and stung. I couldn't go home because my eyes were so red. I thought Mum would know and she'd crown me.

As usual, that unpromising start didn't deter me. The first spliffs I made myself looked like badly bandaged fingers. I hated smoking cigarettes, but marijuana was different. It wasn't like I did a lot, but at a party I would have a go and give it back, just to get in the mood. I could never take much of it.

Then I'd watch the dancing, the skanking, and had to learn that, too. I wasn't born to it, so I had to catch up. I earned the nickname 'Fallyman' – a follower, not a leader, always slightly behind the Dominican boys, who gave me the moniker. Their scene was so cool, fun and different. Strong. And I was desperate to find out more.

Inevitably, with how home was, that soon got me into trouble. My mum loved nice jumpers, ribbed and patterned ones, unisex not feminine, and it so happened that was one of the fashions at the dances I would go to. Naturally, because I didn't have the right styles myself, I'd delve into her wardrobe and borrow one. I'd put it back, dirty, smelling of smoke. She had June and me doing the laundry by now, so I'd end up washing it myself. But it was the borrowing without permission that she had a go about.

Her chastisements were just part of life for me now, though. I never thought to hit her back. I would stand and take it, looking impervious. Then one time I back-chatted her. She was taken aback.

'Who do you think you're talking to?'

'You,' I said, insolently. And this time when she started hitting me, I put my hand up and held her arm.

'Who you think ya holdin'? You think you a big man? You think you fighting me?'

'Nah, I'm not fighting, I just ain't letting you hit me no more.'

So she leant forward and clamped her jaws on my hand!

'You're biting me!' I yelled.

'Well, if I can't hit ya, I bite ya!'

'You're mad.'

This is my mother biting her own son. Eventually, the beatings became a thing of the past. The punishment became to go to my room. No dinner. Pretty soon I was banished more often than not. In a way, this was worse for both of us. It effectively removed me from her control, and it meant that I became a stranger in my own house, shut away from June and Mum for hours. Communications broke down almost completely between Mum and me and we started to lead even more separate lives. She was leaving me to my own devices and lost any track of what I was getting up to.

CHAPTER 6

The First Time

Southall could be a dangerous place in the late seventies. You could easily get bushwhacked on the streets for the colour of your skin. There were around 30,000 people of Asian origin in the area by now and huge tension had grown up between white and Indian and Pakistani youths, especially after a seventeen-year-old Sikh student, Gurdip Chaggar, was stabbed to death by local lads in June 1976. There were demonstrations against the police and authorities in the area that year, demanding more protection for ethnic minorities. The police station was a big focus for resentment. It was happening everywhere, not just Southall.

That August, the Notting Hill Carnival erupted in violence. A hundred coppers were hospitalised along with sixty carnival-goers. Seventeen black kids were charged with rioting, and yet only two were convicted. It fed fears we were being stitched-up – even though the riot started after a kid was arrested for pickpocketing in Westbourne Park and people piled in to protect him.

None of this stopped me going about satisfying my thirst for fun, though. If I was going out, Mum would warn me she was locking the door after a certain time. Sometimes, if I missed her curfew time, I'd end up sleeping in the garden shed. After a while, I found a way round that. I would sneak out of my bedroom window at Cranleigh Gardens, meet up with my Dominican mates, enjoy myself, and sneak back in by the same method when I felt like it.

Back then, Southall, and especially whiter districts such as Hanwell, could be tense places. I was almost fifteen when Alex Haley's TV mini-series 'Roots' was screened on the BBC in January 1977 and you could feel the mood of the area change almost overnight. The story opened black people's eyes to what had happened in times of slavery, hundreds of years earlier.

For a while, following the week when 'Roots' was first screened, it wasn't a good time for any white person to be out and about on the street at night. I wasn't alone in having no idea that white people had treated us like that. It depicted the struggle of generations of black people to earn their freedom from slavery, and showed how they were so badly mistreated by their 'owners'.

I vividly remember the scene where the African, Kunta Kinte, or Toby as the plantation families called him, was punished for persistently running away by having his foot chopped off with an axe. That was unbelievable. It didn't matter that it was a drama, not a documentary – it was based on actual events. I was so angry, and I wasn't the only one. 'Roots' was a complete shock to my system, and contrasted with what I knew domestically. I was aware that Saint-Martin, Anguilla and Dominica were former colonies and that my family's antecedents were slaves. When you watched the TV programme and saw how the old slave owners had worked to break the Africans away from their families, robbed them of their culture, divided and ruled, it was impossible not to consider the damaging impact that had had on Caribbean people. I tried to imagine how I'd have coped with the sort of restriction and punishment I saw in 'Roots'. I'm a stubborn individual. How would I have fared?

One thing I knew – you didn't learn about things like that at school, and that was another shock in itself. How come? Why weren't these things on the agenda? For weeks, 'Roots' was all we talked about in the playground. I've never known a TV programme have an effect like that one had.

In the end, though, for me, terrible as it was, it was in the past. There was no point in trying to take retribution now. But I knew black boys who roamed around at night, keen to beat up white guys because of what was shown in that programme, and for what probably happened to their ancestors. It made me realise that there was a struggle going on out there, and I had no choice about what side I was on.

My new rebellious attitude extended to every aspect of my life. Mum didn't know the half of it. In that crazy period, when I was approaching fifteen, I'd lost my virginity to a woman twice my age.

One Friday night I was at a small house party with cool music and dancing. My friend's girlfriend had a flat in the house, and I got talking to the woman who lived downstairs. She was a slim, pretty black woman with three kids and she had heard that I fancied myself as a cook.

Mum had started me down the cordon bleu route as a chore but by now I was experimenting with every sort of food in the kitchen – Italian, Chinese, West Indian, you name it, as long as it wasn't expensive. So when this woman asked me if I minded fixing up something for her and her three kids, I said no problem. I didn't know what she was after but I liked cooking anyway and thought it would be fun.

So the following evening, Saturday, I turned up at the woman's flat to cook for them. I went straight to the kitchen and prepared their meal, a simple dish of rice and meat, and sat down with them to eat it. It went down well. I don't suppose many kids my age could cook like that.

As we finished the meal my mate came down from his girlfriend's upstairs along with a few others, all of them older than I was. After a little while the woman suddenly piped up, 'Let's play some cards.'

'What kind of cards?'

'Strip poker.'

All seven of us lads in her flat were thinking, 'She's game!'

We started playing, a little apprehensively. Typically, when one of the boys lost, we just plain refused to take anything off. But when she lost a hand, she didn't give a damn. She just stripped off her clothes without batting an eyelid. Just imagine the boys – eyes on stalks, watching her. Then out of the blue she said, 'All right, who's going to warm my bed up tonight?' We all knew what that meant.

The older lads shouted, 'Yeah! I'll do it.' It didn't matter to them that she had three young kids in the same flat. She decided to make us draw lots with matchsticks – the winner got to 'warm her bed'. Everyone picked a matchstick – and I won. At fourteen I was the youngest and least sexually experienced of the lot; this woman was twenty-eight or so. I was shocked and embarrassed at the idea of getting under the covers with her, and yelled out, 'No! No! No! Do it again!' I hurried back into the kitchen to do the washing-up.

While I was doing the pots and plates I was asking myself why the woman wanted me. She was only a few years younger than my mum! I was big for my age, and black kids tended to be more sexually advanced than other teenagers, but I didn't feel ready, and had my mind made up that it wasn't for me.

Fate shifted the ground, though. I heard someone say, 'Come on, we're going back upstairs.' All the boys started off while I was finishing the dishes as fast as I could. So I was the last one left when I made for the exit. Before I could get out, the woman put her arm across the doorway to block me.

'Where you going?'

I didn't know what to do. All the older boys outside in the hallway were hollering, 'Gwan, Fallyman, gwan!!!' If there was ever a day I was nervous that was it.

She said, 'I want you, Paul.'

'What? Yeah?' She pulled me back inside and started to kiss me. Oh my God. I was a bit amateurish. She told me to slow down. It was embarrassing. My head was just going round and round.

Anyway, she put me on the bed and undressed me. I was just thinking, 'Gordon Bennett!'

Then she stripped off and I was wondering what the hell was happening. I didn't know the first thing about women but I was in heaven. She licked me from my toes all the way up and I was kissing her. And then she lay down on the bed . . . and suddenly something clicked and I froze.

I stopped, sat up and said, 'I can't do this, you know.'

'What?!' She was taken aback.

'No, I'm sorry,' I blurted, 'I can't do this!' And I put my clothes back on and ran out to my mates.

'What happened?' They were all amazed I'd come out so soon.

'I couldn't do it.' They ripped into me for that. It was Fallyman this and that. They laughed mercilessly.

The next day, all of us went up to that same house yet again. We were in the upstairs flat, drinking and smoking weed, and the woman from downstairs came up to me and said, 'Boy, what happened?' She was still puzzled about the previous evening.

'I dunno, I just couldn't do it.'

'Would you try it again?'

'Yeah, all right.'

This time, all my mates were on her case, too. She was dancing and rubbing up with all of them. The music was playing and she was full on them and they all thought they had a chance with her. What they didn't know was that she had given me the flat keys.

Eventually, we went downstairs. This time I was calmer. I just laid there and she took control, much like the night before, but all the way this time. Truly. I didn't know it was supposed to be like that. It was amazing. Afterwards I drifted off to sleep and when I woke up I felt like a king. She came in with a tray of orange juice and breakfast cereal, put on the television, and I sat up in bed and thought, 'This is what it's all about.'

The man in me was busting out, even at fourteen. My eyes were opened up. Soon after that, I started bunking off school. In February 1977 there was a teachers' strike and the school closed for a few days, but that wasn't why I stopped going. I took to hanging out every morning with my mates, either at their houses or mine – when Mum was out, obviously. We still weren't allowed friends round. Girls used to come along too and you'd either fool around or have sex with them wherever you could find around the house. I'd say, 'You can use my room, the toilet, the bath, but nobody in my mum's room.' Then we'd listen to music, smoke some weed. It beat maths and biology. I was thinking, 'This is wicked.' I felt I was making up for lost time.

Now, though, I needed money because I had things to spend it on. Raving all night, and chasing girls, came at a price. After a while I became crafty. If I was out and June and Mum were sitting in the front room watching telly, I would climb back in, take whatever money Mum had in her purse and be off without them noticing.

The worst incident was when I was looking in the dirty laundry basket for a spruce shirt to wear out and came across a little bundle. Inside was £340. 'Blood claat!' That was a lot of dosh in those days, especially to someone as much into style and fashion as I suddenly was. I went out with that windfall straight away, pocket burning, and bought designer shoes and clothes – even a Slazenger tennis racket! Some crazy stuff.

What I didn't know was that this was money Mum had allocated towards learning to drive and buying a car. She'd been saving for ages and put it there because she knew we'd look everywhere round the house when she was out, and anything would be fair game. So one day she goes looking for money, money looking for her!

One week went by, nobody noticed it had gone. Maybe nobody knows it's there. That's my head thinking. Two weeks has gone. The world's switched off. It couldn't be anybody's because nobody's said anything. Then it all blew up.

'Paul, I leave some money at the bottom of the basket! I want to know who take it! Did you see it?' Of course I cowered.

'I gonna ask you again, did you see it?'

'Unh-unh.'

'Paul, I ask you again! Did you take all the money?'

'Yes, Mum, yes.'

'Well, what you do with it?'

She couldn't believe I spent all that money for her car on clothes.

'You what? Show me where.'

All this time I'd hidden the clothes and stuff – worn them, taken them off and tucked them away again. Now I had to bring out every item in front of her.

'If you gonna do that,' she said, 'you not gonna enjoy the reward!'

With that she took a pair of scissors and cut up every last piece of designer clothing, shredding it to ribbons in front of me, even the shoes, slicing open the black tops. I bound them up with some tape we had in the house, which was white and looked ridiculous. So I took some black polish and applied it to the tape. I had to go to school like that – I must have looked completely stupid.

I don't know if I thought I'd get away with it. It's just that we never saw money like that and I thought it couldn't belong to anybody in our house. Honestly, who else would have money in your house but your mum? When I realised what she was intending to use the money for, I was ashamed of myself.

It must have hurt her and it was a nasty thing to do, but I enjoyed the money while it lasted. I showed off like I was one of the older boys. My whole bearing shouted, 'I can wear the gear too, you know.'

I was going wrong but we didn't talk over any of these things, ever. I'm sure that's why I was so repressed in my emotions and didn't let things out.

I was just wandering farther away from the straight and narrow. To tell the truth, one of the other things the Dominican kids had introduced me to was thieving. With them I'd started doing little break-ins every now and then, burglaries of houses and shops in the neighbourhood, just to get a little money.

CHAPTER 7

Cricket And The Missed Chance

Mum didn't pay much attention to what was going on in my education, but when she received a letter from the school saying that I'd missed virtually half a term she was outraged. They told it straight. My record was so poor I couldn't take any exams before I left in the summer at fifteen: 'Paul has missed so much, we can't offer him anything.' Report cards had been given to me to take home for her attention but I would never pass them on. Mum was occasionally asked to go in to the school, but I don't think she was aware how bad things had got with the truancy.

When I got into trouble, I would never tell her. She used to find out a long time afterwards. She used to ask me, 'Why didn't you tell me?' And I would tell her, honestly, 'I didn't want to worry you.'

Mum had entertained hopes for us academically. She wanted me to become either a policeman or a doctor. By now, she was leading by example, trying to better herself. She'd always been a smart woman with a good brain and she wanted to study to be a secretary. It would be a more reputable job, better salary, and the hours would be more regular. Secretarial work was what lots of women like her were getting into. So she'd gone to college, and I have to respect her for that. Now she was a secretary with ambitions for her own children. Well, police and me never got on down in Southall. No way was I going to be a doctor, either.

I was always getting into fights in the playground. I didn't pay much attention to anything but PE. I hated English but I didn't mind maths and science, and I really enjoyed chemistry with the Table of Elements and all the experiments. 'Don't touch that . . . boom!'

I enjoyed the social aspect of school, I really did, but all I ever wanted to be was a footballer, and I put all my eggs in that basket. I got on very well with the PE teachers, Mr Uphill and Mr Avery, who tried to help me a lot. They knew I was likely to get into trouble if I was left to my own devices in breaks, so they encouraged me to go to the gymnasium at lunchtime, where they let me play all sorts of sports and coached me on the technical side.

I'd play basketball, football, any sport going. I was good at most of them, especially cricket and athletics – I actually represented the county at 800m and 1500m and was quite tactically aware. I was the sort who stayed tight at the front, watched whoever posed a threat, and then had a big kick at the finish. I didn't have the proper gear, of course.

Boys from the athletics clubs had spikes and flash kit. I used to run in old football boots. Embarrassing!

The opposite sex was never far from my thoughts. I was about to run the 1500m at school once and a girl who fancied me said, 'Paul, if you win, I'll give you a kiss.' I needed no greater incentive and, unusually, set off like a bullet. I came to the line thinking it was the last lap and almost collapsed when I was told I had one more lap to go. I'd put everything in and had to dig really deep to get round and win it and claim that kiss.

It didn't take the promise of a snog to make me want to be a professional footballer, although I soon found out when I was a pro that you didn't have to go looking very far – the type of girl who likes celebrities can find a footballer in a dark nightclub without the use of SatNav. I think they like the toned body as much as the fame and the money, but lots of them are just looking for a trophy.

In 1977, football was the only thing as important to me as girls had suddenly become. It was always the game for me. I just had to make it – I wasn't going to let anything stop me. Mum will tell you, it's all I talked about.

No matter what was in front of me – a tin, a stone – it became a ball. It used to drive my mum mad. As I got older she was supportive of the sport but I don't think she really had high expectations of me. She thought it was good because it kept me out of trouble. She also knew the only way she could penalise me was to stop me going to football practice. I missed quite a few of those over the years. That's the only punishment I really felt.

I loved all sports really, and I was good at cricket, like my dad. I could bowl and field like lightning, but had less patience with batting, and was very raw. That was another reason for me to miss Dad's influence. I'm sure he would have encouraged me a lot more than Mum could or did. Middlesex County Cricket Club took an interest in me as a teenager, and my schoolteachers looked after me for the first stage of trials to join their Colts side of trainee professionals. The trials took place at Drayton Manor playing fields, right opposite my school.

They obviously tried out loads of kids around the county, but I was confident of success apart from one major thing. As usual, I was embarrassed by not having the right gear. You know when you're good, but you still feel bad because you don't have the full kit? These white kids had it all – shirt, pants, box, pads, boots, everything. Mum couldn't afford that and it wasn't a priority. So I'm wearing school pants – black, of course – and black plimsolls. Talk about standing out like a black thumb. The only thing white I had on was my school shirt. I started to bowl, and got to skittle a few batsmen out.

Then, when I was in the outfield, this geezer hit a ball and I ran round, grabbed it and threw it back towards the wicket without breaking stride – it's a typical fielding skill the pros practise all the time. I'd never been coached and it just came naturally to me. In one move I picked up the ball and threw it straight at the wicket – and hit it, bam! Even I was impressed.

Anyway, I was chosen and went straight on to the main

Middlesex trial, which was held on a cricket ground in Wembley. I got to bowl and we bowled them out.

'Get padded up.'

'What for?'

Batting, damn! This was more of a challenge to me because it wasn't about natural athleticism but trained technique. But I was kicking it that day, so eager, and did well enough with the bat for the fella from Middlesex to say, 'Paul, we'd like you to come back again on Saturday.'

I was getting closer to become a trainee pro – amazing. I really wanted this now. I was told to meet one of the PE teachers, who would take me there. Then it was up to me to do enough to get taken on. Not for the first time, Mum put a spanner in the works. It didn't help that I hadn't told her in advance about this final trial. Communication between us was never the best; I'd learned that she wasn't interested in any of my achievements, and I was coming and going as I pleased – for the most part, anyway.

Come Saturday morning, I'm rushing around, getting ready to leave.

'Where d'you think you're going?' Mum was on to me.

'I'm going to the trials, Mum.'

'Not before you do your chores.'

'But Mum, I have to be there in a few minutes.' Even as I said it I knew I was wasting my breath.

'I don't care.'

I couldn't believe it. I had to wash the dishes. I was cursing her. Your mum won't even realise that her child, her son, has this great chance, but if football was irrelevant to her, cricket was even lower down the pecking order. The trial meant nothing to her. I finished the dishes and, thinking I was going to be late, ran all the way down to the roundabout, which was about a twenty-minute walk away, where I was supposed to be picked up by the teacher. When I arrived, no teacher. I was thinking, 'He waited and waited and thought, "Paul's unreliable. He's not coming." And he's gone.' This was long before mobile phones remember. We had a telephone at home, but I wasn't organised enough to have taken the teacher's number.

So I sauntered back home, cursing, deeply upset, but when I got back in the house and looked at the time, I got a nasty jolt. I'd completely forgotten that I'd set my watch ten or fifteen minutes fast to avoid being late! By then, it actually was the time the teacher had said. In desperation, I ran back again. No car – he had definitely gone this time. I must have just missed him. It was just like the school coach a few years earlier – I hadn't learned my lesson. I don't suppose the teachers were very surprised, given my track record of indiscipline at school.

That was it. I didn't make that final trial and my one and only chance was gone. I'm confident if I had made it to the trial, in a few years I'd have been bowling bouncers – and dodging them, too – for the Middlesex first team. It would have been cool, maybe playing alongside their black stars Wilf Slack, Roland Butcher and West Indies pace bowler Wayne 'Diamond' Daniel. I doubt I would have faced the prejudice in cricket that I did in football, what with the world powers being West Indies and India at the time. Norman Cowans and Neil Williams are roughly the same generation as I am, and they both made it for Middlesex and England. When all of them played for Middlesex, they were affectionately known as the 'Jackson Five'.

The county's skipper in the late seventies and early eighties was a clever man – Mike Brearley. He handled them all with brilliant psychology. In any sport where I made it, I would have needed someone who was thoughtful and reassuring, like Brearley. I could have done with him at Chelsea in 1982. And I don't suppose my career at the crease would have ended with a crunching tackle from an opponent!

However close I came to joining Middlesex CCC, though, cricket was always secondary to football for me. Ian Botham played for Scunthorpe in the winter and Somerset in the summer – maybe I could have done the same thing.

I have to face the fact that it was my own fault I didn't have that opportunity with cricket, and no one else's. Mum didn't support my sporting dreams, though, and Dad was never there. Even when I was good at junior level in football and people were telling her, 'Your boy is good,' it made no difference. To me, it goes back to that inability to exhibit affection. She says she didn't want to see me disappointed. There I was, a kid like the others, and all of them had their parents there, backing them. I was the odd one out. I might have been the best boy out of the lot of them, but did I ever have my mother or father there to support me? Never. I was on my own and that really did affect me.

I was committed to football more than anything, and it showed. At fourteen and fifteen I used to play for Hanwell Celtic Under-18s, my little Sunday side. I used to represent the school, Brentside High, or the district on the same day. I had a game in the morning and a game in the afternoon. I don't know how I did it. It also meant a lot of kit-washing for June or me.

Hanwell had half the school team in it. We were 'The Untouchables' and won the league regularly. I found out later that Mum had kept a cutting from 1979 about the *Ealing Gazette* five-a-side tournament: 'Extra-time goals by Paul Canoville gave Hanwell the trophy,' it reads. That surprised me. She actually kept quite a few like that in a folder, so even though she occasionally tried to stop me playing football, she must have been quite proud of my exploits. She just never showed it.

The Hanwell Celtic manager was a bricklayer – Arthur Albert Pettifer, but everyone called him 'Dishy'. In common with all the other teenaged waifs and strays he had to mould into a football team, he took me under his wing.

Dishy was a small guy, a great wicketkeeper apparently, and a Tottenham fan. He liked a drink but was just as happy sitting down with a fag and a cup of tea. His son Charlie played for Hanwell at the same time as I did. Dishy was a typical chirpy Cockney type, full of wisecracks and stories – he needed a sense of humour with so many juvenile delinquents to deal with. He was a terrible driver and had no sense of direction, so getting to games in his van was always a laugh.

The things he had to put up with, though! Now and then when I was in trouble with the police or Mum and didn't have anywhere to stay, he and his family took me in or fed me for the night. It wasn't only me who got into scrapes. We were a tight-knit group of kids. If it wasn't me, there was always another of us in trouble with the law, and he often had to stop by the police station before a match to argue the case for bailing out someone. He didn't care what it was for. He distrusted authority almost as much as we did. I remember one match at the end of a season. We won to take the league title and straight after the final whistle Dishy drove down to the police station to drop one of our players back into custody!

Dishy was a really nice geezer, a proper character. He died in January 2003 at the age of seventy and the memorial service was properly attended. God bless him. A lot of us lads owed him for what he did for us. He was like the father I'd never known.

One incident neatly sums up the difference in his and Mum's approach towards me and my football. One Sunday morning, during the period when Mum and I were leading virtually separate lives at Cranleigh Gardens, I'd been out raving all night and didn't have my boots to play football the following morning.

Dishy picked me and the lads up in his van and I told him I needed to stop off at home for my stuff so – as usual

– I had to give him directions to my house. But when I got there and knocked on the door, Mum wouldn't even answer it – she'd taken my keys from me as a punishment for disobeying her. So I was having to shout to her through the letterbox while Dishy and the boys looked on. This is embarrassing, man. The lads in the team are all my schoolmates. Everyone would hear about this.

'Mum, can I come in?'

'Where you bin?' She's furious with me.

'At a party. I need my football boots.'

'Didn't you know you need your boots last night?' She was right of course. I hadn't considered that.

'Please Mum.'

'If it's a party you bin to, you better go back to it!'

She wasn't going to let me in, but I needed my things for football. So I just shouldered open the front door, ran to my room for the boots and bolted out again. It was a terrible thing to do to your own house but I didn't think about that – I was a man on a mission.

I was walking back to the van with my kit when the lads started kicking off about something going on behind me. I looked around and there was a crazy-looking woman, out of nowhere, running towards me yelling!

The lads were going mental as I jumped inside in the nick of time and Dishy pulled away as fast as he could.

'Who the hell was that woman?' They were all shocked.

'That,' I announced, 'is my mother.'

'Your *mum*?'

Mum had got so fed up with me stopping out that she'd

already dismantled my bed and removed it from my room, leaving only a mattress. Now I'd knocked the door down. Of course, looking back that story shows me how I expected everyone else to fit around my lifestyle, including my exasperated mum. It also suggests I was not taking football seriously enough to give up my all-night raving. Football came first, but only just.

Back then I played centre-half. If you're the biggest at school, like I was, that's where the teachers decide you will play. End of story. I didn't mind. It suited me then. You couldn't get past me. Don't even think about trying to outrun me. And when I jumped for a header, I really jumped.

Like a lot of kids who grew up in the seventies, I loved watching the Brazilians. When I was a pro at Chelsea, Mum was always banging on about me watching videos of them play. It was hard to play samba football when big Mel Sterland was kicking your arse though! What I liked was that wherever they were on the pitch, Brazilians weren't afraid to play their game, even in defence. I empathised with that risk-taking.

I always liked to dribble with the ball, never mind the danger. I would collect the ball in the centre-back position and take on players right from my own box. I remember so vividly one game for Brentside School. We were playing another Ealing borough side, Faraday Comprehensive. It was a really tough school in general, and had achieved some notoriety in 1977 when a BBC TV 'Panorama' fly-on-the-wall documentary exposed how difficult it was to handle troublesome school-leavers of my age. As at Brentside, the PE teachers channelled some of that testosterone into a tasty school football team, and they were big rivals for us.

Our games were always more or less a league showdown, and very tight. Some local youth football organisers were in the crowd watching, because most of the Hanwell Celtic team was made up of players from our two schools. So when I handballed in our area and gave away a penalty, I was mortified. They went 1–0 up and it was down to me.

After that I was trying so bad to get this goal back because I felt I'd let everyone down. I swear Lord, three times I got the ball, took on and beat everybody, but couldn't hit the net. What made it worse was that Faraday's keeper was our goalie on a Sunday. Could I score against him? No!

I don't know if he was brilliant, telepathic or I was a poor shot, but he saved it every time. Our manager said, 'Paul Canoville – damn, if you ever had a finish, you would be unbelievable.' At least I was beginning to get noticed.

Still Mum didn't see any real value in my obsession with football. Once she had worked as a secretary for a while and had a little more money coming in, she tried to get me to take piano lessons every Wednesday. I've always been into music, and the teacher said I had the fingers for piano.

'What music do you like?' he asked me.

'I like jazz,' I replied.

And when he played some jazz, I was blown away. 'Boy, wicked!' But my football team had a cup game the following Wednesday, and it was that or piano.

'June, just tell Mum I went to piano,' I instructed.

I knew the lessons were costing Mum precious money, but I went to the game. I actually went to piano lessons just twice. Don't get me wrong, I love music, but football took first place every time.

Mum had still nurtured hopes that I would gain some sort of academic achievement to get my life back on track, and the school letter about my absenteeism was the last straw for her. With me knocking around with kids she didn't like, going out to dances and standing up to her, she'd had enough, and felt that she could no longer control me. So in desperation she took me down to my uncle, also my godfather, in Acton, for him to look after me. She hoped that being a man and a relative, he would make me see sense, but it was a ridiculous idea. He was a nice enough fella but he couldn't control me – no one could. I was beyond that, mutinous and surly as I was then. I was soon back in the family home, leading my life separately from June and Mum.

Of course, once I left school at fifteen, I was under no restrictions during the day. I was hanging around with my crew, doing whatever I wanted and getting into more trouble with the police – and not just the petty crime that I was occasionally party to on nights out with my mates. Southall was at boiling point.

London's black youth was in the grip of the so-called

'Sus Law', whereby police could stop anyone on the street and search them on the basis of 'suspicion' that they might have committed a crime. That year it seemed as though they stopped any teenaged black kid they saw. They had a massive crackdown, stopping me and my mates all the time. Their targeting seemed so colour-coded. Figures were published that backed up the hunch on the street – 44 per cent of those stopped in London for Sus were black-skinned, although we represented just 6 per cent of the capital's population. It led to a lot of resentment and mistrust of the legal system, especially the cops, and was abolished after the Brixton riot in 1981. Of course, by making the occasional break-in, I had less reason than most to complain about harassment by the authorities.

It was around this time that a new man came into Mum's life, Rendvill Richardson. Mum might have hoped differently but his sudden arrival on the scene did nothing to stabilise things as far as I was concerned. Rendvill really cared for my mother and looked after her very well, and that was what she had needed for some time. But he was hopeless with children – us, anyway. He never showed any respect or liking for June or, especially, me. We were like an unwanted accessory that came with a car he'd just bought. He had none of Henry's charm or small talk either, and spoke about his work – at Ford's near Slough – all the time. I couldn't tolerate him but kept that from Mum – just as I kept all feelings from her.

CHAPTER 8

A Child Is Born

Sometimes in life you stumble casually into a situation that changes you for ever. I am fatalistic about events anyway, never really thinking too much about the consequences before I get into things too deep. *Que sera, sera*. Deal with it afterwards. That was the case when I got involved with Christine in 1978. It started because we were both going to raves run by Fatman Sound.

She was tall and slim, a little older and much more outgoing and confident than I was. I knew her brother. He had a reputation as a bad boy, so you didn't muck about with her. I think she traded a bit on his name and that may have been the source of her self-assurance. I'd seen Christine around at a few raves locally and had even danced with her on a couple of occasions. She was nice looking and strong minded. I was instantly attracted to her, but she always seemed full of herself and I wasn't the most confident kid. So I took my time before I asked her out. I wasn't expecting her to say yes but to my surprise she did. We hit it off and saw a lot of each other. I was sixteen years old and in love. Christine appeared to feel the same way. She was very intense and seemed to want me all to herself. She barely acknowledged anyone else when I was around.

We had sex three, maybe four times, but the next thing I knew she was standing in front of me with the most unbelievable news.

'I'm pregnant,' she said.

I was shocked and absolutely petrified. Then I gathered my thoughts.

'All right. I've got to meet your mum, right?'

I went round to Christine's mother's and I was terrified all over again. Her mum was all right with me, though. I said I wanted to be there for the both of them, despite my lack of standing in the world at the time. When Christine got a flat in Hanwell, not too far away, I moved in there with her. Young as I was, I wanted to commit to our child. I knew how I'd missed out not having Dad around and it was not my intention to repeat that.

Having a pregnant girlfriend wasn't the only way my lifestyle was catching up with me. All my chickens were coming home to roost.

One afternoon Mum came home from work and got the shock of her life. June told her that I'd been arrested. The police had been there and found a stolen television in a cupboard in my room.

To be truthful, Mum was desperate and ashamed – 'How could Paul take a television and bring it up to my house!' She'd striven to be respectable all her life, got herself a proper job, now this.

It got worse. The TV was nicked from our elderly Irish neighbours. Nice people. Mum got on well with them before this happened. It was an opportunist crime. I'd been involved in a few like it.

The Dominicans and I had spotted that they would occasionally forget to take the key out of their front door, and one day when they made that mistake, one of our crew stole it. Two of us waited a couple of days till we thought things had settled down, and then went in to clean up. We took the television, stereo, a few other things and left. What we didn't realise was that we'd walked straight into a trap – and it soon sprang shut on me. It didn't occur to me to question why they hadn't changed the lock, even though their front door key had been missing for two days.

We found out afterwards that the Irish couple had reported the key missing and been advised by the police not to change the lock. They put the house under surveillance and so knew exactly what we had done and where we'd stashed the loot.

It was incredibly stupid. I felt bad that it was so close to home. Mum was humiliated. I had to go to juvenile court over that. I wouldn't tell them my mate's name, or who did what. I went twice in total.

While I was awaiting trial, Mum said she couldn't cope

with me so I had to go into a remand place for young offenders. In actual fact, I thought I was Mr Big, and reckoned it would only enhance my reputation on the street. I think it was in north London because I remember they heard I was heavily into football and some of us were taken to a Spurs game. I suppose it was part of their policy to give kids a glimpse of what they would miss out on in life if they spent it behind bars.

I found the place and the people really daunting – not at all cool, as I'd thought. We all slept in a dormitory and one black guy, a young boy, had violent nightmares every night. He wasn't schizo but he'd be shouting, 'Get off! Get off me!' as if he was being attacked. He was obviously one deeply disturbed individual.

An Irish boy who was there looked not a day over eleven.

'Why you in here?' I asked one day.

'Selling guns.'

'What!?'

The words came out just as if he'd said he had stolen milk. I was shocked to the core. There I was thinking that I was a bad boy because I'd done a few burglaries, but these kids were gunrunning with Uzis – serious! I was straight on the phone to Southall.

'Mum, please come and take me out. I swear to you I won't do anything again.'

'I don't know, Paul, but you just don't want to listen.'

'I'm begging you. I won't give you any trouble. Please get me out of here.'

That was the only time I really felt we were close up to

that point. I realised she was getting me out because she missed me as well. But that place shook me up, it really did. Coming on top of the other reasons, I realised I had to knuckle down and get real.

Everything came to a head in the summer of 1979 – me and the cops, Christine and the pregnancy, Mum and Rendvill. I was now seventeen, but still far from emotionally equipped to handle it all. Then in June that year, just before I faced the magistrates, my first beautiful baby, Natalie, was born. I was really apprehensive beforehand. I'd never witnessed a birth before. People kept telling me about the blood and how painful it would be for Christine. It wasn't far from the truth, but then Christine could be very volatile and wasn't one to hold back from doing what she wanted, including screaming. The whole hospital could hear what she was going through trying to bring little Natalie into the world. When she was born it was incredible to think I was a father, and the baby was so sweet. I was ecstatic.

To show how closed our family was emotionally, I have to tell you I kept all of this to myself, pretty much. Mum knew nothing about it. In fact, I didn't ever let Mum meet any of my girlfriends. She had never made any of my male friends feel welcome, so I never took girls home. I didn't feel any need for her to know what I was up to.

When I reflect back on those years, I don't know what I was doing. I was like a soldier with no mission, a pilot with no training. Dad had never been there at all, and Mum had never been the type to talk over intimate things like feelings or relationships. I had no guidance, I just blundered along all the time, a child leading a man's life. Even after significant things happened to me, I had no one to confide in or ask for advice so I could try to avoid repeating the mistake. The way I was, a virtual stranger in Mum's home, maybe I didn't think I needed anyone.

People may think it strange not to tell my own mother about my first child. Yet when she did find out, she never minded at all. It was no big deal to have a 'babyfather' son. Her attitude was like a lot of West Indian people's – the boys can go out and have children and you don't worry about them, but if the girls get banged up, it's a big drama!

I did introduce June to Christine, though, and to all my girlfriends. But she was a year younger and less worldly than I was. Even though I decided not to tell Mum about Natalie, she found out soon enough, of course, and not in the way I would have liked.

In the meantime, I still had to face the magistrates and the prospect of a more extended detention. Understandably for someone so proud, Mum found the whole burglary thing difficult to deal with and was frustrated that I never listened to her. One person who helped me a lot, however, was Mum's friend from our church in Southall, Stephanie Caton. I always called her Auntie Stephanie. She was one of the few actual friends my mum had. She was raising four girls without a man around the place and the two of them would help each other out babysitting and the like. Stephanie was a rock and very calm and straightforward about things. She always had words of wisdom and seemed a lot more understanding and supportive than Mum.

Mum simply didn't have Auntie Stephanie's patience in those days. Auntie Stephanie would sit down and talk seriously to me about my life – something Mum never did. But at the time – not that I considered it – Mum needed buoying up as much as I did. Stephanie accompanied me to court for moral support. The places she's been with me, she never had to go with her own children!

She was there when I was sentenced by the magistrate to serve a few months in Borstal. I'll never forget, Stephanie sat down with me and laid it on the line: 'You know, Paul, you want to be a professional footballer. But if you keep on like this, you're going to wind up at Her Majesty's Pleasure, not Wembley Stadium, and you won't be able to play no football.'

It might not have sunk in straight away, but I didn't forget. Even now, I still never go by Southall without dropping by Auntie Stephanie's. She's a special woman.

I'll say one thing for Borstal – it gave me the chance to concentrate on my biggest love in life. They had a football team and I played for them. One of the screws said to me, 'When you're out, you should go for a trial at Chelsea.'

'Chelsea?' I said. 'That racist mob?'

Like most black people, I was primed about the club's reputation then for having a lot of bigots among its supporters, and not much time for people of my background in general. By 1979 other clubs, notably West Ham, West Bromwich Albion, Leyton Orient and Nottingham Forest, had had black players wearing their shirts for a number of years. Chelsea had had one black player on their staff, the goalie Derek Richardson, but he never made his first-team debut, and left for QPR.

It was one of the nearest big clubs to Southall and various people knew friends of friends who were linked to their academy. There were rumours on the street that the reserve and youth coaching staff at Stamford Bridge thought Afro-Caribbean footballers were too faint-hearted to perform on a cold winter's night at Oldham. Prejudice was said to be strong on the terraces, too. I'd never been to the ground, but I'd heard about players such as Laurie Cunningham and Luther Blissett being hooted at and the rest, and on the TV you heard a different crowd reaction when they touched the ball.

Chelsea, with more than their fair share of hooligans causing trouble at grounds round the country, always seemed to have a lot of skinhead supporters, too. Rightly or wrongly, people like me associated that look with the kind who beat up people of colour, and who voted National Front. We knew in the mid-seventies that right-wing political organisations such as the Front were deliberately targeting football hooligans, and their disgusting magazines were openly sold outside Stamford Bridge on match days. That's the baggage Chelsea had in my eyes.

The Borstal officer was obviously good at football predictions, though. (I hope he did the Pools.) His words stuck, and I seemed to be on a collision course with Chelsea after that.

Borstal was good for me in other ways. It was out in Ashford, which made a break, and it was very disciplined. It helped bring some order to my personal chaos. I learned how to fold an entire set of clothes into a small square. Your bed had to be sharp. You slopped out. And you had to queue for everything.

I soon learned the price of disobeying the screws on that little rule. We had to line up in the yard outside to use the bathroom and we didn't have the warmest clothes on – I just had a vest. I really feel the cold anyway and was way back in the line, so I decided to stroll cockily to the front and push in. What a mistake. Straight away I was pulled out and slapped in solitary confinement for a week. That was horrible. Don't let people tell you they're soft on young offenders.

Of course, I queued after that. Borstal instilled more discipline into me and deterred me from a serious life of crime. It was being cut off that I couldn't stand. I didn't like being away from my new daughter, family and friends, but most of all I hated being deprived of my personal freedom. I suppose it was a sort of preparation for professional football. I'd never had a job that required regulating your lifestyle like detention did.

Another long-term effect of my burglary was that Mum

was so crushed by what I'd done to her poor neighbour that she decided to move right away from Southall – her home since 1960. She planned to move twelve miles down the M4 to Slough, where Rendvill had a house.

The old Southall she knew had changed a lot anyway in the two decades since Mum had arrived. Racial conflict had exploded on the streets in April 1979. Local black and Asian youth were appalled that the police firstly allowed a National Front meeting to take place at Southall Town Hall on St George's Day, and then created an exclusion zone around the building so it could go ahead without interruption. Nice! Thousands of anti-racist demonstrators attacked the police perimeter with bricks and bottles. Three hundred were arrested. A couple of dozen cops were hospitalised, but the event is mostly remembered because a white demonstrator, Blair Peach, was killed when he was hit over the head with a police baton.

I had other things to think about when I came out of Borstal. I had made a commitment to Natalie and Christine and expected to pick things up again after my enforced absence. I couldn't wait to see them and as soon as I could I went round to the flat. It was great but I needed to get one major thing straight with Christine. We were in the bedroom and I asked her, 'What happened to you while I was inside? You never came to see me or wrote.' I know she was young and had her hands full with Natalie, but I'd written, asking her about our baby and how she was getting on, all unanswered.

'I was just busy,' she said. It seemed to me she wasn't bothered at all.

Then it dawned on me: perhaps there was somebody else on the scene.

Perhaps that's what she meant by being 'busy'. I confronted her with my suspicions.

She didn't seem concerned but I was just blown away by her lack of denial and my choice was instant. 'You know what, fuck off, if that's how you are!'

I couldn't believe she'd do that. It knocked me for six. I was so hurt it was unbelievable. Mum hadn't moved yet, so I just went back there. Damn you, Christine, treating me like that. There was no way back as far as I was concerned. And that's unfortunately why I didn't really get to know Natalie. Mind you, looking back on those events, I was hardly the perfect catch, was I?

Christine didn't let it go, though. She phoned up our house, told Mum about Natalie, cussed and ranted, demanding I return to her. Christine was a tough teenager and she wasn't going to give up easily. Mum would answer the phone and it was for me.

'Who is this?'

'Christine.'

'Leave him alone.'

'Your son wants to be with me.'

It was an awful situation for all of us, tempers flared and lots of unreasonable things were said.

Christine thought it was just Mum stopping me going back to her and Natalie, so she took it out on her, but I wasn't ever going back. Baby Natalie was mine, and I regret not being there for her. But I still don't know why Christine felt so determined to pursue me.

It wasn't just those two relationships that suffered as a consequence. I tell you, something snapped permanently deep inside me on that day at Christine's. At such a tender age I wasn't equipped to deal with the shock and it turned me against all women and closed my respect for them. From then on I treated girls as conquests, and the more the merrier. I craved the intimacy and closeness and to hell with the consequences. If a woman came on to me, I didn't think twice. If we carried on seeing each other, I didn't give two tosses how I behaved at the end of it. I never wanted to experience the intense heartbreak and shock I had felt with Christine ever again. The slightest bad thing my woman did, no matter how lovey-dovey we were, I backed off, left straight away without a word.

Often they wouldn't know exactly what was happening. I'd move on, meet somebody else. When I got bored there, that's when I came back and said, 'Did you miss me?' I always had that charm. I was sweet, I'd make a few funny little jokes, and I was back. I'd never actually ended it, so I thought I could swan back in when I felt like it. It wasn't fair and I knew it.

I don't know if it was how I was brought up, or because I didn't have a man to show me you can't do that to women, but it took years and many more broken relationships for me to realise the error of my ways, behaving in such a callous manner. I know now that everyone deserves to be treated honestly and you need closure when things go wrong between two people. I just wasn't mature or unselfish enough to handle that concept at the time.

CHAPTER 9

Finding My Feet

After the twin shocks of Borstal and the break-up with Christine, I decided to try to earn an honest living and get myself a job. I worked in shops mostly, not very well paid of course, and I never kept one for long. After a while I had enough money to buy some new electricals for my room at Mum's – a hi-fi, a television. Then one day I came home to find it had all been stolen, taken out through the window. How's that for comeuppance! I'd never owned anything like that before. Now I appreciated how it felt to have it taken away. But I wasn't disgusted at the people who'd done it.

After Christine, my affairs with the opposite sex were getting complicated. It was nothing for me to have a number of girlfriends on the go at the same time, moving between them as I saw fit. I'd become a 'gyallist', a womaniser.

And relations were no better with Mum. She had developed this idea that I was making things hard for her deliberately to get back at her. When I had completed her shame by bringing lawbreaking so close to home, she had made a firm commitment to join Rendvill in Slough. When she eventually moved in with him in 1979, she naturally expected June and I to join her, but only June did. Mum could be amazingly unrealistic and blind to reality. I'd just moved on, and I hadn't changed my mind about Rendvill, while she was still hoping that he would provide that positive male influence. One big happy family! What she didn't realise was that the man she chose would deliberately drive a wedge between us.

Whether it was me being stubborn and rebellious, or Mum not putting it to me in the right way, I don't know, but straight away I refused to go to Slough. I just didn't fancy the sound of it. I'd never been the type to discuss my feelings. We weren't that sort of family. For a while I stayed with friends and looked for work.

I was completely adrift a lot of the time. For a while I lived rough on the street, in a hostel for the homeless, and in friends' homes. It was freezing cold, depressing, a struggle from day to day, and dangerous. The street loves vulnerable people. I found that out in a hostel I was staying in that winter. I got to know a girl in there, a white girl, really nice. But one day, I was taken completely by surprise when the supervisor confronted me saying he was about to call the police to arrest me – for the suspected rape of this white girl. That's what she had told him.

Understandably, he was being really heavy with me, but I knew I was completely innocent. I would never have done anything of the sort and there was no way in hell I was going to let that slur stick. When I stood firm, the supervisor checked the story and it all came apart. The girl eventually admitted she was making the whole thing up. She'd been put up to it by a friend who had taken a dislike to me for some reason. He was also staying in the shelter and was a right nasty bit of work. There are all sorts of damaged people in hostels for homeless people. You have to watch yourself all the time. I was sorely shaken up by the rape accusation, and so relieved when the supervisor heard the truth. I didn't blame the girl. She was a weak person who was put up to it and didn't know any better.

All of this gave me a different perspective on life, and sympathy for the downtrodden, those people society leaves behind. I knew what it was like to have nothing and nobody – nowhere to stay, nobody to sit down and talk to, nobody to help turn your life around.

Although I had lots of friends, I wasn't the type to form really strong bonds with others. I wasn't there for them through thick and thin. But wherever I was, however bad, I always kept in touch with Mum, and sometimes at weekends she would come up to town looking for me, chasing me up.

One evening I was on Ealing station waiting for a train when who should be on the platform but Mum, who was supposed to be miles away in Slough. She wasn't even looking for me that time. She was on her way to visit a friend. What made it weirder was that she'd got on the wrong bus, been taken to Hammersmith and had to get another one back to Ealing station. The Lord moves in mysterious ways . . .

I was in a right state and she could see it straight away. She asked me if I wanted to go home with her and I said yes. The only problem was that 'home' meant Rendvill's house in Slough. But I didn't feel I had a choice – it was so horrible living like I was trying to live. It wasn't the happiest time of my life, but at least we were together again. In trying to avoid moving in with him, I'd hit rock bottom.

Once in Slough, it was clear I needed to earn some money. June always says I don't know what work really is and she has a point. I went back to working in high-street shops and then I got a job in the Mars factory. I never stuck at anything for long.

The funny thing at Mars was the induction day. The manager told all us new recruits to help ourselves, eat as much chocolate as we liked. We noshed on bars until we felt sick, which was apparently his intention. It was supposed to cure you of the temptation to eat or steal the products, and it worked with me.

Just once I was justified in not sticking around at a job, and that was when I encountered outright prejudice while working in a shop. A woman there had a problem with black people. She was so disrespectful. She would talk about me like I was her slave, and used to call me a 'little nig nog'. One day, for revenge, I went out and bent the spokes on her bicycle. She got me dismissed.

I could probably have contested the action but, typical of me, and I was ignorant of wider events in the world.

In 1976 the Race Relations Act had made it easier for bosses to be taken to court for victimising people because of their race, creed or colour. I'd obviously been victimised by her with the language she used, and I'd been sacked, but the Act made it a civil offence, not a crime, so I'd have had to take up the case myself rather than involve the police. I don't think Britain was ready for teenagers like me to prosecute their bosses.

It's ironic that Mum claimed later that she moved in with Rendvill almost entirely to try to stop me going off the rails, and for no other reason. She didn't care for him as much as he cared for her, that's 100 per cent certain, although I don't know if he knew it. She desperately wanted this male role model for me, but he was no model I could relate to. She thought I'd look up to Rendvill, respect him and stop my shenanigans. She may have been right in principle, but she couldn't have got it more wrong in practice.

Rendvill worked for Ford's in Uxbridge and was totally wrapped up in his job. He would drink all weekend from Friday until two o'clock on Sunday, then finished. All week he wouldn't touch a drop. Mum found him reliable, and she needed that. He had a lot of good qualities for her, but he had no tolerance of June and me. He had children from another relationship but he didn't ever seem to deal with them. He seemed to have forgotten what it was like to be young. He gave us no leeway and was protective of our mum against us – his only redeeming feature in my eyes was that he genuinely cared for her and treated her well.

I didn't always feel like she was on our side, either, but I guess she was doing what she felt was right at the time to keep a roof over our heads and the lid on the pressure cooker.

Rendvill's house may have been in Slough but, no word of a lie, it could have been the Arctic Circle the way he was with the central heating. I'm a man who likes his warmth, and with Rendvill, if you had the radiators on past a certain time or over a certain heat, he hit the roof. He allowed the heating to be on from six to ten in the evening and in the morning from five, when he got up for work, till eight.

Perfectly normal but, let me tell you, that didn't suit the hours I was keeping at the time at all. I was constantly cold in that house. It didn't matter to me that he was paying the bills when I was shivering in my bed or arriving back from raving to a home that was like a walk-in fridge. Looking back on it now, I can see it was another case of expecting to get my way and getting everyone to fit in with my lifestyle.

As an adolescent I was not helping myself. I had this attitude where I would cheek you back. It didn't go down well with many people and it certainly didn't delight Rendvill. I also made it clear that, although I wouldn't recognise my dad if he passed me in the street, I sure as hell knew that Rendvill was no father figure.

Fights – fists, feet, everything – could start over the tiniest disagreement. Once Mum saw how bad things were with Rendvill and me, she knew the 'role model' idea was out the window and didn't see any point in staying with him long term. We planned that I would find a flat and move in and she would come and join me later.

Things gradually came to a head in the worst possible way for me one day early in 1980. I guess it was a Saturday and Mum was at work. Rendvill and I had a big bust-up about something. I don't remember what it was but it ended with me storming out.

When Mum finished work, Rendvill was there to meet her.

'You know what?' he announced. 'Your son has found a room, so he says, and he's left home – packed all his things and gone.'

Remember, this is a mother who was secretly planning to leave her partner and move in with her son. Now, according to what Rendvill told her, I'd jumped ship on my own and hadn't had the decency to tell her where I was going.

When I came back to pick up some things later that night, she just blanked me completely, obviously angry with me for doing my own thing. I didn't understand that in the slightest. All I could think was that she didn't care what had happened and was siding with Rendvill against me. I felt completely rejected. What I didn't realise was that Rendvill hadn't even told her about the bust-up. So she was furious with me – she thought I was leaving her, without warning, just like that. And when I saw her looking daggers, let me tell you, I didn't feel disposed to talk to her at all.

Of course it was all nonsense, and she was naïve enough to believe Rendvill. She didn't even question him. What kind of man tries to separate a son from his mother? I will never forgive him for that.

The whole situation was totally avoidable. If I'd just spoken to her then and there, explained what had happened, it would have been different. But what I felt when I thought Mum was rejecting me in such a way made that impossible, and scarred me badly.

Once again I had to find somewhere to live. And it was winter. But I was always resourceful and resilient. I could stand hardship if my stubborn head said I had to, and I quickly sorted out some accommodation.

About a month later a neighbour, Cynthia, let on to Mum where I was – 'You know Paul's sleeping in that old abandoned car up the road?' More humiliation for my proud mother, but I already had other immediate concerns on my mind.

The weird thing is that when everything was going wrong personally, my football career had reached lift-off. All the time I was living in a beat-up car, I was playing semi-professional football for Hillingdon Borough, and they were a brilliant club for me.

I had switched clubs from Hanwell because of travelling from Rendvill's house in Slough all the way down to Southall, nearly fifteen miles and a nightmare on public transport. It was just getting too much. Hillingdon was half the distance and easier to get to. I went to West Drayton, and took a train from there.

My first coach at Hillingdon was Colin Barnes, the manager of the youth team at the time. He was the one who looked at my pace, dribbling and attacking instincts (anywhere on the pitch!) and instantly converted me from the centre-half I had been at school to the left-winger I would be for the rest of my playing days. They wanted me to try my skills in a less dangerous area, well away from my own penalty zone. 'Why don't you start from halfway and try again,' was how they put it.

I owe him a debt of gratitude, although I didn't take too much notice of it at the time. To me, it was just a case of taking on players, wherever I was, although the distance to goal was obviously a little shorter now! One thing being a centre-half gave me in my later career was that I was never frightened to track back and make a tackle. I never minded that side of the game, as some wingers did.

Throughout 1980, and especially after I'd been thrown out of Rendvill's house, Borough was one of the few stabilising influences in my life. The higher standard of football meant I had to check my excesses (at least a little) and I made a few good friends who looked out for me there. Derek Harriott was one. One evening, during my exile from Rendvill's, he took me to one side.

'Can I have a word about, er, personal hygiene?' he asked quietly.

Apparently, some of my team-mates had complained

that I turned up for training exuding terrible body odour. He had been given the thankless task of asking me to do something about it. I respected the sensitive way he handled it, but I desperately wanted to tell him why I was like that – I just couldn't get the words out for shame. I wanted to tell him Hillingdon Borough was the only place I could ever get a proper wash down – and only *after* a workout.

Mum claims the BO is genetic – but you can't tell me a regular shower wouldn't help, and you don't get a bathroom in a beat-up old Toyota. When I think back, I was mad sleeping there, but I hadn't developed my usual list of local friends and girlfriends to stop round with yet in Slough. And I was too proud to return to Rendvill's. I caught a terrible cold staying in that car. It mashed up my chest, which wasn't good for my fitness levels, and after a while things were sorted out and I went back to Mum's.

After converting to the wing, I was picked for the Hillingdon Borough first team, which played in the Southern League – two tiers below the Football League – and was managed by Alan Bassett. They were a very good side. Three years before I joined them, they'd dumped Fourth Division Torquay out of the FA Cup on their own ground. In the league we were up against teams such as Dorchester and Dartford, so there were proper away days, much like a professional would have. I couldn't afford proper boots, so Alan took me to buy some and I remember exactly what they were – £70 Patricks. The new kangaroo leather was just coming in and these were beautiful soft boots. Fantastic. Alan was looking after me. He did a lot for me, that manager.

On the field, I needed a different kind of assistance. I was one of the youngest guys in Borough's first team. Don't get me wrong – a lot of players in that league were ex-pros. There were some good boys, tough cookies, and believe me, I used to get these legs kicked. A young black boy with a big Afro like I had was a rarity back then, especially on teams we came up against in less cosmopolitan parts of the south. I would get some pretty bad abuse from them, but I stuck at it.

I was still playing in the youth team for fun as well as in the first team for money. I enjoyed them both, but my preference was to play with my own age group. Football was football really, although the money obviously came in handy. But then the first-team coach laid down the law.

'Tell you what,' he told the youth bosses, 'this is a valuable player. He's staying in the first team.'

They never saw me again in the youth team. A few of the kids my age were not happy. 'Oh yeah? Big time now are we?' It didn't sit well with me, either. I just wanted to play the game all the time.

'Who are the youth team playing?' I'd keep on. 'Can I not play?'

'No, Canners, you can't.'

'Damn, man. If I play, I know we're going to win.'

'But if you get injured, you're no damn use to us.'

I just had to take it on the chin. I'd graduated to playing with the big men only, and I was getting paid. I was in and out of 'proper' jobs outside of football, so to be paid to do what you loved was amazing. It was persuading me I could make a living from the game. I sure as hell wasn't making it anywhere else! Once that train of thought came along, I didn't give a damn about any other work, much to my mum's despair. She still needed convincing it was the life for me. And to tell you truth, so did I at times.

On occasions, things happen to make you wonder why you bother. Soon after I joined them in late 1979, I played for Borough in the FA Trophy. It's a prestigious competition at that level and this was a big game. Early on, I roasted one defender with a move even Mum would've approved of. I was tight on the line in the corner, and I was holding the ball, holding the ball, and the geezer wasn't letting me go anywhere, until I back-flipped it past him, ran on to it and left him for dead with the words, 'See you later.' Maybe that was wrong.

When I next went near him, he cussed me, 'You black cunt.' That was the first time I really felt, 'Whoa, this is bad,' because he was a huge grown man and I was only seventeen. I couldn't believe it. He kept on with the abuse whenever we got to close quarters.

'Yeah, go on,' he said. 'Get that ball, and I'll fucking chop your legs off, you black cunt.'

I was frightened and he knew it. For the first time I was being intimidated and put off my game. When a big old geezer's chatting like that, you've got to be scared. The great benefit of a club like Hillingdon Borough was that they had other black players in the team, people I could turn to for support.

So I called in the cavalry – Francis Joseph, only a couple of years older than I was, but a lot more self-confident. He was a right lad, that boy – big suede coat and always a huge cigar. He was like Shaft. A few months later, in January 1980, he left to join Wimbledon as a striker, and carved out a great eleven-year pro career with Brentford, Reading, Gillingham and finally Barnet in 1991.

'Canners. You all right?' That was Francis. He could see from my face that I wasn't.

'That geezer just said he's gonna "fucking chop my black legs off".'

'What?' So now it was a case of Francis having it out with him.

'Tell him what you told me, mate,' I said.

'What? What?' The geezer's acting all innocent now.

'Don't you try that again!' said Francis.

The geezer didn't want to know about me afterwards. That raised my spirits, but black guys like Francis weren't always playing. I never heard anything racist from my own team. They were a nice bunch of lads, but they weren't all about to ride shotgun for me like Francis. Footballers mostly look after number one.

The physical punishment I received from opponents in the Southern League was worse for me because my game depended on getting past people as much as possible. No defender appreciates that. There was always the opportunity to stick a leg out to trip me, or a stud to cut me.

Still, at my age you weren't going to get done like you could on the streets. I never liked violence and I remember around this time a really frightening walk back from training with Hillingdon Borough one Tuesday or Thursday. Those were the days we trained.

Everyone knew there were lots of racist attacks in West Drayton and you didn't want to be walking late at night on your own. It was autumn, just after the clocks go back and catch everyone out, getting dark an hour earlier than usual.

This particular early evening it seemed to be pitch black, and I was suddenly aware that three white guys were following me. When I walked across the road, they crossed a little way behind me. I was scared. I started walking faster to get to the station, but I didn't want to bolt. The three guys, this must be their area, and they'd know it better than I did.

The walk took about fifteen or twenty minutes. I could have gone round the main road, but I'd taken a shortcut down quieter streets. All I was thinking was that I had nothing to defend myself with. In my sports bag I had boots, I had creams, I had socks and that was it. So eventually I decided to brass it out.

I suddenly turned round and I shouted, 'What's your problem? You fucking want some?' I shoved my hand inside my bag like I was going to pull out a knife and I kept shouting at them like a crazy man. 'You want some!' Luckily, they started to run and I bolted to that station as fast as I could.

I did some good acting there. When I was angry I always looked like a maniac. If they really had confronted me, what am I pulling out? A tube of Deep Heat! I swear to God, in the train station the sweat was pouring off me and I was shaking like a leaf.

I couldn't wait for the train to come, in case they came back. When the train arrived, I jumped on and stood watching through the door in case they suddenly appeared on the platform and jumped in. They didn't. I never went to Borough training on my own after that. I either got a lift or I wasn't going. One thing I was lucky with in life, I suppose. I never really got caught up in any big fights.

CHAPTER 10

Chelsea? Gwaan!

Preseason was an exciting time at Hillingdon Borough. You might get to play a friendly against a league side. I figured in a game against Brentford just before the start of the 1980/81 season. That's when you first think, 'Hell, these are professionals and there's not a great difference.' You think you might have a chance to make it all the way.

By then I was back in the 'family' home in Slough. Mum had finally heard the whole story about the argument and everything, from June. Then she faced up to Rendvill. How could he not tell her the truth? Did he think she'd allow him to freeze out her son? Rendvill had been frightened she might leave too, but he had gone the wrong way about keeping her.

So Mum came and found me and brought me back to the house, but the friction wasn't cleared between Rendvill and me. We shelved the plan to fly the nest together for the time being. Mum was still determined to keep us all together.

Things got harder for Mum to deal with when June revealed her news. She'd been seeing a boy and was pregnant by him. As I've said, for Caribbean families, it's far more serious if an unmarried daughter has a child than if a son creates his own personal baby boom. Eventually, June left Rendvill's home. I just had to dig in, tolerate Rendvill and focus on my football.

Well, it wasn't 100 per cent football. In Slough that summer I became involved with Maureen, who lived in the neighbourhood. She gave me another reason to hang around Slough. Maureen was very Jamaican, even though she was born in the UK. Short and round, was Maureen. I've always fancied fuller women.

When I wasn't out raving and seeing Maureen or other girls, I was striving to make it in the game I loved. It was almost becoming my last chance after the string of jobs I'd left. After two successful seasons on the wing at Hillingdon Borough, where I'd helped the team finish a respectable seventh then thirteenth in the twenty-four-club Southern League, manager Alan Bassett knew I was anxious to turn fully professional. He started trying to fix me up with a Football League club, and before the start of the 1981/82 season I went for trials at various clubs. The first ones I looked at were West Bromwich Albion and Wimbledon. Wimbledon were a Third Division side, heading rapidly up the League. They were known more for their Crazy Gang spirit than big salaries, and their offer of £45 a week wasn't alluring – I could take home more on social security.

Southampton were a more serious prospect – a First Division side with Lawrie McMenemy in charge. His status was legendary after winning the FA Cup with the Saints five years earlier. They also had a few black players coming through and Danny Wallace took part in my trial. I worked really hard and did my best at the trial. I thought I did well, but McMenemy didn't say anything to me so I lost faith in that route.

In the meantime, Chelsea started to show interest, just as my old screw at Borstal had reckoned they would. Ron Suart, the first-team coach, and Gwyn Williams, their youth director and 'Mr Fixit', came and had a look at me playing for the Borough. Chelsea were Second Division then and it wasn't as if they were doing too well, but they had a reputation for giving youngsters a chance.

They had to – everyone was aware that they had spent a fortune on a new stand in the early seventies. The development had been delayed, and costs escalated so much that they were nearly bankrupted. The board had to sell off a lot of the big stars, such as Peter Osgood and Alan Hudson, who had helped win tournaments in 1970 and 1971, and fill their places with young home-growns, such as Ray Wilkins and Clive Walker. They'd been relegated from the First Division, promoted, and relegated again in 1979. Money was still tight, and a lot of the 'youngsters' had grown old. They needed new blood to push for promotion again.

Ron invited me for a short trial at the Chelsea training ground, near Heathrow Airport. Again, I thought I'd done as well as I could, but time passed and I heard nothing. As the days went by I started to get nervous. Had I been kidding myself all along about how talented I really was? I'd given it my best shot at the trial. Maybe, after all this time, my best simply wasn't good enough to make it as a professional. It was a devastating thought. Disconsolate, I went back to Hillingdon Borough and expected to stay there.

In the meantime, I had a feeling of déjà-vu when Maureen told me that she was expecting a baby. I was nineteen and already this was a familiar feeling – one I would experience again and again, the nonchalant way I lived my life.

A little while later, out of the blue, the phone rang and it was Ron Suart. 'What happened?' he asked. 'Why haven't you been back?' They'd been expecting me to return for more sessions. I was relieved. It was typical me not to have been paying attention when I needed to – I was supposed to have returned after the first day. But I did have other things on my mind.

'Paul,' Ron said, 'we like you. We're really interested. Could you come back for a week's training?' Of course I could! This was music to my ears.

So I turned up for the week that might make or break my life. I took the train from Slough to Harlington, where the Chelsea training ground was located. It was just flat open fields with no trees, other than the ones that lined the distant perimeter fences, to take the sting out of the wind. And Lord, there was always wind. From November to March, you often felt it was coming direct from Siberia with nothing in between.

Over the years, I found that in winter the pitches got waterlogged, were cut up, then froze into ridges that I swear you could saw logs on. The dressing rooms and showers were shared with students from Imperial College – they were entitled to push you out on Wednesday afternoons, no messing. There was one payphone, and the physiotherapy facilities were practically non-existent. It was very basic, light years away from the amenities provided for the Chelsea boys now.

But I didn't notice any of that. I was a bit overawed. It was a big club in bad times, but still a big club. For the first few days I just could not be myself in training. I was getting the ball and giving it back, not taking players on. I wanted it so much I was as tight as a drum inside. I was letting myself down.

I'll never forget how some of the lads there helped me. Graham Wilkins was a full-back and a lovely man. He probably came to be grateful that I turned up as fans had someone else to boo! Graham suffered from the boo boys because he could be accident-prone. He was also the brother of one of Chelsea's greats, Ray Wilkins, and suffered in his shadow. But he was the solid sort. Dressing rooms are built around guys like that.

He was about twenty-five when I arrived and he could see I was a young lad not doing myself justice. So midway through my try-out he singled me out during a first team versus reserves game, coaxed me into taking him on and invited me to run at him. 'Come on, Paul,' he kept urging, 'take me on, show your skill!' Simply by doing that he helped me massively. Graham made me play and I came out of my shell after that. He was brilliant.

When the training week was over I was a nervous wreck. I'd loved the work, the people, the vibe ... the prospects. Ron Suart came over to me. This was the moment of truth.

'We like what we see,' he said, and what a sensation I felt in that moment. 'We're prepared to sign you for the remainder of the season.'

I was actually going to achieve my ambition. I was ecstatic. I told June as soon as I could and she was overjoyed. I told Mum, and wanted more of a reaction from her than I got.

The few friends I told were amazed – 'Gwaan!' I was put on £175 a week straight away and started training with the first team and playing in the reserves. Hillingdon Borough received a useful £5,000 for my sale and we played a lucrative friendly at their ground the following preseason.

CHAPTER 11

'We Don't Want The Nigger!'

John Neal was Chelsea's manager when I signed for them on 1 December 1981. He had been brought in in May that year, and would be kept on by the larger-than-life Ken Bates, who took over in April 1982. I didn't have much to do with Batesy, but I could see why he kept the manager, who was a real diamond.

Mr Neal was a Geordie, softly spoken, and about fifty years old when I first met him. He looked older – easy smile, bushy eyebrows, wiry hair with a side parting. He and his Scottish assistant Ian McNeill were hugely experienced – real football men. They weren't the glamorous media darlings that Chelsea had perhaps gone for in better times, such as Geoff Hurst, but the players loved them and they understood the way footballers thought. Mr Neal could make his point quite forcefully when he needed to.

It wasn't easy for him, though. The club had been in trouble financially ever since the stadium redevelopment costs of the 1970s had escalated, and results were still poor on the pitch. They were mid-table in the Second Division when I joined and not looking like promotion candidates.

I suppose I must have been one of Mr Neal's first signings – all the big names of the era, such as Dixon, Spackman, Speedie and Nevin, were yet to come. I had to wait for my chance in a first team filled with home-grown players and seasoned professionals. Even in 1982, when I'd earned a permanent contract, it took a while for me to feel that I really belonged.

Any new young player will tell you about that feeling when you first sit in a dressing room among players you've seen on 'Match Of The Day'. I looked around and there were all these big-name stars – Clive Walker, Colin Lee, Colin Viljoen, Micky Droy – and I was thinking, 'Jesus Christ, what is Paul Canoville doing in this company?'

Micky Droy was the dominant figure, in more ways than one. Man, he was a big fella, standing 6 ft 4 in. in his slippers. But if he was a man mountain on the pitch, he was a gentle giant off it, the quiet force in the dressing room. He was thirty-odd and had business interests outside football, which were just taking off as his time in the game ran out. I couldn't believe the way he smoked. I swear Lord, he could smoke cigarettes like a chimney. I'm thinking, 'This guy's a professional, and they allow him to smoke?'

That was his choice. He wanted to smoke. If it didn't

harm his football, then that was it. Looking back, most of the boys didn't smoke. Or if they did, it was on the sly. Micky was open about it, and I was shocked.

In recent years I've taken fans on stadium tours of Stamford Bridge and the changing rooms are completely different from when I started there – palatial in comparison. Back then, the seating was made from wooden slats, like park benches, and was split up in various parts, so you had different groups sitting together. I was always in a corner. I know why – I didn't want to be noticed. I just got ready for the game and watched everybody babbling away.

'Oi, Bummers, we going for a drink after?'

'Don't know, I've got to see someone, sort out some business first.'

That was the buzz in the dressing room. John Bumstead, Mike Fillery, Gary Chivers, keeper Steve Francis and Colin Pates, the young Chelsea boys, were always on for a booze-up or a party. They sat apart from the older generation of lads who'd come through the Chelsea system – Ian Britton, Graham Wilkins, Gary Locke and Chris Hutchings, who took over as boss of Wigan in 2007.

Then there were the old stagers, such as Droy, Dennis Rofe and Colin Lee, who'd been at Bristol, Torquay and Spurs before us. Everybody knew each other. I was the new boy, just listening, taking in things as they were. I liked observing how the dressing room functioned.

I'd never seen boots the size of Micky Droy's. I'd seen 11s and 12s, but these were huge. Nobody had feet like that. I kept thinking, who's cleaning those damn things? They ought to get paid by the yard!

I was so naïve I actually thought I still had to take my boots home with me and clean them myself.

'What are you doing? A trainee pro's gonna do them for you,' someone laughed.

'What d'you mean?'

I couldn't understand. I had no idea. It was the job of the trainees to clean the pros' boots. Simon Chandler was the one who looked after mine. I was nineteen and he was just a few years younger, a black kid just like myself. He became a friend of mine – a great friend as it turned out. I had much more in common with him than with the first-team players.

He said, 'I take those boots, man, clean them, and leave them in there.' He showed me the boot room. That was an eye-opening thing for me as well. When I saw all the lines of coathooks with numbers for the boots, I was well impressed. This was the proper business.

Some people actually had three sets of boots – rubber soles for dry conditions, and two different lengths of screw-in studs for wet. Norman Medhurst, the physio, asked me, 'What type d'you like?'

'Whose boots are those?' I asked, indicating some neat-looking footwear. 'I'm thinking I'm gonna have a pair like that.'

That's all I had to do. Norman ordered them and I had the boots the next day. So nice. That was new. That was a buzz, man. Two years earlier the Borough manager had whisked me off to buy a pair of Patricks I couldn't afford myself; now I just had to ask for any boots and they arrived straight away.

I felt sorry for the youngsters who cleaned all these boots, though. Simon would ask me which ones I had needed cleaning and I'd tell him just the pair I'd used. Some players always used two or three pairs, just for the sake of it.

I got on with a lot of the apprentices. Robert Isaac was another. Next preseason at Stamford Bridge I saw them carrying loads of decorating stuff and asked Robert what they were doing.

'We're preparing for the season.'

'What d'you mean?'

'We've got to paint the whole of the back of the grandstand,' he said. 'We probably won't finish till seven or eight tonight.'

I couldn't believe it. It was none of my business, but – typical me, always a sucker for a sob story – I asked Gwyn Williams, who was the youth director, why they had to go through all that. Was it fair? I wanted to know more about how things worked round the club.

'Got to get it done, Canners,' he said. 'You know how it is.' Of course, I didn't.

When I joined, I had no idea the apprentices did all the odd-jobs and cleaning round the team, as well as attending school lessons, working on their own fitness and technique and playing matches. It seemed a lot of hard work to me. All I wanted to do was train and play for the reserves, then work to break through to the first team if possible.

So I didn't like to give Simon too much boot cleaning. You had to think about their other duties on top of that. I was remembering where I'd come from and feeling for them.

I'd bypassed all of these apprentice duties by dossing around and coming through the Southern League semi-pro route a bit later. I don't know if I could have done what those young pros had to do. With my attitude, I'm not sure I would have stuck at it. I'd most likely never have received a contract that way. It made me glad I did things my way after all. I'd arrived in professional football the only way I knew in life – by the awkward route.

The scene was shifting domestically, too. Despite all the ructions, Mum and Rendvill had stayed together and in early 1982 they announced they were getting married in the summer. I didn't care about them tying the knot, even though, personally, I didn't trust him. I just wanted Mum to be happy, and if that's what she wanted . . . But pretty soon the sparks were flying again between her fiancé and me. It could be me leaving the heating on, coming in late, or simply not being polite to him. It always kicked off.

One particular incident was like a scene from a 'Carry On' film. I'll never forget it. Mum had had an operation on her bunions and was upstairs in the bedroom with both her feet bandaged up. She heard a loud banging coming from my room, stumbled downstairs on her painful feet, and found Rendvill, Val, his cousin, and me, all kicking the crap out of each other.

She screamed out loud and called frantically for Arthur, a friend of theirs who was visiting at the time, to come quick. Arthur rushed in to see what was happening and called it straight: 'Rendvill, this is not right! The two of you can't be doing that to the boy!'

In the almost laughable rough and tumble going on in the room, suddenly the television fell on Arthur's foot. He ended up being driven barefoot by Mum to Wexham Park Hospital. It was comical when you think about it, but the aftermath was anything but amusing for me. Mum ended up sending me packing out of the front door. She was so unreasonable when it came to my behaviour – I could do no right in her eyes, and was always causing trouble for her. I accepted that I'd created a lot of needless anguish in her life, but even when I was the victim she blamed me for whatever took place.

Apparently, straight after I'd gone, Rendvill suddenly appeared with a hammer saying how he was going to go after me, and what he was going to do to me when he found me. Mum looked at him and said, 'D'you know what you're doing? This "marriage" is over. I don't know if you know it!'

I don't think he believed her. He just didn't seem to get things anyway. Incredibly, having driven her own son from the house, Rendvill all of a sudden asked Mum if she would adopt his son from a former marriage! She thought he was mad.

As far as she was concerned that was it with him and her at that moment, but she was an unpredictable woman.

Things were going much better for me at Chelsea, though. Despite the turmoil at home I was getting to training without problem, playing for the reserves and giving a good account of myself. After just four months in the reserves, in April 1982, I was told I would be on the bench for the first time. That was an amazing feeling after the state I'd been in the year before, living in an abandoned car.

I was given the news after a nice reserve match at Arsenal when I'd done the business and played well. We won 2–1 and on the way back to Slough it was a lovely spring day.

How soon that changed. Soon after I arrived at Rendvill's, he suddenly came to my room and accused me of stealing his food. Yet again it all went off between us. It was like being back in Cherry Avenue with the Jacob's crackers. He was being totally irrational – I always bought and cooked all my own meals, and enjoyed doing so. He was out of order and his timing was just about the worst it could be. I'd had a great day (no thanks to him) but now I was tired and I'd really had enough of him bullying me day after day. I went downstairs to the kitchen and picked up a knife.

'You want to fuck about? Come on! I'll fuck about with you today. I've had enough of your shit!' Then I thought again, put down the knife and said, 'Come on, let's go!'

That was it. We were grappling, laying into each other,

tearing, punching, kicking, rolling out the front door. The next thing you know the whole of the road was out on the street watching.

I don't remember how it ended, but when it did, that was me away again, out of the house and off to stay with whichever friend or girlfriend would take me in, homeless once more, two days before my debut for the Chelsea team. Not the ideal preparation for the biggest moment in your time on the planet. What craziness it all was.

Then, on top of all that, came the shocking response to me warming up as a substitute at Selhurst Park on that Monday night, 12 April 1982. It was supposed to be my special time. I was twenty years one month and one week old, and about to represent my club in the Second Division of the Football League for the first time, against Crystal Palace, and supporters were baying, hooting like mocking monkeys and throwing bananas at me from the stands. I was on for three minutes and it seemed like the longest torture of my entire life.

I was playing on the right, next to the wankers who were abusing me. I didn't move away from them the entire time I was on the pitch. If I think about it now, I realise my mind still echoes with every single line I heard those bastards say.

At the final whistle I ran straight off down the tunnel as soon as possible. I was so glad none of my family was there to hear my magic moment disgraced. I was shocked and distraught. What happened there? Did I just hallucinate all that? I made my debut, but a banana landed in front of me . . . I've been called a 'black fucking so-and-so' . . . They chanted 'We don't want the nigger!' and I was that 'nigger' they didn't want. That's what really hurt me above all. It wasn't the away supporters. It was our own fans.

I was muttering to myself. I knew that the manager had done – for me – the worst thing by taking off their hero Clive Walker, the blond, flair player, the man who had scored the only goal of the game. But what do they want for their team? What did I do so wrong? No one can help the skin they're born in.

I don't really remember the players coming over to me after that disgrace, just John Neal with a few words of wisdom that, typically for him, meant little at the time but more as they sank in, and a team-mate or two asking, 'You all right?' But I was in the corner, head in my hands, dazed. It wasn't the experience someone who'd just made history should expect. I'd just become the first black footballer to play in the first team for the club of Tommy Lawton, Jimmy Greaves, Terry Venables, Bobby Tambling, Peter Osgood and Ray Wilkins. But congratulations were out of the question.

If you're hurt, or even if you're sent off, there's usually a 'How are you?' or 'Mate, how are you feeling?' Support. Something. I don't know whether other players were as shocked as I was, or they just didn't know what to say. Maybe they'd heard it happen to Luther Blissett and Laurie Cunningham already and it didn't concern them that much.

All I was sure of was that I had been out there and made my long-awaited debut. I think I even got one or two touches. I was struggling to come to terms with everything else that had happened. It was a horrible blur. So personal. So hurtful. The hatred of scores of my own supporters would ring in my ears for years.

It's extraordinary when I think about those few days now, and I don't know how I was able to deal with the double blow of the violent bust-up with Rendvill at home and the annihilation of my life's dream.

Typically for me, everything came together in one fell swoop. I didn't change, though. I just carried on with life regardless. I was homeless, staying at my sister's hostel. They weren't supposed to have men in there – just another ridiculous scenario I'd got myself into. I'd sneak through her window (old habits die hard) and sleep on her floor. Then I'd leave early in the morning and go about my business. Mad. I was so upset about Rendvill and what I'd had to resort to in order to put a roof over my head, but the important thing was what was happening for me at Chelsea. That was what I focused all my energy on. I was just determined to achieve my life's goal. And Mum still married Rendvill in the summer.

Obviously, I had to sort out some accommodation. Bunking in and out of my sister's room was never going to be a long-term solution. And you can't have a professional footballer moving from floor to floor. I started looking with a vengeance for a proper place up in Hackney, determined to get us away from Slough and Rendvill as soon as possible. Even though she'd married him, Mum was going to join me once it was sorted.

She was worried about me again. Despite the success with football, she thought I was in danger of throwing it all away and there was no way she could leave me to my own devices. That's how the family eventually moved up to London, away from Southall, Slough and all the baggage of my teens.

I went up to London with a girlfriend from Slough, Annette Brooks (now passed on, but always remembered), and eventually found a place with Ujima, a black housing association, and told Mum.

Mum kept our scheme secret from Rendvill for fear of how he would react. She wasn't worried about him being physical, just that it would make life miserable. Instead, one day after he went to work, Mum just packed up her things and moved out, just like that. In due course she joined me in Hackney. It was finally goodbye Middlesex, and maybe even good riddance. But in the summer of 1982, that was still to come.

CHAPTER 12

The Wider World

After the turmoil of my debut in April, I didn't play again for Chelsea until the last two games of the season. We lost 1–2 at home to Luton Town, with me coming on as a sub for right-winger Peter Rhoades-Brown, 'Rosey', but drew 1–1 away to Blackburn, where I started instead of the same player. I knew my best position was on the left wing, but the main man there at Chelsea was Clive Walker. He was lightning fast, a good crosser of the ball, a goalscorer and the hero of the terraces.

He wasn't the only one, either. Some other younger wingers were there ahead of me at Chelsea. On the right, Rosey liked to run with the ball and Phil Driver was a speed merchant. Mike Fillery played wide left midfield, although he wasn't the same sort of player as I was. It wasn't like I was going to walk into the team and it took me a while to adapt. Over the summer I resolved to make an effort to get to know the first-team boys a bit better when we met up again, and fit in with them.

My first preseason was an eye-opener all round. I was still only twenty, and very naive in lots of ways. I knew the street, but I didn't know the world. I hadn't travelled abroad for years. I'd been to France a few times as a child with Father Morgan back in Southall, and to the Caribbean, but not since I was a kid. I wasn't used to going on holiday every year.

When they told me I was going on the preseason tour of Sweden before the training sessions Chelsea always had in Aberystwyth, I had to confess I didn't even have a passport. No sooner had I told them than my new passport appeared. The club sorted it. I was well impressed. It was like having a butler who waited on you and did all the fiddly things in life on your behalf.

The day we were leaving for Scandinavia we had to meet at the ground where the coach would collect us and take us to the airport. I got my stuff together and reported to the stadium with the others, then realised I'd forgotten my passport. It was still in the drawer at Mum's in Slough. I couldn't believe it. It was a hell of a dash, and I ended up having to meet the rest of the squad at the airport. There's always one, but sometimes I wish it wasn't always me.

Once I'd settled in on the flight, though, I started to think, 'Gordon Bennett, Canners, you're travelling away on tour as a professional footballer.' I was wide-eyed. It was another thrill for me.

We flew to Stockholm in July and faced four little local

teams in a week. I played left-wing in every game, with Phil Driver down the right and Clive Walker inside us. I got two goals in the third match, which we won 8–0, and one in the last. It was a good start.

I remember it was so hot and I noticed one bloke I was up against kept disappearing. He was there at my side one minute and the next thing the shadow had gone. Water in little containers was provided at the side of the pitch and he'd gone for a drink. That's the first time I saw guys doing that. It was a tiny thing but as the sweat was pouring off us, we could see the logic in it.

Sweden was a big learning experience for me – in how you should look after yourself and prepare for a season, and how to carry yourself as a pro, especially in a foreign country, with nice hotels, restaurants, receptions and the like. This was a level of luxury I'd never been exposed to.

It was great to think this was what my life was about now, playing football and travelling. It was nice seeing other countries. Sweden was the cleanest place I'd ever come across. You can't be antisocial there and it isn't even the police who enforce that code of conduct, it's members of the public. 'Oh, um, a man there told me you dropped litter,' someone said to me. I'd seen canals and rivers, but I'd never seen a stream where the water was drinkable. It was so clean and I thought, 'Why can't England be like this?' Off the field, things warmed up on that tour, too. That's when I started to let my hair down, really. I opened up with the boys and felt like I was part of it all. I'd earned my position.

We had a dinner in the hotel, quite formal. After we'd finished eating, we were just sitting and talking among ourselves, when I said, 'What's that? What's going on?' A DJ was playing tunes and the music was rank. At that time Michael Jackson was hot, and so someone asked him to play some Michael Jackson or Stevie Wonder, a bit of soul.

Suddenly a George Benson track started playing – 'Give Me The Night' or something. Yeah! The hips and shoulders started twitching and that was me started. I decided to show the boys a few of my moves. 'Come on, boys. You lot are moving like you're stiff or something! Get on the floor.'

A couple of the boys started off – 'Come on, Canners, give it the moonwalk!' So I was giving it large. The music was playing, the boys were egging me on – 'Go on, Canners!'

Next thing I knew, I got the tap on the shoulder and it's a woman. All right, all right. Who's set me up now? But I didn't want to stop there because I was trying to impress them, show a bit of the real me. 'Come on then!' We danced together, and everybody joined in. That's when I realised the allure footballers have for women. I wasn't the only one who had a Swedish lady sidle up to them, asking, 'D'you really play for Chelsea? Oooh.' It must have been true what they said about Scandinavians being more upfront about sex. A few of the boys pulled, including me, and the atmosphere from then on in with the boys was nice.

I always looked forward to the overseas breaks. On another trip, this time to Spain, a top Scottish team, and all their wives and girlfriends, were staying in the same hotel. John Bumstead and I were looking out of a window and a couple of the Scottish women were opposite getting changed. We knew they knew who we were, and could see us watching them.

Did they stop? No. They undressed completely in front of us in their room. My eyes were popping. Then we started thinking. The last thing we wanted was to be caught by some nutty Scottish footballers ogling their wives. But it was good fun while it lasted.

Each preseason, Chelsea had a training camp by the sea in Aberystwyth. We'd stay on the student campus, train and socialise. It was a bonding exercise and never mind the stinging wind that blew over the sand dunes, even in August.

Aberystwyth 1982 was my first experience of preseason training and I had no idea what to expect. At Hillingdon we'd trained on Tuesdays and Thursdays and that was it. We reached Wales by coach and our camp was right by the seaside. The sea was absolutely freezing but the salty air was the first thing I noticed. It always seemed windswept. Johnny Neal absolutely loved it there. 'Yeah, get that in your lungs, boy!' he'd enthuse in his soft Durham burr.

We exercised on miles and miles of seashore and dunes. It was a typical British bay, where when the sea's gone out you've got all these wooden barriers, or breakwaters, along the beach. To locals they were groynes. To us they were hurdles. When we were running, we had to jump over them, which was all very well when you'd got fresh legs, but hell when you were tiring. And we'd run for ages, trying to build up fitness to last the whole season ahead.

You really had to move your feet to get up those dune hills, and no walking or drinking was allowed. Before I arrived, Phil Driver was king of the cross-country runs but now there was a new boy on the block – Canners, Brentside High's very own Sebastian Coe! Phil and I would be up the front and when we glanced back, the rest of the boys would be straggling out for hundreds of yards.

It was murder for some people. I remember my mate Keith Jones one time. Sometimes we'd do a group relay. The first group would go round the circuit and you'd touch hands on your return. The last man to touch from the first group set off the next one.

On our leg, we could see poor Jonah, as Keith was called, struggling and when we came out from behind the sandhills, there was no sign of him. The rest of the boys behind us were running and waving. So we went back to investigate and found Jonah completely shattered and in a right state. I watched the Chelsea players training under José Mourinho, and there was hardly any running without a ball at their feet. The fitness came from working on actions and skills and developing intuitive play, like when you were a kid on the street. Back then, we were of the old English school of thinking, that the perfect preparation for a nine-month campaign was to run the legs off a player till he was sick.

'I can't move!' said Jonah. Someone picked up his leg. I swear to God, it looked like it had no bones in it! He was so drained he'd turned to jelly. We laughed so much. We couldn't believe it. That was how preparation for a long season of professional football was in those days. I had no problems in that respect. I could run till the cows came home. But I just know I would have loved the modern, Mourinho method more.

I was always buzzing in preseason, especially that first one. An overseas tour, then two weeks spent just getting fit. Fantastic.

The campus in Aberystwyth was a good place for it. You had your own room, there was a dinner hall, and a funfair on the front. I didn't go out like some of the others, but tried to integrate myself with the boys where I could. We'd sit, chat, read the paper, talk about music. I'd never played cards but I tried to join in and they taught me how to play a game called hearts.

By eight o'clock, I was tired. And you knew the next day you were going to be knackered again. So that was it for me. Sometimes there was a curfew, other times not, depending on how the manager had seen things going during the day. He knew people had to let off steam sometimes.

But how anybody could have gone out on the lash was beyond me. I didn't get why they would do it. I could rave all night but I never really drank. I never drank lager. I hate beer. My dad apparently used to love a tipple, but not me. I may have been tired the next day but I was never hung over. Apart from that, it wasn't my scene at all. I was never a pub-goer like the white boys were, and I didn't smoke cigarettes. Some of these boys would get caned when they were supposed to be getting fit. There was a big drinking culture at Chelsea at that time. They loved their beer and that was their life – down the pub or wine bar, loads of parties. Propping up the bar all evening just didn't appeal. When I went out back home it was to my usual haunts, and for music, mates and women, not to get hammered into oblivion.

To me it would have been like starting from scratch every morning. You'd just worked yourself silly to reach a certain level with your body, then had a booze-up and put yourself back almost to square one.

As far as I was concerned, each workout I was building my fitness, day on day, feeling like I was getting ready for the start of the football. Aberystwyth wouldn't always hold happy memories for me, but that first trip was special. I'd connected with the other players much more and that carried over into the 1982/83 season.

CHAPTER 13

Bench-warming Blues

The reality of my situation was soon brought back to me, however. Playing for the reserves I hadn't been getting any racial abuse from fans. I suppose only the true supporters, diehards, would go to watch some of the teams we faced, such as the 'stiffs' of Orient or Plymouth Argyle. The idiots would find their voice in a big, anonymous crowd. On any level you take it, it's unjust; it's not right.

To have your dream shattered so horribly takes a lot of getting over. I don't know that I ever did. No matter how well integrated I was becoming in the dressing room, my first appearances in home games at Chelsea were just as bad as at Selhurst Park. The fence round the front of the stands was put up a few years later when Ken Bates was tackling the hooligans – I could have done with the security protection in 1982, I can tell you. Bates even claimed recently that he received razor blades in the post when he spoke out in my favour, but I wasn't aware of anything like that at the time.

Stamford Bridge is a magnificent stadium these days, but back in 1982 it was a wreck, despite all the money they'd spent on development in the early seventies. The old greyhound track was still there, between the pitch and the front of the East Stand, where the dugouts were.

When I was a substitute, after a while John Neal would say, 'Go on, Canners, warm up,' and I would get up and start to jog along in front of the stand. As I went past I'd hear the racist shouts, 'What's wrong with you, golliwog,' 'We don't fucking want you,' and all the rest.

After the first few experiences of that abuse I just wanted to get past them as quickly as possible to the south end, where there was a big area out of earshot. I would stay there, warming up until I knew I'd overdone it. I just didn't want to go back and hear this cruelty and viciousness again.

But of course, I always had to run the gauntlet back to the bench. Nobody could miss what was happening. Not even the decent people who silently turned the other cheek. There was so much hatred and hostility. 'Go on, fuck off back home!' But everyone else carried on regardless as if it wasn't happening. It was like one of those nightmares where no one believes your story.

I was physically scared, too. The abusers were right there next to me as I jogged past. There was nothing stopping them jumping on me. I was seriously imagining they might come off their seats and attack me.

Every single game I expected somebody to jump down and hit me. I don't know how I would have reacted had it happened, if I would have retaliated. There were a lot more of them than me. This is not four or five people. This is maybe fifty or sixty. That was a frightening thing.

Even when I went off it was, 'Get off, you black cunt,' 'Get inside and stay in there!'

That's the reason I always kept my head down, never looked at them. I didn't want to push it. I knew if I'd faced them, seen what an individual looked like when he said what he said, I'd have had to respond. I'd have hated him and I'd have gone for him. It was better not to give it that focus.

Another thing that always killed me was when the teams were read out before the match. As a footballer, you should love to hear your name called out. It's a small perk of the job when you're acknowledged by your supporters, and it marks you out from a Sunday footballer. I just wanted to hear a small show of appreciation. But it was, 'Number ten David Speedie' . . . hooray! . . . 'Number eleven Paul Canoville' . . . boo! *Boo-oo, oo-oo!*

I didn't even want to hear my name after that. Imagine that. I took to coming out late for the pre-match warm-up to rob the idiots of their moment. I used to run out at the last minute, just get a feel of the ball and then go back in. I never was out there longer than that. I just didn't want to come on the pitch and hear that abuse.

It made a big difference that manager John Neal made it clear he knew I was getting the stick because I was black. It gave me strength.

'They're against you simply because of your colour and we're not going to stand for prejudice like that,' he said. 'I'll take the abuse if you'll take it. We'll see it off together.'

He said if I walked away, the bigots would have won the day. I agreed, but it was never easy being the first – a trailblazer.

I never mentioned any of this to Mum of course. Didn't want to worry her. It wasn't like that when she attended her first ever football match. That was when I was about to sign forms back in 1981, and Mum had been invited along to a game at the Bridge with me. She had come round to thinking I could maybe make it after all. It was Chelsea v. Grimsby in late November 1981 and we drew 1–1, but when Grimsby scored, for some unknown reason she decided to jump up and shout, 'Very good!' Then everyone started giving her dirty looks. It didn't help that she just happened to be wearing a scarf in the away team's colours – black and white. She hadn't done it deliberately. She'd just pulled it out of the cupboard and put it on. She said later that she felt sorry for the visitors because they were getting a hammering and no one was praising them. 'What you doing, Mum?' I joked afterwards, 'You trying to get me lynched?' I didn't know how accurate those words would feel for me a few months later.

I was well aware that many teams had a crew of hardcore racists back then but hadn't realised how easy it was for them to whip up others when the barracking started. At Stamford Bridge, the stands did not look anything like the multicultural streets outside – just a sea of white faces watching matches. Other London clubs had black players, but never Chelsea's first team. Some coaches there in the seventies had fallen for the common stereotyped rubbish that black footballers were fast and skilful but didn't have the heart for a battle and were not to be relied upon. They didn't see it as racist, just fact. I knew all that before I went there, but actually experiencing it was something nobody could have been prepared for.

You didn't get the impression that the club saw any of this race-related stuff as a problem at first, what with the National Front magazine being sold openly along the Fulham Road on match days (as it was at Leeds' Elland Road and several other grounds). Midweek games were the most intimidating. Walking through those crowds as one of the few black faces, I'd watch my back because you never knew whether someone would have a go at you.

Like a lot of black kids, I had a soft spot for West Bromwich Albion. In 1978 they'd become the first English club to field a trio of black men in their team – Cyrille Regis, Laurie Cunningham and Brendon Batson. Ron Atkinson, the manager, who was later disgraced for making seemingly racial slurs against Chelsea and France defender Marcel Desailly, dubbed them 'the Three Degrees'.

A popular reggae tune by Dennis Alcapone summed up what a lot of black people thought about English football. It was called 'World Cup Football' and gave some half-serious guidance to the FA about how to succeed going into España '82.

'If England want to do some good,' Alcapone sang, 'gimme no Ron Greenwood' – the manager at the time. 'Forget your pride and your prejudice,' he continued, 'and carry the man Cyrille Regis. Take out your likkle likkle book, and write down the name Garth Crooks.'

Half joking he may have been, but Alcapone spoke for a lot of us when he suggested there might have been more black faces in the England squad that summer. As it was, only Viv Anderson made the cut, and he didn't play a single game.

That's how divided things were then. Of course, plenty of white kids were into black culture – ska music, Specials, Madness, the Two-Tone thing going on was massive – but that didn't mean the NF and others weren't listened to when they screamed about black and Asian immigrants stealing jobs and houses. There were lots of white bigots around and some of them became footballers, as I discovered. But this was my one and only pitch at the big time and I didn't want to think about negatives. What would be would be.

As it turned out, I had found the club and its staff to be mostly welcoming, and from the little group of young black kids in the youth side, some did break through. Simon Chandler and Rodney Beste didn't get professional contracts at Chelsea but made their way in football elsewhere, while Keith Dublin, or 'Dubbers' as he was known, and Keith Jones made the first team.

Central midfielder Jonah's first game was away at Barnsley in March 1983, a year after my start, and Dubbers, a left-back, made his debut against the same team at the Bridge a year after that. I may have borne the brunt of the hatred from a minority of supporters, but at least it opened the gate for them and many more Afro-Caribbean footballers with the club.

When Jonah and then Dubbers made the step up, they no longer trained with the reserves but with the first team. That made three black faces and on more than one occasion there were altercations with one player who obviously had a problem with black men. It was always dealt with properly, but as if the colour wasn't an issue. Of course it was. Back then, casual, institutional racism was displayed at almost every level of the club – not so much that you would quit over it or kick up a rumpus, but enough to make you feel different and an outsider most of the time. It was the sort of problem official inquiries have accused organisations such as the police of having in recent years.

Coming through the youth team set-up as they had, the younger black kids had seen things at Chelsea that I didn't know about. I'll never forget Simon Chandler telling me what it was like to sit in the East Upper stand at Stamford Bridge, all the apprentices together in their club kits, and hearing a load of Chelsea supporters shouting 'black bastard!' at me while I was playing on the pitch. And those were the posh seats.

This is the club the young trainees were supposed to dream of playing for. They heard that crap and they couldn't say anything because the whole stand would have got on their case. Simon said he couldn't express, even to the management or senior players, the overwhelming joy he, Dubbers and Jonah felt when I did well, scored a goal or set one up. There was silent unity.

Probably some people didn't want me to do well. Simon always says there was deep-seated racism at Chelsea – that was his experience. People of colour had to be that much better to succeed.

Simon had played with other black kids in the Chelsea junior team that won the South East Counties League and League Cup final, 6–2 against West Ham, in 1984. And he, Dubbers and Jonah were in the team that had competed against an Arsenal youth side that included David Rocastle, Paul Davis, Paul Merson and Martin Keown, and got the better of them.

But whereas the Arsenal lads formed the backbone of their successful side of the 1980s, Dubbers and Jonah both played sixty-odd times for Chelsea and drifted away. Jonah is still reckoned by Gwyn Williams, who nurtured him, to be the best prospect for his age in his time at Chelsea. He had great lungs, could boss midfield and had a great range of passes. Dubbers was strong, athletic and fast. But as soon as either of them made a mistake the crowd was on to them, slagging them off. There wasn't the same open racist abuse I received, but still the tolerance threshold was low, as much in the coaching staff as the crowd. Simon and several others never got far enough at Chelsea to prove themselves.

Simon reckons one incident probably ended any chance he had. One day in the dressing room – I wasn't around at the time – he had run a bath and cleaned the boots of a first-teamer. That wasn't enough for this player, who seemed to have a problem with blacks.

'Get me an ice orange drink,' he ordered. There was an ice machine at the training ground and you could crush the ice and add juice to it. It was refreshing, but a bit of a chore. And it was said so rudely.

'Get it yourself,' Simon responded. He had taken enough bossing around. Trainees weren't supposed to talk to pros like that, though.

'You black bastard!' And with that this senior player actually spat in Simon's face. He was older, bigger; he was a bully. It was disgusting. Simon wasn't taking any more of that. He reached into the laundry room nearby where the kettle was kept for making teas and coffee. He picked up the kettle, still full of boiling hot water, slightly splashing poor Millie, the old laundry lady, who was everyone's friend. Until now no one had realised what Si was about to do, but when he started to lunge at the senior pro all hell broke loose. Suddenly, all the other players jumped on Si – God knows what damage he would have done if he'd clobbered the other player with a scalding kettle.

Then a youth team coach intervened. He said the first-teamer was in the wrong, but Si was too. He announced that John Hollins, who had returned to Chelsea as a player and a coach, would deal with the incident later, but he demanded that Simon apologise. Si didn't see why he alone should have to apologise, so he flew off the handle again.

'Apologise? Me? Why? He's the pro. He abused me. He spat at me!'

Simon was humiliated and angry with the club, and did everything he could to get away after that. In the end he only hurt himself. That's how it works. Dubbers and Jonah knew the score and they told him to bite the bullet. You couldn't react to things or you'd be out. That's probably why they progressed into the first team. They were good role models. It was the only way to be at Chelsea back then. There were undertones of prejudice in what quite a few players said or did, but most of the time everyone did their best not to allow them to surface.

Of course, it wasn't just about race. There was a social hierarchy where trainees were subordinate to pros, and they had to respect that whether they liked it or not. Another time, Si nutmegged a Chelsea centre-back in training and made the mistake of joyously shouting 'Nuts!' as he did so. Justice was soon exacted on him – he got a punch in the face for his cheek.

Simon told me about what one or two of the Chelsea staff would say, little anti-black gibes all the time. For instance, when a new white kid joined the juniors, the coaches would nod towards the black guys and joke to the new boy, 'Watch your valuables with this lot,' and worse.

When the Chelsea lads talked to other apprentices, those boys couldn't believe what people got away with at the club. I knew nothing about that – no one at the club ever said anything like that to me anyway. I don't know whether they thought the same way but didn't feel they could get away with it in the senior game.

I certainly didn't get the impression the staff and players were racist when I used to bring my mate George to the Harlington training ground. He was a big black geezer, 6 ft 4 in. I was hanging out and going raving with him at the time. Hollins used to welcome him with open arms and the lads adored him being around – he lightened the mood. Despite him being clumsy and totally useless at football, they'd throw him a training kit and get him to join in. He'd be thundering round the pitch alongside household names such as Kerry Dixon and Pat Nevin, with his arse popping out of his too-small tracksuit bottoms.

One incident made me feel really bad, though. Soon after the start of the season I was struggling with a niggling injury, and spending time on the treatment table. The physio Norman Medhurst had an Irish assistant called Jimmy in to help him out. He was a nice geezer, good company. While he was treating me, he happened to mention that he was thinking about going to the Notting Hill Carnival that weekend.

Personally, I don't go to Carnival. I went there once and that was it – too much stress. But I wanted him to enjoy himself at what was basically a large black street party. I told him he ought to go. 'You should enjoy yourself there, Jimmy,' I said.

When I saw him after the August bank holiday he was a little quieter than usual.

'How d'you get on at Carnival?' I asked, smiling.

'It was hell,' he said. 'I got mugged.' I felt so bad. After all, he'd gone there on my recommendation.

'They stole my camera,' he explained. 'Took some scissors and cut the strap off from round my neck.'

I was embarrassed, even though he wasn't the type to look at every black man in the same way. I sometimes had the feeling I had come to represent the whole black race in the first-team set-up. There I was driving around in the classic 'black man's wheels' – the BMW with the pumping stereo. They knew all about my womanising and turning up late every now and then. I wasn't being a great ambassador.

When I was older and more confident, I wouldn't stand for the nonsense I did then. Maybe I would have stood up to it and probably got thrown out for my sins, like Si. Ask my mum, ask my sister. I'm so quick-tempered. Sometimes I don't believe I let that abuse go on without saying anything, but I know why I did. It was because I so wanted to be a footballer and I knew I had to be stoical to make it. I didn't want anything at all to come in the way of it. That's why I never reacted. I would have lost everything I'd fantasised about and worked so hard for.

Such was the experience of the black pioneer at Chelsea Football Club. I didn't feel like an historical figure, a champion of a cause. I was me, a victim of arriving at the wrong place at the wrong time. It's only when I look back, or someone tells me what a contribution I made, that I realise how I helped to usher in gradual and positive change at Stamford Bridge.

I have a letter from Leon Mann of the Kick It Out anti-racism organisation. He describes how his father had become a Chelsea fan when he moved to the area in the sixties, and how he walked out of a Chelsea match and never went back in protest at the racial barracking I received.

'My dad was so ashamed that fans could abuse any player in this way, let alone their own,' he said. 'I strongly believe many fans also walked away and never returned.'

I didn't have that option. I had to trust the fact that either I'd win the boo-boys over or, more likely, the decent fans would make their voices heard.

I bore a lot of the pain of being racially abused in the way I'd been brought up – by myself. I wanted to be a success so much that, like Dubbers and Jonah, I always tried my best to fit in, but I never compromised and I never forgot who I was. Unlike a lot of today's black footballers, I was very much into my community, and I had a certain status in it. If you went to my barber's at Stamford Hill on the day of a game, I'd be there handing out tickets to the match to friends.

I was always out and about on the club scene. Playing football, playing out. I'd come back from a match at Liverpool and that night you'd find me raving in Hackney. The rare groove, the hip-hop. The ladies. It never affected my performance on the pitch. I was naturally fit. I was hanging out with two guys who ran a sound called Casual Affair, later to be GQ. If I wanted to get on a nightclub or rave guest list, there was no problem.

I was a sharp dresser at Chelsea, too – crocodile skin shoes, snakeskin shirt, Pierre Cardin, Cecil Gee, and a white gold ring with little diamonds marking out my initials 'PC'. I used to kiss it before I ran on to the pitch.

At some stage I earned the nickname 'King Canners' – after King Canute as much as anything. I liked it and used it myself. Nice dressing-room banter.

I'd say, certainly in my second season, I suppose I'd become a bit of a character in the dressing room. And on match days I had to get on well with club secretaries Sheila Marson and Theresa Conneelly so they could help me out with tickets. They helped me juggle the seating positions of the various women I'd invited to games – to make sure they weren't next to each other, or all hell would break loose!

Around this time, completely out of the blue, Christine turned up again for the first time in years. Probably because she knew I was a footballer and must at last have some money. She started coming to the Chelsea ground. Her line was, 'I know Paul Canoville's here and I ain't going till he sees me!' It was the same sort of stubbornness she had given Mum and June in 1979 when I left her.

Not unreasonably, she was claiming maintenance for Natalie, who was a toddler by then. I regret not getting close to Natalie. She doesn't know me, she really doesn't. But with the circumstances of our split, it was a difficult situation. Natalie couldn't make any choices then, and I wasn't forcing anybody. If she wants to know me now, that's OK.

When I saw Christine she'd bawl at me, 'Your daughter needs this and that.' I did have to pay maintenance for Natalie and I didn't mind that, but I wasn't happy with how Christine went about it. That wasn't the end of it.

When the stories about Christine were passed around the club, it must have made people laugh, sigh and see just another Afro-Caribbean stereotype. As the only black man in the first team it wasn't like I had a lot in common with the other players. I was into my black culture, and it was of no interest to them. The majority of them were from the London area or home counties, but not many of them had grown up with black friends. Harlington didn't help. There was nowhere really to sit and socialise after training, no nice cafeteria. As soon as it was over I was away in my motor, off to see a woman or another friend, back to the world I was accustomed to.

So I made an effort to get to know my team-mates better. When we came back from an away game it might be one o'clock in the morning or later. I would be worried about how the hell I was getting home, but they were up for it. 'Canners, we're going out man, come on,' they'd say and at first I'd knock them back, but once I'd resolved to fit in more I sometimes went with them and had a good time. We went and got a drink and it wasn't in a bar, it was an all-night café on the Fulham Road, just down from the ground where we were dropped off. You could catch a meal, a drink, breakfast, or a hot chocolate. I was hungry that first time. One thing they did there I remember was chips with mushy peas. Mum made it difficult to enjoy chips, because she hated us having them from a fish bar out of paper so much.

'Wait till you get home!'

'But Mum, that's what you do with chips.'

'You're not having chips on the road. Wait till you get home.'

I'd never come across that other stuff. Mushy peas? Unbelievable. The lads loved it at the Up-All-Night after an away game. We all wanted something proper to eat, nice food, a hot chocolate, even if we got there at four or five o'clock in the morning. I carried on going there on the odd occasion, just to link up with the players. I hear it's changed its name now, but the current players still sometimes go there after an away trip, the same as generations did before them.

I discovered a few overlaps of interests with the other players. John Bumstead, a midfielder from Rotherhithe, south-east London, who was three years older, was a big cricket fan. If England were playing the West Indies, others would join in, but Bummers and I would keep up the cricket banter a lot of the time. He was a decent player too.

Music was a different matter in our dressing room. I was a lone voice there. All the others knew about was the pop and soul stuff of the early eighties – The Police, Billy Joel, The Jam and bands such as Imagination or Kool and the Gang. The closest they came to my taste was George Benson or Bob Marley. They knew nothing about the deeper music that was the soundtrack to when I was growing up – reggae, jazz-funk and now rap. For away games, the lads would bring in tapes to play during the coach journey. I liked to make cassette compilations and bring them in to listen to myself, but I didn't think the boys would get on with my taste in music if I kept putting it on the coach's sound system. That would have been too much. Nowadays, advertising companies base whole campaigns for big household-name products around rap or ska music or Caribbean slang. In 1982 black culture was still far from mainstream, still in a 'ghetto'.

On the playing side, I was becoming far better integrated. I got my first proper run in the first team at the end of the 1982/83 season. I'd played six games in the autumn of 1982 but was asked to play on the right wing and started or finished on the bench in half of them. It meant that I was always trying to make a big impact as soon as possible. With my pace and ability to get round a player, though, it was going pretty well for me. Even though we lost at Derby in the League and Notts County in the League Cup, I felt I was starting to have an effect and create openings for us. We weren't a team blessed with speed so I could make a difference, especially against tiring defenders. I could cross and had shots too.

Then just at the wrong moment a thigh injury ruled me out and I didn't start again until March 1983 – my usual bad timing.

Mike Fillery was the schemer in the team then and he was left-sided, wearing the number eleven shirt. He was a brilliant young player and a laid-back type. When he was on form he was unbeatable. You knew he had it, but it was a matter of confidence whether the things he tried came off. He'd get downhearted and play the easy ball.

At the start of the season we had been hoping for promotion, but results had been pretty dreadful over the winter. My chance came that spring after Fillers was moved inside to see more of the ball and Phil Driver and Peter Rhoades-Brown, both right-wingers, hadn't worked out. I started down the left against Charlton. We lost 2–5 but John Neal showed faith and stuck with me and it all came together between Fillers and me in April at Craven Cottage.

The pitch was cut up, and Colin Lee partnered David Speedie upfront. Fillers was so on form that day he made it easy for us. I fancied my chances against Tony Gale, never the fleetest defender. It finished 1–1 and I scored our goal. Fulham's manager, great goalscorer Malcolm Macdonald, would have been proud of my acrobatic volley. Things like that started to encourage more backing for me from the supporters and helped drown out the morons, whom I could still occasionally hear hooting among the general noise.

I enjoyed being more involved in that match. I liked the responsibility I was given at set-pieces; I didn't normally do that. We'd worked on corners and I started taking them, and being involved in the plays as well.

I suppose it was because if a cross came to me on the edge of the box I was useless, but the manager said to me, 'This time, go to the back post, and as the corner's being taken, fall back so if anything does come over the top you can have a chance.'

The plan came off straight away. I was on the back post, dropped off the markers, the ball flicked off Micky Droy's head, came to me and I just hit it full into the net. That was John Neal's set-piece. He knew what he was talking about, the boss. I was made up. When the volley came off just as we'd planned it, I set off on a long celebration run. I didn't get far, though – tripped up and landed flat on my arse in a puddle.

Good as this opportunity was for me, there were still difficult days ahead for the club. That draw with Fulham left us thirteenth in the Second Division, five points away from the relegation zone, but with no real thoughts of the drop.

Then we went on a disastrous run of six games that brought three defeats and no wins. I played in all but one of them. The worst was the desperate 0–3 defeat by fellow strugglers Burnley that dumped us into the bottom three for the first time. There were now four games remaining, against Rotherham, Sheffield Wednesday, Bolton Wanderers and Middlesbrough. Out of these, Wednesday were the only ones in the top half of the table. The others were all in the mire with us.

Players will tell you that it's much easier to step into a successful side that's playing well than it is a struggling one fighting for its livelihood. You learn about people at times like that in football. It takes personality to overcome really bad situations. I found I could deal with the pressure and always tried to do my best. I was so hungry to succeed.

In the dressing room, we had some big personalities, ever joking but always there to have a quiet word or dish it out publicly when needed. Joey Jones was loud, boisterous, getting everyone going; Colin Pates and Micky Droy, too. Importantly for the run-in, Steve Francis, who was a good young keeper and one of the lads, had returned at Burnley. Some other players you wouldn't want next to you in the trenches. Through it all, although he must have been feeling the pressure, manager John Neal hardly changed in his approach to us, still calm, organised, reassuring.

At home to Rotherham, I looked round the dressing room and felt the tension. I was a sub. When we came out for the start, there were not even 9,000 people in Stamford Bridge and it was hard to get going. Our defenders stood off Rotherham, hesitated, and they scored after less than a quarter of an hour. This really was turning horrific.

I came on for Joey Jones when we needed to take a few more risks. The equaliser was fortunate. Gary Chivers knocked in a free kick, Micky Droy glanced it on and Clive Walker stabbed it in. A 1–1 draw was poor, but it was still something. Afterwards, in the press conference, with journalists baying for blood, John Neal made a typical cool joke. 'It's a bit claustrophobic in here,' he remarked. That's what he was like. Understated.

Two days later we managed the same result against Sheffield Wednesday, but I didn't feature. David Speedie got our goal. It wasn't getting any better for us. The newspapers, TV and radio were writing our obituary, talking up the sad demise of a once great club. Chelsea had never been lower than football's second tier in its seventy-eight-year history, and we were damned if it was going to happen for the first time now.

Even so, you needed a maths degree to work out all the possibilities of who might get relegated. With two matches remaining in the first week of May, even Cambridge United, in twelfth place, were not out of it.

Our final two games were away at Bolton and at home to Boro. The three of us were still desperately scrambling for points. Speedo was suspended and I was recalled for the visit to Burnden Park in grey Lancashire. The weather had been awful in the week before and it rained constantly on the day. I liked that sort of weather. The ball sped up, defenders slowed down, and it gave you a chance to use your pace and tricks to full effect.

When the Chelsea boys ran out this time, even though there were only just over 8,500 fans in the stadium, it was an impressive sight. Somehow it seemed like half the stadium was wearing blue and singing their hearts out for the team. It gave us a huge lift before kick-off.

I was playing midfield, with Clive Walker wide left and Mickey Fillery on the other flank. Tails up, we ripped into them in the first half but couldn't make it count, although Colin Lee had a few chances. The ball kept sticking in the mud and puddles and it was a typical scrappy relegation battle.

John Neal was calmness itself at half-time. He just went

through a few routines and had a quiet word with one or two players. Keep going and it will come.

With just under twenty minutes to go, Clive broke through from the left and found himself in space outside the corner of the box. The ball sat up for him and he fired a scorcher over Jim McDonagh in the Bolton goal, sending the players and the fans into ecstasy. As one of the eleven who played that vital game, I was a Chelsea hero of sorts now.

For all the joy of winning cups and gaining promotion, there's something extra special about escaping a catastrophe in that way. The win rocketed us up the table. We were now fourteenth, six places and two points farther away from disaster.

When Middlesbrough visited a week later, both sides knew a point would keep us up. We were unchanged and I kept my place in midfield. In front of almost 20,000 fans, it was a nothing game, as you might expect, and at the end there was a pitch invasion. While the supporters revelled on the pitch, we headed straight down the tunnel. Great as it was to stay up, most of us felt ashamed for getting into the mess in the first place.

The longer summer progressed though, the better the achievement seemed. We were looking at still playing in a good league, and suddenly an influx of keen, quality players from Neal and McNeill's network of contacts arrived. The new men included Eddie Niedzwiecki, who was a star keeper for Chelsea until injury ended his career five years later. John Hollins, who was still a legend at the

Bridge from his exploits with the Cup-winning teams of 1970 and 1971, returned as a right-back who did some coaching. The new arrival who stole all the headlines, though, was goal-machine Kerry Dixon from Reading for a fee of £150,000, plus £25,000 if he played for England (which, of course, he did). He was less than a year older than I was and had a far bigger reputation in the game, based on bagging 51 goals in just 116 games for the Royals. Now it was royal blue for him, and what an amazing career he had at the Bridge. Unfortunately, he and I got off on completely the wrong footing in preseason 1983.

It was Aberystwyth again and he'd joined up with us for the first time after signing. We'd finished training and I had run a nice hot bath for myself. I'd forgotten my toiletry stuff and towel, slipped off to get them and when I came back, who's just about to get into the bath I'd run? The new golden boy!

'Hold on, Kerry,' I reasoned, politely, 'that's my bath.'

'Can't see your name on it,' he sniffed, and stepped into it.

That really annoyed me. I thought it was disrespectful and rude. There were loads of other baths free that he could have used if he'd been arsed. I tried to talk him out but he wouldn't move.

I wasn't going to let him get away with it. I had limits. So I decided on the most drastic course of action and climbed right into the bath with him. Wooah! You should have seen his face!

So it all went off. Micky Droy came rushing in to be

greeted by the sight of two naked angry men shouting and shoving at each other. Just as Kerry landed a right-hander on me, and before I was able to retaliate, Micky, who was built like a Hummer, grabbed hold of me. We were still yelling at each other but Micky wasn't interested in what caused it, he just didn't want two players scrapping. It could have been much worse if he hadn't been around.

We both had to go and see John Neal about it. After what I'd been through at Chelsea by now, all sorts of things were going through my feverish mind. Kerry got the first punch in – that's what I was so vexed about. I was thinking how I could get my own back. But there was no way we could stop passing to each other or anything like that. That would just be stupid. OK there was unfinished business, but he was a team-mate, a geezer I would be locked together with in the group. We had to share training, changing rooms, a football pitch. It didn't make sense to plot vengeance. That train of thought showed I'd grown up a little, and could put professionalism above retribution.

We would either be a team or we would be against each other. We didn't have to be best mates – and I didn't really get into bonding with him – just team-mates. I only had to befriend him on a certain level – on that pitch, you cannot be separate individuals. That was a lesson football had taught me. In the end, as usual, I just had to bite the bullet. John Neal talked to us briefly about the incident and asked us to shake hands. That was it. We were fine after that.

It made a big difference to know you were playing well, and were part of a club that could be going places again. With confidence boosts like that in my mind, I started the new season, 1983/84, in pole position on the left, even though another brilliant new player had arrived in September in the form of £90,000 talented fellow winger Pat Nevin.

Although our tastes were very different, music was a common bond for Pat and me because we were both so passionately into it. I'd ask him to bring me in a mix tape and I'd do the same. And that's when I got into music by Cat Stevens (now, of course, Yusuf Islam). When I heard him for the first time I asked straight away, 'Who is that?' He was folky but he could write a tune and had a groove to him. Having that point of reference, I came back at Pat with Bill Withers' 'Ain't No Sunshine'. It got him at that part where it goes, 'I know, I know, I know, I know ... Ain't no sunshine when she's gone'. He just loved it. After that he used to say, 'Come on man, you've got to show me some music, Paul!' I played him a few more tapes, some early rap, but for him it was never going to replace those bands he heard on John Peel's show on Radio One. He was so passionate about obscure indie rock bands. There's a story that in October 1983, when we played at Fulham and won 5–3, Pat actually asked to be substituted before the end. John Neal asked him why, was he injured? 'Nah,' said Pat, 'the Cocteau Twins are playing at the ICA tonight and I don't want to miss the start.'

He became like an icon to me. Pat was always the

person who had a book on the coach, sat by himself. No playing cards for him like the rest of the boys. It was an opportunity to educate himself and I had total respect for him. He was completely different from everyone else, intriguing. He could switch on, switch off. He did that in a game, too. Give him the ball, 'Go on, Pat!', and out of nothing he'd beat four players and get a goal.

I loved to watch him play. The way he collected the ball, controlled it – both feet – you just loved to be on Pat's side. When you were winning, Pat held on to that ball. He was unbelievable. Little as he was, you'd think he'd get knocked about, but he was agile – great user of the ball, too. He had this move where he used to scoop it over defenders. Wicked.

He'd say to me, 'Canners, I'd love your speed.'

I'd say, 'Pat, I'd love your skill.'

Pat Nevin was a good team-mate and did a lot for me at Chelsea. He is the only one of the players who spoke up publicly about the way some fans treated me. I don't think the others did because of how they would have looked, sticking up for a black guy against white blokes, threatening as they were. I was part of an Afro-Caribbean world that most of them knew only bad things about through the media. Possibly some of them may have held racist views themselves. Those supporters, abusive though they were to me, had been fiercely loyal to them all this time. How would they react to being criticised? I have to look at it that way.

It was a football club, not a university. Nobody

discussed issues such as racism. Once some of the guys got in an argument with Pat about apartheid in South Africa, but they just did it as a wind-up. You'd talk about incidents such as the Brixton riots when they happened, but mostly you kept to the game, or lighter stuff.

Pat was philosophical. He was a smart guy, a proud Scot, and he was also an outsider. He read proper newspapers, had an encyclopaedic knowledge of clever pop stuff, always had an intellectual take on the latest news, and never hung out with the other players. He'd never be at the Up-All-Night café after away games – he was out doing arty, Bohemian things instead. He could leave the others gaping when he joined in a debate sometimes. They didn't really understand his take on life, and I don't think they understood me, either. Although a lot of them were from broken homes and working-class backgrounds, I came from a different culture and perspective, moulded by my experience, and I lived an opposite lifestyle to them.

My problem with the fans wasn't theirs. It clearly affected me – they could see that – but not them personally. Hadn't Graham Wilkins got stick for giving the odd goal away? I think most of the players thought I just needed to ignore them, as Graham did, work hard, and hope for the best. They weren't concerned with understanding me and what I was going through. 'Canners, you're all right, mate, you're with us . . .'

I didn't want it to become a big talking point anyway – that's how I was. But Pat, he would take it on, say his piece and let them know how serious it all was. Really, I suppose, it should have been me, but I didn't want to rock the boat. It had been hard for me to get where I was and I didn't want to blow it. Football was the big hope for me to make something of my life.

If I'd kept kicking up a rumpus about the abuse, it would have seemed like I was instigating trouble. Next thing, the chief would get to hear about it. 'What's wrong, Paul, have you got a problem?' I could hear him saying. I just didn't want to escalate it.

The boss knew how I felt, anyway. I didn't see it as the players' job to do anything. There were only a few times when I really lost my rag with the lack of support from Chelsea. The first happened when I was playing for the reserves at Millwall. During the game, Dubbers said to me, 'Have you looked up there on the terraces?' And in among the small crowd of people were three geezers wearing Ku Klux Klan hoods, home made out of pillow cases or something. No one was telling them to take them off or anything. After I saw them I went berserk on the pitch. I lost my head and was flying into tackles dangerously after the ball had gone. It was unprofessional of me. I could have done real harm to a completely innocent party. What I should have done is calmly complain to the referee or a stadium official or mention it to someone on our bench.

After my response on the pitch things came to a head. Whether he was aware of the Klan headgear or not, the referee walked over to our bench and told them to substitute me or he'd have to send me off. I didn't mention it to anyone.

The second time was when we played at Brighton in September 1983. Racist hooting wasn't the biggest problem at Chelsea in those days. Hooligans – black as well as white – purporting to be fans, used to tag along to matches for a good punch-up. Every club had its 'firm' but Stamford Bridge was right up there with Millwall, Manchester United and West Ham for the most regular offenders. The worse their reputation got, the more they liked it. It didn't need a spark to set them off, just an opportunity. Before that Brighton match, 125 supporters were arrested outside the ground, and as the whistle blew on our 2–1 win, a huge pitch invasion started, in which four coppers were injured and the goalposts were broken. You can see why I had been worried about being attacked.

But at the Goldstone Ground I was far more concerned by what their right-back did to me on the pitch. I was giving him a hard time, beating him regularly, so he took the law into his own hands and clobbered me in a tackle. The foul was given, and as I stood up, he spat in my face. I was disgusted. Of course I retaliated and laid into him, and that's all the linesman saw, so I was sent off. I scrubbed myself over and over in the shower to remove the memory of his saliva on my skin.

Our players were sympathetic, as was manager John Neal. 'If that fella had spat at me,' he said, 'I'd have spat at him and knocked his head off.'

I cried when I got sent off. I couldn't believe it. I was shocked. Being spat at is the worst humiliation of any. It's a denial of your humanity and robs you of your dignity.

It's pure filth and the ultimate disrespect. Call me all the bad names under the sun, I'll take that all day in comparison – it's only words in the end – but never spit in my face. I wanted to kill him.

After that incident I had to go to Lancaster Gate and appear before the disciplinary committee at the FA.

'You admit you did it?'

'I did.' And I'd do it again.

'Why?'

'Because he spat at me.' I got a three-game suspension. Bastards.

I was the only black guy in the first team at the time. Don't get me wrong, I wasn't over-sensitive. You could have a joke with me about black issues. I found it funny if it was funny. But if I didn't find it funny, if it over-stepped the mark a little, you'd see it in my face. 'What's wrong, Canners?' 'I didn't find it amusing.' And it would stop there; they were sensitive in that respect.

To be fair, I think most of them meant no harm at all; they just had little or no experience of being around or dealing with black people. They didn't know how a black man plaited hair, for instance. I used to have an afro, then I started to put my hair in braids. That fascinated them.

'Gordon Bennett, how long did it take you to do that? Who's done that?'

'My sister.'

You could see they were genuinely intrigued, it wasn't a wind-up. It told me how little they knew other than what they read in the papers or saw on TV – when black people were in trouble or starving in Africa. Some of the London boys – Patesy, Fillers, Bumstead, Dale Jasper – they'd grown up rubbing shoulders with the Afro-Caribbean community. I got on well with them and they would never antagonise me. I didn't always find the same thing with the lads from other parts of England, especially the less cosmopolitan areas, where ethnic minorities were more thin on the ground and isolated. Once, when one such senior player was injured the same time as me, the physio said he'd got passes and we should both go down to this swimming pool because it was good exercise for our condition and non-load-bearing. After he'd gone, this geezer turned to me in all seriousness and said, 'You're not going are you, Canners?'

'Why not?'

'Everyone knows black people don't float.'

CHAPTER 14

The Golden Age At Chelsea

If I had a bit still to do to win over every racist in the Chelsea crowd, at least my coaches and most of my team-mates were backing me on the pitch.

John Neal's signings were working like magic from the start of the 1983/84 season. David Speedie, the fiery little Scot, had great touch, vision, and an excellent shot on him. He was forever whinging on the pitch, demanding the ball and reacting when you didn't pass to him, and he could be a truculent whatshisname off the pitch – Kerry and Pat also found him hard going but seemed to have built telepathic connections with him on the field. He was a brilliant player for Chelsea in my time there, and one of the most difficult forwards for any defender to deal with. Seventies legend Alan Hudson was re-signed at thirty-two. He was good with the reserves – always telling the keeper to roll the ball out, not hoof it, so that the team played more football – but he was never fit enough for the first team and left in a year.

One of the shrewdest signings was Nigel Spackman, 'Spackers', from Bournemouth. What a bit of scouting he was. At just £35,000, he was the business. He could trot around all day, box to box, tackle and short pass. Spackers was a major part of our achievements in that season and a nice guy. He went on to have a fantastic career at Liverpool and Rangers. Ironically, after seeing what happened to me, he saw the same thing occur with John Barnes at Liverpool and Mark Walters at Rangers.

The funniest thing with Spackers, though, was in the first match of this new-style Chelsea, at home to Derby. He was one of four players making their debut and after five minutes he picked up a loose ball from a corner and whacked it in from outside the box. Hello, we all thought, dark horse for the golden boot! How wrong we were – he got just twelve in his four seasons at the Bridge.

We absolutely slaughtered the Rams 5–0 and it was soon pretty obvious this side was a very different prospect from the one that had only just avoided relegation the previous season. We were serious candidates to win promotion to the First Division come May.

By the autumn I felt I was really playing my part at Chelsea. Even better, I could sense that people in the crowd were warming to me. It wasn't raucous or obvious, just a new buzz of anticipation when I got on the ball. After what had gone before, it made me feel wanted and gave me an extra yard of pace.

In October I got my first goal of the season in a 3–2 win at Huddersfield Town – it was their first home defeat in eighteen months – but it was overshadowed when we heard that a Chelsea fan, a twenty-year-old student, had been beaten up in the street by Yorkshire fans and killed. That's how things were in those days. Like racial jeering, it was a sinister part of the national game, but a part of it nevertheless.

At the same time the newspapers were full of the fact that one of the major shareholders at Stamford Bridge, David Mears, had sold his lot to a property development company, Marler Estates. His great grandfather Gus had started the club eighty years earlier, and now they were saying he'd cashed in to kill it. But I was a footballer and until it affected me directly, I didn't pay it any heed. *Que sera, sera*, as the Cup anthem went.

The Saturday after Huddersfield we returned to a place I always enjoyed, Craven Cottage. I had a great time against Fulham's Paul Parker, who became England's right-back a few years later. He was small, nippy, but I got plenty of change out of him that day. Kerry and Pat were linking well and I remember Pat, playing down the right flank, going on one amazing run, like a Brazilian. He ran through the middle and beat virtually every Fulham player. Twice! By the end of it he looked as knackered as they did, but Colin Lee nicked it off his toes and slotted it home. We won that one 5–3. I was buzzing.

The same month we went up to the Midlands for a Milk Cup first leg to face Leicester City, then bottom of the First

Division. It was a real chance to test our mettle against a top-flight outfit and we fancied ourselves to progress because their defence was quite lumbering.

Kerry easily outpaced their backs and converted a long clearance for the opener. It was like that all night. I always knew my pace could surprise people, and when a Leicester defender knocked a short back-pass to his keeper, it was suicide. I was able to nip in, lob the ball over the keeper and head it into an empty net. Our travelling fans went wild as I ran past them.

Despite one or two annoying muscle injuries, things were turning round big time for me now. I netted my debut hat-trick in a Chelsea shirt on 6 December 1983, and that was a proud moment. It was against Swansea City and I got the first goal after eight minutes when I latched on to a rare mis-kick in front of the goal by Kerry, hit it first time and saw the net ripple. After that I was flying all evening. Some games you just feel as though you can zip through defences. It was a weird game because they were so weak. Any time we attacked we could have scored.

My second came after typically fluent approach play. It was a perfect example of how that team played – with pace, accuracy, directness. John Hollins at right-back, Kerry and Speedo combined to lay it on a plate for me from a yard out. My third came in the last ten minutes when their keeper carried one of my crosses over the line. It was that sort of day.

I'd been a professional footballer for a little over eighteen months and I'd got my first hat-trick. I was given the match ball to take home and keep afterwards, signed by all my team-mates – I didn't know that was the tradition. It was an honour. You've achieved something, scored a hat-trick in your professional career. Not every pro can say that. I'm not a great one for records, mementoes and stuff, but Mum still has that ball.

In January 1984 I faced another challenge. John Neal was reunited with one of his former players, Mickey Thomas from Wrexham. I should have been anxious about that, angry even – he was another winger to add to the collection, and a fellow left-footer – but I just couldn't dislike him. What an amazing personality he has, like a cheeky schoolboy, talking twenty to the dozen, non-stop entertainment. He's a great geezer to have around.

Mickey was best friends with club captain Joey Jones, another ex-Wrexham lad, and they were inseparable. I loved those Welsh boys. The two of them were up to mischief all the time and would sometimes sleep in the offices at Stamford Bridge if there was nowhere else – they both still commuted from Wales. Mickey would disappear for hours, seeing women, drinking. He had a real problem sleeping and used to make himself busy whatever the hour. He was hyperactive twenty-four hours a day and had little respect for club rules, especially blackouts.

'Canners, come out and have some fun, man,' he'd say, but I couldn't trust myself to do that before a game and still perform amazingly well, as he did.

'We can't do that, Mickey, there's a curfew,' I'd reply.

They were great characters. And Mickey could run all

day. I don't know if he had beans in his pants, but that boy was unstoppable. Apparently, he had an oversized heart. He had an engine, I know that, and he was box-to-box all match.

With him and Pat around the club I played in spells, then got dropped or injured. It was still a fantastic campaign to play in, not that my performances on the pitch had won over everyone in the stands. We had played Crystal Palace at Selhurst Park and Pat scored the winner that pulled us up to second place in Division Two with six games remaining, odds-on for promotion to the top flight. I had come on as a second-half substitute for Mickey Thomas and, incredibly, there were still a few morons prepared to hoot and boo when I ran on.

That was 14 April 1984, two years after my debut against the same team. Shows you how long I went through that crap.

I'll never forget that Pat came out publicly and, as only Pat could, attacked those last few fans who were abusing me. At the after-match press conference, he told the assembled media representatives that he didn't want to talk about his goal, he wanted to talk about my treatment. It made all the papers the following day and probably shamed a few Blues supporters. He said he loved and respected Chelsea's fans, but he was disgusted at some of them for subjecting a black team-mate to racist barracking.

The game after that, at Shrewsbury, Pat made sure that he, Kerry and Speedo ran out alongside me in a show of support. I think that helped a lot by giving right-thinking fans confidence at last to shout down the idiots. Recently I was told about John Drewitt, a supporter who had a season ticket in the West Stand in the eighties, and who still goes to games. After I'd made my debut he found himself surrounded by a small pocket of neo-Nazis, hooting and swearing at me, calling me 'coon' and 'nigger' as I ran down the left-wing for their team. John Drewitt was a big white bloke who didn't like what he saw and wanted to make a stand. So one time when I was taking on the opposition down the flank in front of him he stood up and yelled out, 'Skin the white bastards!' It was a clever way to have a go. He was making fools of them and they didn't like that one bit! There were too few making a point like that back in my first few years at Chelsea.

Nevertheless, our 1983/84 promotion run-in was a great time for me, especially after the shows of support from my team-mates. It was a complete contrast to the relegation struggle the previous year of course. One of the main reasons was the form of Kerry Dixon. The tall, fast, powerful, blond-haired, goalscoring golden boy got an incredible thirty-four strikes that year. He was a legend for Chelsea and I'm full of pride that I helped load a lot of the bullets for him with my crosses from the left.

At the end of April, we beat Leeds 5–0 at home in one of the most amazing games I was involved in – amazing for all sorts of reasons.

I'd always actually supported Leeds as a kid. I liked the football they played, they had neat kit design ideas, including the ridiculous vinyl tassels on their socks, and they were successful – obviously, I thought, partly because of the tassels! I didn't have anyone in Southall to influence me in any other way, so I went mine. Leeds it was. Ironic, later, that I went to Chelsea, because those two sets of fans absolutely hated each others' guts as a result of some big battles in the sixties and seventies, especially the 1970 FA Cup final and replay, which Chelsea won 2–1 after extra time.

The scenes with the fans at the 1984 game, though, were incredible. Hooligan culture was strong then and the kids on the terraces didn't give a damn. It was spectacular to watch but quite scary, especially when you were sitting on the bench, or warming up, like I was as substitute.

We were buzzing, almost certain of promotion. The Stamford Bridge crowd was huge – over 30,000 – and the mood was very boisterous. Even before kick-off supporters had been encroaching on the pitch.

We mashed what was quite an old Leeds team and every goal was given the same treatment – invasion of the grass and mobbing of the players.

When I came on, because of all the invasions, I was under strict orders to enjoy myself but not to score another goal. 'Canoville came on to add the fifth with a powerful run,' *The Times* said. Never mind that I'd ignored instructions, I ran through their side to score the last goal of the game. I was completely swamped in the crowd invasion. Considering what I'd been experiencing, I was more than a little apprehensive. But this time I was mobbed, patted, hugged. No abuse.

The ref was worse off. He was knocked over and

eventually called a halt to the game early. It was the wise thing to do but his whistle was the cue for the terraces to empty once more.

This time Chelsea fans took issue with the few remaining Leeds fans and it turned ugly. A Leeds fan found a piece of wood from somewhere – Stamford Bridge was a right dump back then – and started smashing the electric scoreboard at the away end. Madness. Chairman Bates called it 'just excited and boisterous', but one copper had to be revived after being hit by an object and forty-one people were charged afterwards for threatening behaviour, wilful destruction and being drunk and disorderly.

A week later we went up to Manchester City and won 2–0. I came on as a half-time sub and produced a cheeky flick, a bit of Canners magic, to put in Speedo. He crossed for Kerry to score. They were promotion rivals and this was a big result.

All I ever wanted was to play for a professional team and influence the outcome in some way. I was using my assets, beating players, stretching teams, getting in crosses, corners, deflections, anything that made things happen.

We were a genuinely strong side now. We'd beaten almost everyone in sight and got promoted from the Second Division as champions in May 1984. It was a dream come true.

The only cloud on the horizon was the condition of John Neal. He had been taken ill with a heart problem as we were on the promotion run-in but kept it quiet. It was more serious than he'd thought. He'd been such an influence on my career. I had no idea at the time how important his absence and eventual retirement a year later would be to me personally.

That summer of 1984 was fantastic. I had moved to Hackney by now, had my own flat and felt much more at home there, and we were looking forward to life in the First Division.

When the fixtures were published it was a fantasy start for us. The opening game was at Highbury against Arsenal, our London rivals. Our fans were especially pleased. Chelsea and Arsenal had been nip-and-tuck in the sixties and seventies before we'd fallen on hard times. Here was a chance to pit ourselves against the best in the capital again and see how we measured up. There was an extra zip at training in the build-up to that one. John Neal was recuperating and less involved. First-team coach John Hollins had stepped up and was doing a great job in training with his usual enthusiasm for the game. Along with assistant manager Ian McNeill, Holly was going to take a far bigger role generally until Neal was fully fit and healthy again.

Everybody was working hard just to get to play that game at Highbury. I was with the reserves and we played a practice match against the first team, which now included Doug Rougvie, a big, lovable, daft summer signing from Aberdeen. The match was designed to help the 'probables' get organised and work on their set-pieces. Playing on the 'possibles' side, I was going all out to force my way into the team. I'd been a pro for two years but still had a lot to learn.

I was playing on the left wing and Colin Lee was playing right-back. When it came to training, I was on form – the smell of new-mown grass and all that. The surface at the start of the season at Harlington was lovely. It was drizzling and the ball was skidding.

Colin was no spring chicken, so every time I got the ball I was roasting him. *Phtt*. Gone. Flicks past him, the lot. We changed over for the second half, and I did a trick that nutmegged him. The ball went past him, I ran on and crossed it. It went for a corner, I went for the ball and a challenge came in on me that wasn't the type you expected from a team-mate in training. It was Colin Lee, one of the senior players and not one of the most enlightened.

As usual, Micky Droy observed what happened and came over to me.

'Take your time,' he said quietly. 'Be warned, mate. He's not liking how you're taking the mickey out of him and he will break your legs.'

What? Damn!

He'd seen the way Colin was looking at me, and he'd seen the way he didn't like to be made a fool of. Micky may have been exaggerating with the leg-break business, but the whole thing had just passed me by till he pointed it out. Micky knew you couldn't be doing that to a fellow pro without him taking a lump out of you. He was the senior player marking my card. He did it properly, quietly, a word in the ear. I respect him for that. I took his advice and toned down the tricks in training.

You felt you could show off a little when you were in the

reserves, playing against the first team, though. You wanted to shine so you took the kick. To make it worse, we also used to support each other – 'Well done, Dubbers, well done son.' We'd rub it in for the first-team players. That's what they didn't like.

One time Speedo was ready with a tackle and I could see him coming a mile off. I had to jump to avoid him – 'Unlucky son, but here we go, come on.' We used to wind them up something chronic, but not everyone could accept that, as Micky rightly pulled me up about. I looked at it as a learning curve really, I just watched myself. I even eased up on Colin a bit. By then, I'd done enough, anyway, because I was included in the team to play Arsenal.

Life in the mid-eighties was generally pretty good for me. I was living near my second son, Dwayne, who was born in that area so north London was pretty much the focal point of my world, without the baggage of Southall and Slough. And it was all coming together at the start of the football season. All my mates were Gooners, and I was playing against local rivals Arsenal for my first-ever game in the top flight of English football. We were the new kids on the block, an old London rival very much on the rise again. Chelsea hadn't played Arsenal since 1979 and, although the red team had finished sixth in the League and won no Cups the previous season – a disaster for the 'bank of England' club – they nevertheless boasted a team full of household names. I was really looking forward to playing at Highbury. It felt like I was playing on my home patch, and I was far more excited than nervous about the result. We had just been promoted and had nothing to lose.

As I lived locally, I asked if I could meet the team down at the ground. The manager agreed, so I made the most of the opportunity. It was a boiling hot day in north London but I was really spruced up for the game. For style reasons, and despite the temperature, I had on this bad-boy overcoat with standout white pants. I wanted to look a bit flashy, stylish.

I borrowed my mum's car and drove down to the ground. I was surprised as I got close. Firstly, I had never seen so many Blues fans in my manor – they were literally everywhere you looked – and secondly, I thought the ground looked a bit old from the outside. The Stamford Bridge stadium had charm but was quite decrepit because Chelsea had been skint for a decade; Arsenal had no such excuse.

But it was still a thrill to be playing there. I would be facing the people you saw on the telly – Paul Mariner, Pat Jennings, Brian Talbot, Viv Anderson.

Kick-off was unusually early, 11.30, because of fears of hooliganism. Once I'd parked up, I strolled through the crowds and found the players' entrance. For once, I wasn't late. I was shown the way to the dressing room, which was again old but very grand and impressive. It looked very classy, very First Division. I remember thinking that it was going to be a good game. Things felt right. The team was right, the buzz was right . . . I was right. I belonged here. Then when I began to strip ready for action, I took off my shoes and noticed something disarming – the floor was warm under my feet.

'What the hell's going on with this floor?' I laughed.

'They've got under-floor heating,' came the reply. It wasn't such a novelty to some of the lads.

'You're joking,' I said. 'Why hasn't Chelsea got some of that?' Unlike Stamford Bridge (and especially Harlington, the God-forsaken training ground) you could take your socks off, walk about and not get frostbite. It was good, man.

So I went out on the pitch to soak up the atmosphere that was building for this big capital clash. I was going to be performing in front of 45,000 people. Wow! It was a tiny pitch, but for me it was ideal – lovely playing surface, cut inside the full-back, one pace and you're in the box – mayhem. I was gagging. You just give me the ball and I'm off.

When we lined up I was pitted against their right-back, Viv Anderson. I'd never met him but he was an idol to lots of black kids, and I had a lot of respect for what he'd put up with when he started. He was twenty-eight now, but back in 1978 he'd broken new ground by becoming the first black footballer to play for England. Respect to him for that. Viv had been rejected by Manchester United as a fifteen-year-old and had almost given up his dream of being a footballer and found other work, but Nottingham Forest – his hometown club – scouted him and signed him up in the early seventies. He won the League and the European Cup with Forest, but wasn't immune to racial abuse from the same sort of morons I knew about. It was a big day for him too – his Arsenal debut. I was twenty-two and chomping at the bit.

I did all right against him. The first half wasn't too good. It was close, tight. Viv liked to attack as well as defend. When he was ready, if you gave him space, bam! Doug Rougvie was asking for me to help because he was off running at him again and again.

We gave them a hard time for the opening twenty minutes, snapping at their heels and not letting them settle. But Mariner opened the scoring against the run of play with a header. We were really up against it, 0–1 down at Highbury. But boy, we gave what we got.

Kerry knocked in a rebound from his own shot three minutes later. Second half I started to open up. I swear to this day I was brought down in the box, but they didn't give anything. Typical of Highbury.

Pat Jennings was like a don. It was an honour to see him play live. He made things look so easy. Paul Davis was immense in that game for them. He shielded the ball and didn't make a mistake. It ended 1–1.

It was a great performance from us, a statement of intent in the top flight. But the pride in that game, for me, was to come back to Hackney that evening. I went raving as usual with my north London mates.

'All right, Canners?' They were nodding, smiling, respectful. 'Yeah, your boys did all right.' Too right we did. The club was in better shape all round. After the Arsenal game, Ken Bates announced a profit of £185,000 after a huge loss the season before. It was all looking up.

The baby King Canners on his throne.
Probably outside Albert Road, Southall.
Don't mention the hair.

Me and June,
looking very
cute, around
1966. Better
hair!

Above: The kids' Christmas party at Mum's work. June's in the middle – I'm the one with the attitude.

Left: At a family wedding around 1972. Mum looking glamorous with June a bridesmaid and me uncomfortable in a tight-fitting suit.

Right: The Caribbean island of Anguilla, where my mother grew up, looking nothing like 'Little Slough'.

Left: Under-18 5-a-side cup winners: the successful Hanwell Celtic side of 1979. That's me, aged 17, with the afro and the glare.

Below: My first full season. The 1982/83 Chelsea squad that narrowly avoided relegation. I'm back row, far left, sharing a joke with Bummers.

Right: A typically restrained Canners celebration, after the goal that earned a priceless point at Craven Cottage in April 1983.

COLORSPORT

COLORSPORT

Left: Taking on Ray Houghton. Fulham again during the early days of the great John Neal Chelsea team of 1983/84.

Below: Back in the big time, August 1984, and putting everything into robbing Arsenal's Brian Talbot at Highbury.

COLORSPORT

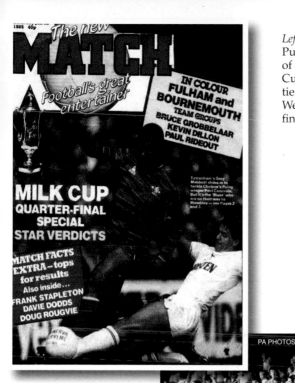

Left: Front cover star! Publicity ahead of our epic League Cup quarter-final tie with Sheffield Wednesday, my finest hour.

Below: Great days. Me and the boys (including Joey Jones, Kerry and Mickey T) celebrate promotion with the fans after beating Leeds 5–0 in 1984.

Below: Talk about frustration. My shot fizzes just wide, on the night Sunderland dumped us out of the 1985 League Cup in the semis.

HAVE FUN NOW
YOU ARE
6

You've been framed! I had no idea my image had been used on
cheesy greetings cards until someone bought one for me.

Right: Much appreciated. A lovely message in the benefit match programme from the biggest Chelsea fans group.

CHELSEA INDEPENDENT
supporters association.

THANKS PAUL,
For some great moments
Very best wishes for the future

P O BOX 459, LONDON E7 8LU

THE ROYAL
PROGRAMME: 20p

READING F.C.
1871

PAUL CANOVILLE'S BENEFIT MATCH

READING v CHELSEA
Saturday, August 13, 1988
Kick-off 3pm

Above: The programme for my benefit game in 1988. That's Lee Dixon (then of Stoke City) turning his head in the photo.

Right: Looking anxious coming away from Old Street magistrates after the hearing about the 'offensive weapon' in July 1985.

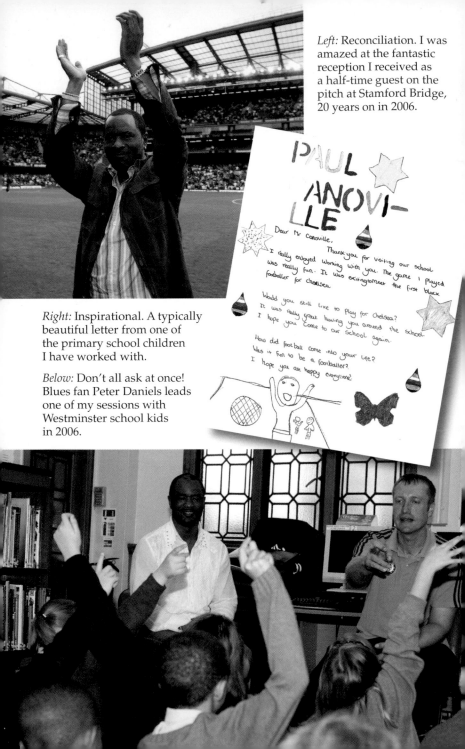

Left: Reconciliation. I was amazed at the fantastic reception I received as a half-time guest on the pitch at Stamford Bridge, 20 years on in 2006.

PAUL CANOVILLE

Dear Mr Canoville,

Thank you for visiting our school. I really enjoyed working with you. The game I played was really fun. It was exiting tomeet the first black footballer for chelsea.

Would you still Like to play for Chelsea? It was really great having you around the school. I hope you come to our school again.

How did football come into your Life? Was it fun to be a footballer? I hope you are happy everytime!

Right: Inspirational. A typically beautiful letter from one of the primary school children I have worked with.

Below: Don't all ask at once! Blues fan Peter Daniels leads one of my sessions with Westminster school kids in 2006.

Two days later we had our first home game of the season, against Sunderland, a mid-table team the previous season destined for relegation at the end of this campaign. It was another stretch along the learning curve for us – even also-ran teams were going to come to the Bridge and give us a problem. Clive Walker was playing for the Mackems – he'd been sold in the summer after nine superb years with the Blues – and they had Barry Venison and Gary Bennett in a five-man defence that was tough to break down. Even so, the livewire Speedo had the ball in their net after eight minutes, disallowed for offside. Then four minutes later, Speedo flicked a brilliant chip between two of their back line straight into my path, just like I loved it. I raced past the two defenders and broke into the box, hitting left-footed from the angle across goal. Their keeper Chris Turner got a palm to it and it seemed to take for ever to trickle over the line. It proved to be the winner, though, and we went fifth. Amazing.

The next game was a novelty, enforced by the demands of live television – we faced Everton at the Bridge on a Friday evening. I was a doubt with an injury but made it, for what it was worth. We had chances we didn't take in a poor game of football, and the millions watching worldwide were treated to one goal by Everton, ending our run of nineteen league games unbeaten, and a stupid scuffle between me and their bogbrush-haired full-back John Bailey.

Fit-again Mickey Thomas came on as a sub in that match for young Dale Jasper and was soon starting games ahead of me. I was back on the subs bench for our trip to Old Trafford and came on for Mickey to help see out an honourable 1–1 draw at the start of September. After that, when Mickey was available, it was hard for me to find minutes on the pitch. I couldn't complain because the on-field telepathy between him, Kerry, Pat and Speedo was really doing the business. Again, I just had to make an impact when I had the chance.

Jonah had broken into the team by now. He came into centre midfield for Johnny Bumstead and more than held his own, scoring twice in a 6–2 demolition job on Coventry City in November. A month later came one of the best victories Jonah and I were involved in at Chelsea – the 3–1 topping of a Liverpool side including Grobbelaar, Neal, Lawrenson, Hansen, Kennedy, Nicol, Molby, Wark, Johnston, Dalglish and Rush. They were probably the best side we faced that season going forward but we were more than a match for them on the day. Speedo was simply immense, really dishing out a torrid time to Lawrenson, who lost his rag and should have walked for one too many illegal tackles. Grobbelaar was a joke, at fault for most of our goals, including leaving one of my crosses for Joey McLaughlin to head into an empty net. Kerry brushed aside Hansen to score his twentieth goal in twenty-two games. 'Unbelievable defending,' as the man himself might say with his TV pundit's hat on. Of all Liverpool players, Dalglish was amazing, a pleasure to watch with his cleverness, close control and economical passing. There were 41,000 at the Bridge to see it, and a great atmosphere.

I enjoyed myself again at Sheffield Wednesday the next weekend in a 1–1 draw. I think I got the better of their full-back, Gavin Oliver, and felt at the peak of my game. My touch was spot-on, I was full of tricks and could run all night.

However, in yet another example of bad timing, in mid-December, just as I was coming on strong, I took a knock in another draw, at home to Stoke, and started just two more matches for the remainder of the season.

Around the same time it came out in the papers that Noel Blake, the Jamaican-born full-back Portsmouth had bought in the summer, wanted out of the club. The reason? Racial abuse from his own fans. He was quoted as saying what I never had: 'I don't care where I go from here just as long as I get away. I have had enough of this crowd.' The Pompey chairman came out strongly, called the fans' behaviour 'disgusting' and swore he wasn't going to allow Blake to be driven out by racism. He even said he'd go on the terraces and root out the offenders. What the two of them said seemed to shut up a few people and Blake stayed for several more seasons, becoming a crowd favourite, before moving on. (In 2007 Blake was appointed FA National Coach, working with the nation's kids. Again, it shows how things have changed, even if it didn't happen overnight.)

With me at Chelsea, acceptance had to happen of its own volition. It never ever crossed my mind to walk away.

CHAPTER 15

A Legend Is Born At Hillsborough

Chelsea, the club with the well-earned reputation for being up and down, had suddenly become very consistent in the League – with or without me in the side. In Cups we still displayed the old capacity for unpredictable glory or unmitigated failure. I had some of my best and worst moments in knockout competitions. For a long time – until José Mourinho came along – Chelsea were brilliant against the big teams, which were Sheffield Wednesday, Arsenal and Liverpool, in my day, but when we got to the little teams, leagues below us, it was totally different.

I see why there are upsets. You know in your mind you should beat these smaller sides. You're even reminded beforehand, 'Do not take the mick and think these boys aren't in it. They're playing for keeps and they'll have you. You hold that ball or they're in.'

We'd think, 'Yeah, yeah, yeah,' and before you know it, fifteen, twenty minutes and you're in a game. They're 1–0 up with probably five chances where they could have scored.

If it hadn't been for Eddie Niedzwiecki, that scenario would have happened to us a lot more. Brilliant keeper. He saved us enough times. We played Mansfield Town, Wigan, Walsall, Notts County, Shrewsbury and were always getting into trouble. You used to hear of Mansfield losing 0–2 and 0–3 in their own division. And then we would go there, they'd play proper football and you really had to work. It was a mindset thing with us that nearly always put us in difficulty.

We had the leaders on the pitch, but it wasn't enough. Everybody needed to be pulling up their socks and saying, 'Take these as a Liverpool, not a Mansfield.' Guess what? These teams are fighting for their lives, man. They've got a trade, too. They're professionals as well. They don't give a fuck. They play their hearts out. And so it's right, man.

Every time we played a lower league side we were rubbish until a wake-up call. All right, we'd get away with it, 1–1, do the job in the next game, but we could have done the job first hand and we failed almost every time.

Shrewsbury Town gave us grief in the FA Cup in 1986. I remember thinking, 'This is Shrewsbury, it's a Cup game, what the hell is going on here? They're flying. Buck up, man, because we could be out.' We won that one 1–0.

You never saw that complacency at Chelsea under José Mourinho, or now under Avram Grant. They're doing the job right. Don't take it easy. Beat them and beat them good – 3–0 up, that's it. When you start to score, that drops their heads. With us that was always the intention but we needed something to motivate us – maybe the shame of losing, but a wake-up call every time.

With Mourinho you got the feeling that the players didn't want to lose partly for him. They were loyal to him. Was that the same for John Neal?

I don't know if it was for everyone. For me it was because I was given my chance by him, and he would take me to one side and talk to me. So would his assistant Ian McNeill. Some of the boys did things their own way if they didn't get looked after. I don't know if John Neal was trying to avoid upsetting any of them. He wasn't that kind of a motivator anyway, nice as he was. He was the gentlemanly, old-school type who'd put a hand round your shoulder and have a quiet word. There were no smashed tea cups with him. He'd gone through football in that fashion with a fine managerial career at Wrexham and Middlesbrough, and you had to respect him for that. But when players started to think they were bigger than the club, oh boy.

By the mid-eighties there were more larger-than-life personalities in that Chelsea dressing room than in the 'Celebrity Big Brother' house. And the best example of what they could produce when it came together right was the game I'm always remembered for, the Milk Cup fifth-round replay at Hillsborough against Sheffield Wednesday, 30 January 1985.

I remember it just as much for another reason. It was also the night I met my father for the first time in twenty-one years. As it happened, he was living in the area at the time. He'd been in touch with Mum just before and contacted the club to ask if I could get him tickets for the match, which I arranged. It was all a little strange, our first meeting being at a match, but I didn't know what else to do.

I didn't meet him before the game. I'd left the passes for him on the gate, while I was down in the dressing room getting myself psyched up. We'd see each other afterwards.

That day, I was totally filled up in every way. We did light training in the afternoon and ate something around three o'clock at the hotel in Yorkshire where we were staying. It must have been good food because I loaded myself up. I seriously overate. I suppose it was the tension of seeing Dad that evening.

I was rooming with Keith Jones and told him, 'Jonah, my stomach's so full!' He said, 'Sleep it off, man.'

When I woke up later, I felt no better and I was thinking, 'Please be sub, please be sub.' I could hardly move. Sure enough, I was named on the bench.

I was still full as we sat down in the dugout and watched Wednesday storm into the lead – 1–0, no problem. But when it went to 2–0, then 3–0, I was thinking, 'Damn, we're finished.' We were close to the crowd and a woman supporter with a broad Yorkshire accent behind the dugout was really revelling in Chelsea's plight, taking the mick out of us and handing out sweets to Jonah. At 3–0 she was rubbing it in again. 'Don't worry, lads, there'll always be a next time!' There wasn't much we could say. We just had to grin and bear it.

On the pitch, Wednesday's Andy Blair had been giving an earful to Mickey T. That sort of thing goes on all the time, but Mickey wouldn't forget it. When we won a corner at the end where our noisy away fans were packed, Mickey Thomas decided it was payback time. Just before the kick was taken, he sidled over to Spackers and asked him whether the three officials were looking in his direction. Spackers told him no, so Mickey turned round and bashed Andy Blair, who fell to the floor, laid out and needing treatment. All the Chelsea fans were laughing their heads off. Micky Lyons and all of the Wednesday boys rushed over to Mickey and started shoving him. The ref of course hadn't seen anything, so he went over to the linesman, who hadn't seen anything either, and then to the other linesman. While this was going on, the Chelsea fans, who of course saw it all, started singing: 'There's only one Mickey Thomas!'

Talk about giving the game away! Mickey was signalling to them to hush. The modern-day video panel would have had an open-and-shut case with that one. Luckily, Mickey got away with it; otherwise it really would have been all over.

We'd played the first game just two days before at the Bridge and it had finished 1–1 thanks to Speedo. It was always a fight between our two teams.

It was miserable at half-time. There was bedlam in the dressing room. Everybody was wound up. Certain individuals supposedly weren't doing their job, according to some of the louder players. Joey Jones was shaking his fists, tattoos flashing around. He'd always go out and lead by example. He'd take the first man out with the ball. There was no such thing as a fifty-fifty tackle with Joey. He did not give a damn. Bam!

Big Joe McLaughlin was up there shouting. When a dressing room has two loud Scotsmen in it, they become louder than loud.

'Fucking get a hold of these men!' That was Joey.

Then John Neal came in, quietly asking, 'What's going on?' But he already knew we were upset and sorting it out. So he just left that area alone and went over the set-pieces with Pat and Kerry.

'Start using that ball over them. Right, we've got some space over there. This fella isn't getting to him.' We could see that it was up to us now. We'd be more serious in the second period. We'd rip into them when we came out.

Then it emerged that Colin Lee had been injured in the first period, a muscle strain. All I heard was, 'Canners, get warmed up right away.'

'All right.'

It was our kick-off from the restart and Joey just launched it from the back towards Kerry. I didn't expect that, to tell the truth. When I set off, I was watching the ball and it was like an up and under. With me, though, it was a case of always gambling in case Kerry knocked it on.

I was just running. Kerry flicked it on, I saw the ball and it fell between me and a Wednesday central defender. I just nicked it off the boy's foot.

It was a first-time shot. It wasn't a case of just hitting it, but hitting it right. The left-foot shot bounced just in front of keeper Martin Hodge and gave him no chance to save. Eleven seconds after kick-off Wednesday were pegged back to 1–3.

And after that, I thought we were going to score with every attack. It felt that way. I think we reacted so much as a team when we were down. We always had to let the opponents score first before we got a reaction out of our team. A little later, Kerry beat the offside trap and picked up the ball on the edge of the 'D' with Hodge desperately trying to block him. Kerry coolly took it wide to his left and stabbed it right-footed into the open goal. That was 2–3 and I thought, 'You know what, we can do this.'

We were buzzing, man, and soon we had pulled it back to 3–3. Pat broke into the box on the left, swivelled and laid it square to Mickey, who clipped it sweetly into the top left corner from the edge of the box. God knows how good that was if you were in the Chelsea end.

Then, with full time approaching, came my moment. Kerry, Mickey, Pat and I were causing havoc, dodging through them, and I kept looking to go wide and cut in at the angle. So when Pat got hold of the ball in our half and ran with it for most of the field before passing to Kerry on the right corner of the box, that was it. I was calling to

Kerry to pass because I knew he liked to take that ball for himself, like all great goalscorers, but I was completely unmarked and running towards the penalty spot. It must have been eight times I called, 'Kerry! Kerry!' I was sure he'd look for some angle to shoot himself, so I was really shocked when he passed that ball to me, but he did.

And when that ball came to me, I just thought, 'I'm hitting it, I ain't placing nothing.' When I saw the ball bounce under Hodge on the wet ground, I willed it in and it skidded under the keeper. As it crossed the line I was thinking, 'Oh my God! This is the winner.'

In my mad celebration, pointing and waving my arm around, I ran to the bench, looking for Jonah. I was going to see the woman in the seats behind the dugout and say, 'Give us one of those sweets now!' But I didn't see her. Jonah said from 3–3 she was quiet as a mouse, did not say a word.

Joey Jones had grabbed me on my run and screamed, 'Go on my son!' His fellow Welshman didn't hold back, either. Andy Blair, having recovered from Mickey's first-half bashing, had kept on at him again, so when we went ahead, Mickey gave him some of his own medicine, and a lot of our players joined him!

So now it was 4–3 with a few minutes remaining, but while Doug Rougvie was our left-back they always had hope. Sure enough, Mel Sterland went on a run out of nowhere. I didn't mind my defensive duties and I was chasing back to help cover as he approached the box. I was yelling to Dougie, 'Don't touch him, Doug, don't touch him!' But he did. He tripped Sterland and gave away the penalty.

They equalised of course and it ended 4–4. All that hard work had been undone, just like that. It was a magnificent match to be part of, though, one of the all-time great comebacks. Indelible.

Afterwards, with all those personal vendettas to settle, it nearly all kicked off in the players' bar. But as a few large, diehard Chelsea fans had found a way in there, the Wednesday players obviously thought better of starting anything.

Anyway, my thoughts had turned to linking up with Dad. I was a little frightened of meeting him when it finally came down to it. I had no idea what to expect.

For twenty-one long years Dad had been completely absent from my life. I was still upset that he hadn't been there for us since I was two, and I knew in my heart that it had affected my life in a lot of ways. He had left a big empty void. I didn't even have an image in my mind to pin the resentment to. Mum had removed any pictures of him from display around the house straight after he'd gone. He was 'missing without face'.

Of course, I knew I looked like him because people were always calling me 'Vernon bwoy' around Southall. Then when Mum, June and I went to Dominica in 1974, people in Mahaut, where Dad's family is from, would kiss their teeth as I passed and call out his name. Everyone knew Vernon. I must have looked a lot like him but I'd never seen him. As it happened, his parents, my grandparents, still had a framed photograph of Mum and Dad's wedding for us to look at. After the years of being recognised as his son and not being able to agree, I finally got some relief and saw what they meant.

That's the only reason I was able to recognise him in the players' bar at Hillsborough – apart from the fact that he was the only other black guy in the whole room, of course. He was pretty conspicuous once I got inside. He called me across, and I looked at him slightly dumbstruck. After all this time, his 'bwoy' finally got to meet Vernon.

All I could say was, 'How are you? What's happening?'

'Want a pint?'

'Yeah, OK.'

And we started chatting, just light things. Nothing deep. How long had he been in Sheffield? What was he doing for work?

No recriminations. I'd had a really good day. It felt like a breakthrough match for me. I didn't want to disrupt that feeling.

We couldn't chat for long because I had to get the team coach back to London. I was so glad I saw him, though. It felt like a locked door had finally been opened, even though it still hurt when I thought about him not coming to see June and me before. He asked me to come up and spend a longer time with him when I was freer, and I did. He's not much of a football fan, though. He never came to watch me play again.

Since that day we've spoken almost every other day, on and off, and it's been the same light chat each time. I never put him on the spot. I don't ask him questions about the past. That is a period I can't do anything about. It was just how things were at the time. It's up to him to talk about it if he wants to get something off his chest.

Brief as it was, I took the reunion in my stride. Back then my life revolved around being a professional footballer. I was feeling so good after that Sheffield Wednesday game. I'd arrived as a footballer and I made headlines in the next day's papers.

Typically, as I've learned, when I'm on a high, fortune always steps up to slap me down. The day after the Wednesday game and meeting Dad again, the phone didn't stop ringing with radio, magazines and tabloids wanting interviews with me. Buoyed up, I went out to chill a little at a place called George's Pool House, down an alley near Wired For Sound on Mare Street in Hackney.

I drove down there in my BMW and parked right outside the record shop. In George's all the tables were taken, so I nipped into Wired For Sound instead to hear some of the latest beats. I was in there no more than ten, maybe fifteen minutes when someone came inside and asked whose Beemer it was outside because the cops were looking it over like they wanted to dish out a parking ticket. The car was on a yellow line, so I resolved to move it before the law made their move. As I got in and started it up, I was suddenly surrounded by coppers. Now I had a problem. In truth, I hadn't just gone to George's to shoot pool, but to score £10 worth of weed. Unprofessional, I know, but just a little celebration.

You can imagine what was going through my mind at that precise moment. They'd been staking out the joint for drug pushers and here was my name about to move from the back pages to the front, and for all the wrong reasons. Just what I needed.

One of the coppers started off.

'Sir, we have reason to believe you have just fraudulently used a pension book to withdraw funds from that post office,' he said, indicating a place a few doors down. I was relieved but baffled.

'You got the wrong man. It wasn't me.'

'The man's appearance matches your own and he was witnessed getting into a green BMW the same as yours.'

I repeated my innocence but realised I wasn't going to get off that lightly because of the matching descriptions. I was taken, complaining, down to Hackney nick, there to be picked out from a line of people by someone who worked in the post office. The woman never materialised but I was still charged with fraud. They had now also worked out who I was, and didn't they like that! Worse still, while searching my car they had found something else to interest them. No, not the weed, but a small spring-loaded cosh that was honestly just a memento from one of our preseason tours and that I carried around in case of muggers. The coppers loved it. That, me old mate, was classed as an offensive weapon. I was charged, bailed and told to appear before magistrates in the summer.

The deception charges around the pension book would be dropped completely, but I was eventually fined £150 for possessing an offensive weapon and the damage was done. There's a photo of me taken when I was on my way to Old Street Magistrates Court for the hearing a while later. Head bowed, looking sad and sorry for myself.

The story about the case was everywhere, and was broadcast on a TV sports show that same evening by Malcolm Macdonald – bad news certainly travelled fast where Hackney Old Bill was concerned.

But it could have been much more damaging. Luckily, the £10 of weed had not been left in the car when the police pounced and searched it. After I bought it, I'd actually hidden it inside one of my trainers. How I got out of the station with it still tucked away I'll never know. Of course, I never told Chelsea that part of the tale. I must have been mad to do such a silly thing anyway.

Although the fraud charges were dropped by the police, my team-mates wouldn't let me off so lightly. I was playing in a reserve match shortly afterwards when one of them sidled up to me at a corner.

'Canners,' he said, 'something just dropped out of your shorts – is it a pension book, mate?' Raucous laughter erupted all around me.

Joking aside, it was one of the worst moments of my life, but oh so typical for everything to happen at once. How to switch from hero to villain in twenty-four hours! The calls for *positive* interviews ended immediately. It was a disaster, especially after the Sheffield match the day before had put me right where I wanted to be.

History is kind, however. The police business has been

forgotten while the Hillsborough epic is a legend. It even turned my biggest lifelong critic into a supporter. On the back of my breakthrough in the Milk Cup game, Mum was interviewed by the official Chelsea newspaper, *Bridge News*, and when I saw a copy I was amazed. It was the first time I'd ever heard her be so positive about me playing football. I made the front cover and there was a full page inside, a photo of me with my arms round June and Mum, a headline – 'Well done, my son!' – and a sub-heading that still makes me laugh: 'I advised him to buy the Pelé video'.

The article was an eye-opener for me as Mum was saying some things in print she would never say to my face – same way she would talk us up to friends and neighbours when we were kids, but never praise us when we were on our own.

'The children are very close,' it says. 'Paul was always looking after June. He's a very soft-hearted person. Anyone can give him a sob story and he'll feel sorry for them.' She was often critical of how I gave things to my girlfriends, handed over money, bought furniture for a home and left it there, but often they were looking after my child! She even doubted some of the children were really mine.

'Even now,' the article carried on, 'I can tell when he's feeling hurt after having a bad game. He's not a poker-faced person. He withdraws into himself and is miserable. I don't need to ask him the result. I just look at his face to see how they have done.'

She talked about my school football, too. 'He was always in three or four teams,' she said. 'In the beginning, it used to be a headache, with all the dirty boots and washing. But after the start Paul was ever so good because he would do it all himself.' Too right I did.

She was asked about my first chance with Chelsea when I was semi-pro at Hillingdon Borough. 'I wasn't too excited,' she answered, 'because he had a few disappointments with other clubs, like Wimbledon, before that. But when he signed, I felt great, because I thought at last football seemed to be paying off for him. And he deserved it, because as a boy he used to go out in all types of weather to play and train.

'I was still a bit worried for him,' she continued, 'because I knew it was going to be tough.'

I'd never seen Mum watching or listening to me play, but she talked about it in *Bridge News*.

'During those games [she watched live] I bite my nails and clench my fists and afterwards it takes me hours to calm down, so I try to avoid it.' I had no idea it meant that much to her. 'If I'm at home watching the telly, the neighbours at the other end of the street can hear me, especially if he's missed one.'

Mum was asked how she reacted to the abuse I got from fans. 'I don't,' she said. 'Paul doesn't pay any attention to it and he told me not to take any notice of them. He hasn't let it dissuade him from getting there. I think the people who do it are just uneducated louts. Some fools have to show their resentment for anything. For instance, it used to be the Jews who got the treatment.' I couldn't have put it better myself, really.

After that it was classic, embarrassing Mum: 'I was saying to him recently that he's not as good as he could be. He probably needs a little extra help. I know he goes training a lot but I suggested he should get the [Pelé] video because it might aid him.' Jeez, thanks for putting that last bit in print for every Chelsea fan to see, Mum.

The great Brazilian himself would not have been too upset to have a game like I had at Hillsborough, though. In fact, that famous 4–4 draw is still the match every Chelsea fan I meet mentions to me, even though it ended up a draw – thanks to Doug Rougvie.

No one gave Dougie any stick in the dressing room, as I remember, even though he'd effectively thrown a famous victory away. As fellow pros we just supported him. Doug was a big geezer as well!

We won the replay 2–1 a week later. I missed a sitter in that one. It went through my legs. I couldn't believe it. I made the corner for Mickey Thomas's winner, though.

All of us realised we had a good chance to go all the way to the League Cup final when we drew Sunderland in the semis. They were really struggling in the First Division.

But we lost 0–2 up at Roker Park and then 2–3 at the Bridge and I was only a sub. Oh that was a gutter. I felt hurt about that, and Clive Walker, of all people, played a blinder at our place.

He killed us. You'd have thought our boys would have known all about him. You know, I don't think he ever got the testimonial he was due from Chelsea before he left. He deserved it. The guy was a hero at Stamford Bridge.

We finished sixth in the First Division that season, a brilliant return for a newly promoted side. I was involved in 24 of our 42 league games and was proud of my contribution, especially as I had a lot more to unlock inside me. Thigh and groin injuries were one annoying recurrence. But I wanted to convert many more chances into goals, and I still needed to turn in top-drawer performances week in, week out. There was a lot more room for improvement, and I liked that.

CHAPTER 16

The Writing On The Wall

After a successful 1984/85 season, my profile was the highest it would be as a footballer. It was known I lived in Hackney so I started to get offers from the council and local voluntary groups to work with kids over the summer. I enjoyed it so much. I remember I took a load of boys, aged ten to fourteen or so, for soccer skills training, and taught one session in Millfields Park, Clapton. I also backed a few initiatives the mayor had with disadvantaged children and it felt good to use my experience and status in sport to try to give troubled kids some inspiration not to go wrong. I'd been there and I knew it wasn't the way forward.

As far as my football career was concerned, the summer of 1985 suddenly brought a big step backwards for me to be truthful. John Neal had never fully recovered from his heart problem, was forced to retire from the manager's job and went upstairs to become a Chelsea director. Personally, I missed his reassuring day-to-day presence a hell of a lot. John Hollins, already virtually the manager, was confirmed in the position and made changes that weren't good for me. He bought Jerry Murphy from Crystal Palace. Murphy wasn't creative, lacked pace and wasn't so much of a team player. That's not me talking, that was the opinion of fans at the time. Murphy was a left midfielder, and serious competition for my position because the new boss had brought him in.

You're always told as a player that the good times are shorter than you can believe, and it is so, so true. If I'd come through in football fifteen years later, the wages from my time at Stamford Bridge would have set me up for life. Back in 1985 there wasn't anything like the amount of money from Sky TV, manufacturers' sponsorships and image rights, and nothing like the number of agents and advisers you hear about now. The few who were around would have been sniffing around the stars, such as Kerry Dixon, goalie Eddie Niedzwiecki or Pat Nevin.

I had 'negotiated' all my own contracts, simply because I didn't know any better. I wasn't the assertive type, and none of the other players ever mentioned to me what sort of add-ons they were getting – bonuses for goals, for being high up in the League, doing well in Cups and stuff. I was totally ignorant of all that. So when Chelsea talked to me about money, I was thinking about it just like a normal salary in any old job, with no little extras. Everyone else was getting them. I didn't ask. I didn't know anything at all about lawyers or agents. I didn't have a Pini Zahavi sitting next to me at the Royal Park Hotel, or the PFA talking me up to get a better whack out of the Chelsea board. Other players did. The way I was, it was easy for the club to take me for a fool when we faced each other over a desk. It wasn't a familiar or comfortable situation for me and I had to be happy with what I was offered. They didn't ask me what money I wanted, they told me what I could have. When I first signed in November 1981 I got something like £175 a week for the last six, seven months of that season. My reaction was, 'What? £175? Love it. Thank you.'

Of course, I didn't know the wage structure. I was still an outsider in the dressing room. The next contract they put to me in summer 1982, I sat there reading the offer – three years, £300 a week. 'That's pretty good, yeah!' Not thinking, 'Now hold on Paul, are you sure?' I wasn't equipped to deal with the intricacies.

None of the others came up and said, 'Are you sure you're getting what you deserve?' Why should they? Dressing rooms aren't like that. I wasn't one of the boys and everyone was looking after himself. It wasn't like each player's deal was pinned on the noticeboard for others to take a good look at – 'He's getting a top-three place bonus – I'll have some of that!' Ultimately, it was down to me to look after myself rather than expect others to look out for me. I should have been more organised, but I wasn't. I still couldn't believe it was happening to me, and everyone knows you don't try to intervene in dreams. You simply lie back and let them happen. If you try to force them, they fade away.

Eventually, I picked up snippets and it gave me ammunition. When Jerry Murphy came in from Palace as John Hollins' first signing in summer 1985, there were rumours what starting money he was on and it was many times more than I was earning. But he'd been at Palace when Ernie Walley was manager and he was a free transfer, so some of the money saved there would have been offered as wages in order to entice him. I was really angry, though. Jonah and Dubbers had already complained that it was harder for us to get the sort of deal we wanted.

I didn't mind Mickey Hazard coming in, which he did later, and being well paid – he earned it, a class act.

But Jerry Murphy – I'm sorry. He never made a through ball, he couldn't run. Yet he could pick up ten times more wages than I was on. I rated myself at least as good as him. They paid him great money, with no work-rate, and they wouldn't pay me. I saw that as favouritism, taking the mick.

At the same time, my contract with Chelsea was coming up for renewal. John Hollins told me, 'Right, Canners, we're going to give you £400 a week plus £9,000 signing-on fee for three years.' If you read the newspapers, you saw what other people were getting out of the game. At Manchester United it was revealed that Bryan Robson was paid around ninety grand a year. The rest of the squad earned between £30,000 and £70,000. I'd been at Chelsea nearly four years and was being offered around £23,000.

A cricketer – albeit one of the best ever, Ian Botham – was earning £300,000 a year in 1985. Maybe I'd chosen the wrong sport all those years ago after all.

'All right,' I said, but I was thinking, 'I want to buy a house now.' So I asked, 'Do I get the £9,000 upfront?' It would be a good deposit on the property, which was on Dyson's Road, near Northumberland Park – and a stone's throw from White Hart Lane stadium, would you believe.

'No, we'll give you three grand every year for three years.' So by the time the tax came off it we were looking at just over two grand right away.

I said, 'It's gotta be three now, because I want to get my house.'

'I'll go back to Mr Bates and ask him what he thinks.'

Batesy refused. No reason. I tell you what, I had to borrow the £2,000 just to put down a deposit to get the house. I paid that back religiously every month without fail. Over the years, even when it was tight, they took that payment out. I refused to sign Chelsea's contract.

It made me consider whether I had done enough in my Chelsea career. I never thought I was about to join the ranks of Stamford Bridge immortals (and did not even really appreciate my special place in the club's history books at the time). But when I played I always gave 100 per cent. I did what defensive duties I was asked to do, got my crosses in for Kerry and Speedo. I'd always felt I didn't get enough goals, and I wasn't always at the peak of my game, which was frustrating. I'd had quite a few niggling injuries, usually just as I was getting a run together, which hadn't helped. I was still only twenty-three, a few years from my prime, and could definitely improve. The best was yet to come, I was convinced of that. Whether that would be at Stamford Bridge was open to question now Jerry Murphy had joined the procession of rivals for my left-wing slot.

I was still learning my trade, but I was starting to recognise my market value and wondered whether I had to move to realise it. I'd had a few good spells at Chelsea, when I was in the starting line-up, but never the sort of long run in the side when you really show what you can do. I knew there was nothing Murphy had over me. It was frustrating.

But he cost money, was recommended by Hollins' new coach, Ernie Walley, who had worked with him at Palace, and was always going to play.

Worse, I was sidelined anyway from the start of the 1985/86 season and the Blues started reasonably well without me.

Murphy, however, despite being in pole position, wasn't doing the business, which allowed me to step in again in early September. I started to get a few chances from the bench, and now the Chelsea supporters started getting right behind me whenever I replaced Murphy.

That was especially obvious at the Tottenham away

match. Glenn Hoddle was right on his game and we were 0–3 down in the first half and reduced to ten men after Patesy had seen red for two quick lunges on John Chiedozie. That was the scenario when I took over from Murphy, who had done absolutely nothing.

I went for it as soon as I came on and tore into Spurs' defence, having a part in Kerry's goal for us. But we didn't get the breaks and they made it 1–4. The Spurs game was always one of the biggest on the calendar for Chelsea fans, and I think they respected how hard I'd tried to restore some pride for when they faced their workmates the following morning.

I got my first start at home to Southampton. The match came straight after famous Scottish manager Jock Stein had died and we had a minute's silence at the Bridge for him that was immaculate. This was my second top-flight campaign and I was starting to apply the experience gained in the way I played. But home-grown winger Kevin McAllister, another Scot, made his debut as a sub and almost stole the show, running at their left-back and murdering him with his pace and dribbling.

It was a relatively easy 2–0 win for us. Kerry tapped in from close range and towards the end I thumped one past the legendary Peter Shilton.

It was Arsenal at home next and another fantastic performance by the Blue boys against our cross-town rivals. I started again, and Hazard made his first start, barely fit and looking it in the second half. (He'd been brought in to replace Nigel Spackman, which was flair replacing reliability, and out of step with Hollins/ Walley's usual taste. Perhaps it was Mr Bates who picked him.)

McAllister was on the right – and didn't their left-back Kenny Sansom know it – but the game belonged to Pat Nevin, playing centrally behind Kerry in place of Speedo. Pat scored the first – an equaliser for Charlie Nicholas's goal scored against the run of play – and won a penalty when he completely fooled Arsenal centre-back David O'Leary with a wicked check and turn. Spackers, on for Hazard, put it home for the win.

After the game, Pat was so funny. In the press conference he was asked lots of positive questions about his performance and influence, and the goal, and he complained to the reporters that the interrogation was all too easy. They were bewildered at first, then one of them chirped up about his contract dispute with Chelsea. 'Ah!' he smiled, 'that's more like it.'

That result put us third behind Liverpool and Manchester United. It was such a good squad we had, even if John Hollins kept tinkering with it. I'd got away from Viv Anderson a couple of times, and done my best as always, but it didn't count for much in the long run. There were so many pros to keep happy you had to be on your game, every game.

Four days later we travelled up to Mansfield Town for the Milk Cup. They were a Fourth Division side pushing for promotion. They'd defeated Middlesbrough in the previous round, so a top-flight club held no fear for them.

They also had a little-known but in-form keeper by the name of Kevin Hitchcock, who joined the Blues a few years later. I was trying to use my pace against their sluggish defence, but nothing was coming off, and Spackers came on for me. We were lucky to escape with a 2–2 draw, both coming in the last fifteen minutes. (We won the replay 2–0 at the Bridge.) I wasn't the only under-performer, but I felt singled out for stick.

At the same time, off the pitch, life was getting ever more complicated as a result of my wayward love affairs. Now I was a footballer, I had a woman in every port. My third son, Jermell, was born in May 1985 in Lewisham. My second daughter, Lorreen, had been born in April that year to Marsha. Marsha was a sweet girl, curvy and light skinned. She was the sort who would do anything for anyone and as a result had any number of men chasing her – so they could be mothered by her. I suppose that includes me. It didn't work out with either mother long-term – although, as usual, I never strictly speaking ended the affairs – and I didn't have any more children with either of them. That was me then. I was a one-man population explosion. I now had five children. The way I behaved, flitting around, I was with all of the mothers and none of them at the same time. In many ways, I must have been a nightmare but I tried my best.

One difficult relationship I hadn't walked away from did finally click in September 1985 – my personal rapport with the Chelsea fans. It happened when we were playing at Watford. Some time in the first half I slid in for a tackle on their star player, England's Luther Blissett, who also happened to be black, and took him and the ball out.

I still remember it all so vividly. I come into the changing room at half-time, and the other players are all going mad, absolutely buzzing. They're shouting at me. Had I heard the fans on the terraces? After all this time! The fans are singing my name! And after the crap I had to put up with, this is a laugh to them. It's a joke. They're so happy for me, though.

Yeah, of course I heard it! That provoked a wry smile. 'Can-o-ville, Can-o-ville, Can-o-ville . . .' What a great feeling, at long last. Check that out!

But at the back of my mind was the realisation that I had to kick a black boy to hear them call my name. It was as if I'd had to do that to get acceptance. They were seeing me finally as one of them. I tackled a dark-skinned man like myself, so suddenly I'm playing on their side.

That was a big breakthrough for me – acceptance, feeling wanted. It felt good. After that I noticed another nice difference. When they called my name out over the Tannoy, there was a cheer. Not a loud one, but a cheer nevertheless. I would come out on to the pitch with everyone else to warm up after that. The minority of fans who had been abusing me seemed to have been silenced.

During that period, I had met lots of decent Chelsea fans. The most dedicated among them used to be waiting for autographs by the stadium gates. They would tell me to ignore the abuse. 'They're not truly supporters of the club,' they'd say, 'but we are.'

Early on I remember one fan used to offer me some Wrigley's chewing gum, but to start with I thought it could be poisoned. I really didn't know who to trust back then. As nice as she obviously was, I swear to God I didn't know at first if she was genuine. When she kept offering it every game, eventually I said, 'Oh, yeah. Thanks.' I built up a rapport with her and talked to lots of others fans who were great people.

That's where I found proper support, genuine fans, home and away followers. 'Do you know how long we've been coming here? Since the day before that there' – they'd point at the old Shed stand, built in the thirties. That opened my eyes to the dedication. Wow, this is really what fans are like. It made me a little more determined to prove the idiots wrong. Those people are there through thick and thin. The rest of us, players, managers – even, I hope, bigots – were passing through.

When I was young and supported Leeds, I wasn't that bothered about going to see them, even when they were in London. And when I was older and had a little money, it wasn't a big thing for me either. I didn't have the same obsession as the fans around the gate at the Bridge. I was glad to watch Leeds on the box, but had no inclination to travel all the way to see them live. These people would go everywhere, every game.

Those are the people I class as true supporters, not the hooligans, and not those people who carried on at grounds like they did, abusing me and other black players. Were they really supporters of the club or just a nuisance? I reckon a lot of them were supporters but they just had the wrong mindset and were easily led.

After a win over Manchester City in October, McAllister was on the bench as much as I was. I knew I finally had the backing of the Chelsea fans, but I couldn't say the same about the staff. They weren't doing a bad job generally, but I lost my place and was back playing in the Football Combination for the reserves.

I was disappointed with myself, but happy that the first team was still doing well in the League. I kept trying to impress but it was hard with the number of midfielders vying for four positions running into double figures. I'd had a few injuries early that year as well, but I thought I deserved to be given the nod when I was ready for action again. Holly used a huge number of players that year. It was as if he couldn't make his mind up whether to stick or quit with anyone, especially me.

I earned a recall in the Milk Cup to face Fulham in a 1–1 draw at the end of October, and played in the replay a week later, 6 November. This is the game best remembered as keeper Eddie Niedzwiecki's finest hour. At their riverside home he was like the Thames Barrier – parrying, blocking, stretching, clutching, stifling, diving as Fulham watched in disbelief. We won from Kerry's twentieth-minute tap-in, but I was taken off injured on a stretcher. Nightmare. Even when I was fit again, I didn't hold up hope for a swift recall.

I said as much when I featured in the Chelsea programme player questionnaire around Christmas. 'I'll just have to work hard and wait and see,' I was quoted as saying. 'I can't argue about not being selected as the team have done so well [we were fourth at the time]. It would have hurt more if I wasn't playing and the team were losing but at the moment I can have no complaints.'

Other revelations from the mind of Paul Canoville, 1985 style, were that I wanted a year's subscription to *Ebony*, the black American lifestyle magazine; the musician I'd most like to swap places with was Roy Ayers, the jazz-funk vibraphonist whose concerts were as funny as they were funky; and that my pre-match superstition was to kiss the signet ring on my right hand (taped over during the game of course) just before kick-off.

When asked how I would 'improve today's society', I replied: 'Change the government.' I meant it. I hated the mean-spirited Thatcher years and what she did to the inner cities and vulnerable people. Unemployment had peaked at 11.8 per cent of the working population in 1985 and the TV news had been filled with stories about the hardship of the dole and about the government's conflict with the striking miners, who were struggling to save their way of life. She also did nothing to improve things for black people, and there had been riots in cities across the UK. Meanwhile, rich City workers, Yuppies, were absolutely coining it so she wasn't great for the poor either. The divide was too great and as someone who'd been unemployed and living on the streets in the past, my sympathies always lay with the underprivileged.

As the season progressed I was wondering about

whether I might end up another of Thatcher's statistics myself. I was so often on the Chelsea bench I could tell you the names of all the woodworms off by heart.

One incident shows how desperate I was. I was living in Stamford Hill and the night before a game against Tottenham I slipped in the bath and hurt my rib. I rang Gwyn and told him I was in agony but John Hollins asked me to go on the bench. I was strapped up and hardly able to move, and there was no way I could play, but the boss still asked me to warm up by the side of the pitch as if I was about to come on, just to gee up Spurs.

Now, though, Canners the man with responsibilities saw that as appearance money, and even that was no longer regular by now. I wasn't struggling for money but I obviously had commitments. I had recently got together with Maria Samuel, who was taking most of my attention at the time. She was full-figured, as I like my women, a good laugh, but a born worrier. Maria was much more of a home girl than I was used to. She was reliable, had a big heart and did the right thing.

I looked after most of my children and their mothers and now I was looking to buy a property – something I never could have seen my teenaged self doing – so money and a future was now an even bigger issue.

I'd come through so much to be an established player at Stamford Bridge. Now it seemed that, after the huge progress I'd made, my career was suddenly and unexpectedly falling apart before my eyes. It wasn't right, and for the first time in my professional life I was actually getting very low about football. Problem was I didn't have anything else to fall back on. This was all I'd ever had and the old doubts from before my Chelsea days were re-emerging. I didn't know what I had to do to improve things.

It wasn't that the team were doing badly just yet, despite loads of dissent behind the scenes. I had to admit the team didn't miss me as much as I missed playing. Even after our brilliant keeper Eddie Niedzwiecki was seriously injured in March 1986 and first Steve Francis then Tony Godden had to step in, Chelsea were getting results.

But for me, with John Neal gone and the new regime in, I felt I had to be twice as good as anyone else to get a chance. Even when I performed, they still didn't look on it as important when their bought-in men were available. They'd pigeon-holed me as 'droppable'. You could still take liberties with me and I wasn't the sort of person to rock the boat. I'm just not like that – until I can't take any more. And that's the state I was arriving at now.

That's the point I think I knew I had really matured in some ways. I had to stand up and say something on my own behalf.

I was fed up with being used like a robot. My game had been reduced to running down a line helping out in defence. Hollins had been a leather-lunged midfielder turned right-back. He didn't trust flair and wanted everyone to stick religiously to their position. It seemed to me that he stifled players such as Pat Nevin – already a legend to fans – and then started dropping them. I wasn't free to stray or switch over to the right flank. Pat Nevin and I did that a lot – 'Canners, now, switch.' At first I wondered what I was doing there, but it made a difference because now if I got the ball, I could dip my shoulder and go left. I could never shoot from the left because it was the wrong side and better to cross for someone else. Switching to the right was another exciting part of my game then. Now push was coming to shove for me at Stamford Bridge.

I was still acting professionally, training and playing hard. Then all of a sudden, John Hollins asked to see me. He said, 'I got a letter from your girlfriend, Paul, and I do understand. You're working hard and playing for the club . . .'

What a shock! Without me knowing, Maria had written a letter to the Chelsea manager on my behalf. She explained that I was depressed. 'Give him a chance,' she wrote, 'have faith in him and he'll play well for you, do the business.' I was shocked and hugely embarrassed. She did it for the right reasons, though.

Even after that heartfelt plea, John Hollins didn't really offer me much comfort. 'I've told Adidas,' he said, 'that you are a valued player and that you're under contract, so you are now sponsored by Adidas.' So I'm not getting games, but I'm gonna get some Adidas kit? I'm supposed to be happy with that?

I didn't actually get another start in the first team until the visit of Liverpool in May 1986. By then we'd resorted to being a long-ball side. My role was reduced to that of a greyhound, chasing balls over the top. I'd always preferred receiving it at my feet where I could try to use my ball skills as much as my pace. It was even more soul-destroying now, trying to make an impact while chasing so many lost causes.

In that game, player-manager Kenny Dalglish netted, giving Liverpool the League Championship and the first part of a domestic double. Speedo came closest to scoring for us but it was like gatecrashing someone else's wedding. After that, with one match left, there was nothing for us to play for. We were confirmed in sixth position again – one place above Arsenal – which was a very good return, considering how divided the camp was on occasions.

My last official game for Chelsea came two days later, a really disappointing 1–5 defeat at the Bridge by Watford – for whom Luther Blissett and John Barnes starred. I suppose that was quite fitting.

All in all 1985/86 had been a pretty gutting season for me and, rightly or wrongly, I didn't feel I was being treated fairly. I knew the writing was on the wall for me at Chelsea. Maria's well-meaning letter hadn't had the effect she naively expected – in fact, it must have made me appear a little desperate.

Then a couple of incidents occurred that didn't help my case, even if I had been inclined to stay. One was a foolish moment when I gave Hollins' Welsh assistant Ernie Walley some backchat. It was so trivial I can't even remember what I said, but he acted like a sergeant major with us, and never forgot defiance. You just didn't cross him if you wanted to play. That was the case no matter how soppy you thought some of Walley's training routines were.

Ernie was a stockily built fella with deep-set eyes. He'd been temporary manager at Crystal Palace in 1980 when Terry Venables left, and lost seven of his twelve games in charge there. He was now in his fifties and his strict approach and 'modern' outlook on how efficiently the game had to be played were at odds with the core of the team that had been promoted as champions and brought a sixth-place finish in the First Division under John Neal. We liked to have the freedom to play our game and show a bit of flair. Walley and Hollins wanted a more direct, orderly style of play, which would eventually alienate some of our key players. His sessions at Harlington could be weird.

Famously, he would organise eleven-a-side training matches played minus one obvious requirement – a football. I just didn't 'get' him, and I wasn't alone in that. The other problem was that John Hollins didn't seem to know whom he wanted in the team and whom he didn't. He kept chopping and changing, using thirty-odd players in the League, and over a year or so we lost our way. Even so, I shouldn't have cheeked Walley if I wanted to stick around; it only served to weaken my hand.

The main problem started on the last day of our 1986 preseason training camp, again in Aberystwyth. I spent most of my time in the company of the younger black kids,

Jonah and Dubbers, both of them now pretty regular first-teamers, and Rodney Beste, who seemed on the verge of breaking through but never did.

As I wasn't part of the drinking culture, I always liked to relax and try to get my head down when we were working up to fitness.

There was supposed to be a curfew at around nine or ten o'clock by which time everyone should be back in the building. After midnight we heard a racket outside. We were in Jonah's room and looked out of the window to see a group of the lads rolling back to face a right rollocking from Ernie Walley. They'd just come back from the pub and it looked as though they had had far too much to drink. They were raucous and slurring their words. When Ernie had finished with them, one of them heard us up at the window giggling and laughing at the state of them. He didn't like that one little bit but when he started to call me 'black cunt' and stuff like that, he was way out of order. That was outrageous to me and I wasn't going to take it from anyone any more. He was still a team-mate, though, so I gave him a chance before sorting him out.

'You're drunk and don't know what you're saying. Get up to bed and sleep it off.' Drunk as he was, he wasn't taking the hint, and kept on repeating all these vile racial insults.

'Come down here,' he yelled, 'if you want to do something about it.'

By now I was really angry. As I started to head down Jonah and Dubbers were urging me not go, but my mind was sent on confronting him. Enough was enough. He'd had his opportunity to slope off without a pasting.

So I went downstairs, outside, stood toe to toe with him and faced him off.

'Go on, say that again.' And he did!

Without hesitating I knocked him out flat there and then with one solid punch, and stood over him considering a few follow-ups. Jonah pulled me away.

I think what upset me most about the whole incident was that the others stood next to him, looking comparatively sober, while he was dishing out this racist rubbish, and none of them had the wherewithal to tell him to stop. To me, that meant they either didn't consider it that offensive or didn't care for my feelings. Apart from anything else, it was unprofessional of them.

No one said anything the following morning. No apology was forthcoming. It was the problem that dare not speak its name at Chelsea again. Then as I was queuing with the others in the canteen for breakfast, holding my food tray, Jonah suddenly looked alarmed. He was in front of me and looking round behind me.

'Don't turn round, Canners,' he whispered. He told me my 'mate' from last night was coming straight for me and he's got a golf club in his hands.

With that I told Jonah to hold on to my glasses, waited till I was certain he was within range, then turned round and held up the tray in front of me. I managed to parry the club as he brought it down with full force towards me. Then I grabbed him and got him up against a wall, restraining him by the neck. Everyone piled in to stop us.

The training fortnight was over anyway, and I was bundled into a car and taken back to London separately by Norman Medhurst, the physio. It was a sombre journey, and I spent it wondering what next for me at the Bridge. We didn't discuss the incidents, but when I found out that my adversary had been allowed to travel back with the rest of the squad on the coach, I was absolutely furious. He gets to stay with the management and team-mates, playing cards and joking, after what he'd tried to do to me! It was just like it had been when I was a kid – no matter whose fault it was, I was always to blame. I've seen the same thing happen with bullying incidents at school; the victim gets asked to spend playtime in a quiet room with a book while the bully stays out in the playground. It's always easier to deal with the weaker person than it is the tormenter, but it's a sign of weakness in the institution too.

I suppose the management simply saw me as another troublemaker after all that. I had also been stalling on the new deal they had offered me, which I considered insufficient. I could imagine them thinking, 'What's going on with Paul Canoville? Fighting, giving backchat to Ernie Walley, now he's not signing his contract. What can we do with this geezer?' In their minds the reasons to let me go were piling up. How I wished John Neal's steady hand was still at the wheel. But he was rarely seen, and had taken a place on the board of directors.

When it seemed there was no way back for me at Chelsea, I began to look for other clubs. I was told by Ian

McNeill that Millwall were interested in me, but I only had to think of the Ku Klux Klan nutters at that reserve game to answer, 'No can do!' Then I learned that Brentford were coming in for me, and they asked if I would go to see them.

So I went for the tryout at Brentford and immediately recognised Roger Joseph, the younger brother of my mate Francis from Hillingdon Borough. Francis Joseph had stood up for me against the racist defender at Dover that time. Roger had a good career himself, being a regular at Griffin Park and with Wimbledon before finishing at Orient in 1999. He was a really nice guy.

He would have been around twenty back in 1986 when I saw him at the Brentford trial, and when I lined up for the training match, I realised he was playing right-back and I'd be directly up against him. They were in the process of converting Roger from midfield to defence and he wasn't altogether comfortable in the new role, but I couldn't hold back, no matter how nice a geezer he was. I wanted the move. So I kept taking him on, using my pace and his unfamiliarity, and absolutely roasting him. Their manager Frank McLintock, the former Arsenal hardman, was trying to coach Roger to deal with me, and in doing so was praising me up. He kept saying, 'This is what I mean by a quality player, this is what he does. This is what I'm trying to say to you . . . Show him inside, if he goes inside, we could swallow him.'

Every time Roger tried to force me into the middle, I just dropped a shoulder and was gone past him. I had to do it. Then Frank would be off again: 'This is what I'm saying, can you not understand. This is what a quality player can do . . .'

I felt sorry for Roger but I wanted to show what I could do and nothing was going to stop me. Frank was impressed enough to make me an offer immediately.

'How much do you want?' he asked.

'I want £400 a week and a £20,000 signing-on fee.'

I knew Frank really wanted me and this was a fresh start. I wasn't going to make the mistake of underselling myself as I had done at Chelsea.

'You got it.'

It was all agreed. Amazing. So that's how you do it. Nothing was actually signed yet but I shook on a deal and that was that. The only issue to be settled was that Brentford and Chelsea had to agree my transfer fee.

Then all of a sudden a new club cropped up – Reading. Their boss was Ian Branfoot. He'd been assistant to Lawrie McMenemy when I'd spent some time at Southampton before the Chelsea deal five years earlier. Apparently, he'd recommended that the Saints sign me, but they already had Danny Wallace, Andy Rogers and George Lawrence on the left at the time.

Knowing I had the Brentford offer in the bag, I went to Reading and tried out anyway. I did well and Branfoot was already half-sold on me, so he said he wanted to sign me and asked me the same question Frank had. He got the same answer – £400 plus the £20,000 signing-on fee.

'I've been to Brentford and they'll give it to me,' I said. I was mastering this negotiation lark at last.

'We'll give you £15,000 and a company car – sponsored.' Reading, supposed to be losing £1,000 a week at the time, were trying to limit costs. They wanted me to have a motor with one of those stickers down the side – 'Joe Bloggs Autos, sponsors of Paul Canoville'. I was damned if I was going to drive around north London in that! No way.

'Just give me the £20,000,' I told him. 'I'll get my own car.' We settled.

Frank McLintock was furious that I'd shaken on a deal with him and the Bees, only to switch at the last minute to Reading. 'I am absolutely choked,' he told the press. 'Canoville had signed with us.' The man from the Football League disagreed. 'Brentford said it was a conditional transfer and if they did not agree with the valuation they could pull out. On that basis, anyone is free to speak to the player.' The problem for Frank was that Brentford were disputing my fee with Chelsea and it had gone to a tribunal. In the meantime, Reading had stepped in. That was all to do with the clubs, not me.

I was grateful to Frank for showing faith in me, but Brentford were Third Division and the Royals had just been promoted to the Second. I felt guilty that he found out from the press notices that I'd gone to Elm, not Griffin, Park. I had phoned to tell him and apologise but he already knew. I should have rung him before. I suppose players have agents to do all that kind of housekeeping for them now.

It made me reflect on my first club. First Division Chelsea were offering me a £9,000 signing-on fee at the time. I had been thinking nine was maybe the top whack for me – my full worth – and that's a lot of money. But two lower league teams were more than happy to pay me £20,000. That shows you what was going on for me at the Bridge.

What was even more galling was that my old club valued me at £125,000. Although it wasn't a fortune in 1986 – Barcelona paid Everton £2.4 million that summer for the services of Gary Lineker – it meant they priced me at fourteen times what they were prepared to pay me as a signing-on amount. Eventually, Reading haggled them down to £60,000. (Brentford had offered £10,000, hence the tribunal.)

My departure was a further sign that John Neal's mid-eighties side was being broken up at Chelsea. The powerful but volatile Scots striker Gordon Durie had arrived from Hibernian for £400,000 in May. In February 1987 Nigel Spackman would be sold to Liverpool for £400,000 – Steve Clarke, José Mourinho's assistant and a great servant at Stamford Bridge down the years, arrived at the same time. Flair players such as Pat Nevin were asked to knuckle down and do the donkey work. Chelsea would finish fourteenth at the end of the 1986/87 campaign, then eighteenth in 1988, by which time first Ernie Walley then John Hollins had been replaced.

I played 103 times for the Blues between 1981 and 1986, and scored 15 goals. In a Chelsea book published a few years later I'm described as 'gifted and mercurial', and a loss to the squad that summer, 1986. There was no mention of my small but significant honour as a race pioneer in the club's long history. That was something Chelsea still had to come to terms with.

CHAPTER 17

Rupture

The move to Reading in 1986 was a liberating one for me. I was older now and felt really comfortable in myself for possibly the first time. I felt I'd shed a lot of the baggage from my childhood, and the racial abuse I'd received in the early days as a professional footballer at Chelsea was in the past. Michael Gilkes, the big friend I made in my Reading days, would tell you I was the original raver, sound man and footballer. A chaotic private life aside, I had it all, and would give you my last penny if I thought you needed it, especially if one of my children or their mother needed anything. But there was never a dull moment with Gilkesy and me.

He was actually trying to break into the first team when I arrived, but still told me that when he found out I was joining Reading, his initial thoughts were, 'What a great signing.' Then it sunk in that I was a left-winger, like he was, and that I would be the manager's first choice in that position as he'd just bought me, and he realised it would limit his starting opportunities even more.

After a while, he told me that the first time he'd noticed me as a player was away in the League Cup at Sheffield Wednesday. He was very complimentary, saying how unbelievable I was and how he'd been thinking to himself he wished he could play football like that. To be honest, I felt like I was better equipped than most at the time to play that position. I was big, strong, quick and very brave.

Even though we were chasing the same starting slot, we became really close friends. As it turned out, he outlasted me at Reading, and he got to play two games as a sub on loan to Chelsea in 1992. Great geezer.

In 1986 Gilkesy was living at his mum's in Leyton, east London, and I was living in my new house in Tottenham, north-west of there. We travelled into Reading together for training and matches. What journeys those were!

We'd mainly use the old North Circular Road, which was always rammed with traffic. We would be breaking all speed limits whenever possible. We broke a few sound limits too because I had the fattest Alpine music system and the biggest JBL speakers possible that would still fit on the parcel shelf of my BMW.

I always looked forward to the journey home from training. That was always nice and relaxed, listening to the latest tunes from a sound system that was louder than the public address system at Reading's Elm Park.

Coming back into London, we'd hit Hackney early

afternoon. Stop off at Kingsland High Street, Stamford Hill, for some proper soul food. I'm talking good wholesome fare from the Caribbean restaurants there – ribs, rice and peas, jerk chicken, fried fish and dumplings. I know the modern Chelsea chef, Nick, wouldn't approve. Too much fat and protein makes you less able to exercise. Back then no one cared too much as long as you ate enough.

Gilkesy and I didn't share much time together on the pitch but we made up for it socially on the Hackney club scene, although I was a few years older than he was. Musically, the mid-eighties focused on the rare groove scene for me. Lots of DJs had grown tired of the modern electronic stuff and looked back to the past for inspiration. Rare groove was what it said – records that were hard to find and may have been overlooked when they were first released in the 1970s when disco was king. The sound was typically funky, soulful and jazzy. The tunes were catchy, danceable and non-electronic – organic. Ravers couldn't get enough of it.

People would travel to the States and search obscure racks of vinyl in the hope of finding a tune no one else had heard of that would slay the dancefloor. Everything from forgotten cuts by the godfather of funk James Brown's backing band – I'm talking Maceo & The Macks' 'Cross The Tracks' – to groups you'd never heard of such as The Jackson Sisters and their tune 'I Believe In Miracles'. Illegal raves started being held in abandoned warehouses all over the place every weekend. The whole scene was exploding.

It was a wonderful time to be young in London. Well, it was for me.

Maria didn't go out as much as I did, especially as she was pregnant, but she knew what I was like. I hadn't changed my Mr Loverman act yet. Don't get me wrong. By then, like everyone else, I was aware of the risks of sleeping around. Everyone in the UK had been sent literature about HIV and AIDS. I practised safe sex until I was comfortable with a woman and knew them well enough.

These were truly some special times in my life. I was confident, buzzing. Gilkesy and I were nearly always late turning up for training and the traffic was no excuse. I must have spent half my weekly wages on fines. The captain at the time, Martin Hicks, used to love collecting my money.

You had to be a character to survive a training pitch full of big personalities, including Steve Moran, Billy Whitehurst, Keith Curle, Hicksy and Stevie Richardson. I reckon the wit between footballers is as sharp as it is in any tabloid newsroom. Believe me when I say there was no place to hide. It really was a man's game. The big difference at Elm Park was that I'd arrived on a fee. The club had paid good money for me and the manager was going to back me. On top of that, I had a couple of years' First Division experience. That doesn't come off the shelf in bottles. I was older, more sure of myself, my talent and my future. I was a well-regarded professional footballer. I was established.

Remember, I'd first entered the Chelsea changing room

as a callow youth and run up against some big personalities in my time there, no holds barred – Kerry, Patesy, Joey Jones, Mickey T, Joe McLaughlin, Dougie, Speedo, big Micky Droy, Nigel Spackman, Pat and the rest. You didn't get through with that lot by hiding away.

But the dressing room is one thing. You gain respect by what you do on the pitch first and foremost, which I believe I did – that's the training one as well as the match-day turf. If you've got the banter as well, you can always hold your own. Ever since I was a child I've liked to play the clown. I'd do mimicry, funny little commentaries, always playing the fool. People tell me it was a shield. It's just how I've always been.

Now I could walk the talk. At Reading even more than Chelsea I was always killing the boys about their gear and lack of dress sense. To be fair, I was right. Some of them were shocking. I called Trevor Senior 'King of Millets' and it stuck. At Reading I was appreciated for what I could do. Manager Ian Branfoot had shown £60,000 worth of faith in me. This was a fresh page I'd turned. I felt so comfortable there, partly – I realised – because the baggage of the racist chants had gone from me, like the burden had been left at Chelsea. For one reason or another, I always had to prove myself there. At Elm Park I was taken for who I was – a highly rated player.

I struggled in the first few matches because I'd joined on 1 August, two days before the first game of the season. I wasn't used to the guys or how they played – they were more long ball than I was used to at Chelsea, apart from towards the tail-end under Hollins. But once the ball started arriving at my feet I began to play well. Branfoot wanted them to play football. He saw it didn't work when the ball was pumped over the top for me to run on to. He told them to lay it on for me as I wanted it. I felt influential.

There were some effective players there, too. Trevor Senior wasn't a great footballer but boy could he put the ball in the net. Get it anywhere near him and he'd score. Soon I was scoring goals like I'd always promised myself I could. At the end of September and start of October I scored in three consecutive games against Crystal Palace, Grimsby and Blackburn. I was becoming a major player for the Royals.

Things were going well for me all round now. I was twenty-four, still to peak, doing what I'd always wanted to do, and playing probably the best football of my career. As soon as I arrived at Reading, the enthusiasm of the crowd and the local press towards me was amazing. Suddenly I was this 'exciting winger from Chelsea' and their 'star player'. I was riding on the back of the faith shown in me. The step down a level had allowed me to get my confidence back and defences were that bit easier to get behind. Now the goals were coming too.

With Gilkesy's advice I was even getting my financial affairs in order. I didn't have any personal insurance, and one day he fixed for me to meet the fella who provided his cover. I'd decided to go down the same route. The very next day, Monday, 21 October 1986, we travelled up to Sunderland for a match on the Wednesday night.

We stopped at a chip shop in Wetherby on the way up – we only did that after away games with Chelsea. Trevor Senior had curry sauce on his and fell ill. Ian Branfoot joked that the place had been recommended by Sunderland's coach Lew Chatterley! Gilkesy was rushed up from Berkshire on the day of the match as cover.

We took the lead after half an hour when Jerry Williams hit the ball into the roof of the net. I'd already been on one run, done a few tricks, shot against the post, and just before half-time I hit the side-netting from another chance. In the second half, they equalised through Dave Swindlehurst.

He was going to have an even bigger impact a little later. I think it was Gordon Armstrong who hit a bad Sunderland back-pass and one of our guys latched on to it and hit the bar. The ball came out some way on the rebound and I went for it. As I turned on the ball, Swindlehurst was also contesting it and caught me sideways just above the right knee. Crunch. I fell to the ground in agony.

I didn't know straight away how bad it really was. I'd had injured joints before of course – it's part of the game and you rarely play without some sort of pain. Some injuries hurt a lot to start with but fade after a short while. This didn't. It felt like the knee had opened up and when I looked down I was shocked – there were lumps where there shouldn't be, my knee cap had been pushed completely to one side and where it was supposed to be there was simply soft flesh. I went into a panic and our left-back Steve Richardson really had to work hard to calm me down. The knee cap had trapped a nerve and the pain was shooting all the way down to the tip of my toe. I was in pieces. I felt sick. As they took me off on a stretcher I was distraught, partly with the extraordinary pain, and partly thinking what this would mean once the pain had gone.

It was bad timing again. A few weeks earlier it had been announced that Glenn Hunter, whom Branfoot considered to be 'the best physio in football', was quitting Reading. A new physio, John Hasleden, had been recruited to replace him but he was not officially due to start until a few days later. He happened to be up there at Roker Park, so his first job was to help carry me off the pitch.

I was taken to Sunderland hospital, and to his credit Swindlehurst came to see me and apologised. I had no issue with him after that. I have to laugh now when I read Sunderland boss Lawrie McMenemy's post-match comments: 'The incident certainly took the edge off Swindlehurst's goal for him.' How did he think I felt? (Oddly enough, Swindlehurst went on later to become the assistant manager to Francis Vines at Crawley Town. When those two were sacked in 2005, the man who'd ended my Chelsea career, John Hollins, took charge.)

After one desperately long day, I was flown down to the Royal Berkshire Hospital back in Reading on the Thursday, where it was easier for people to come to see me. That's where the surgeons opened me up. As I knew, the knee had dislocated, but that was the minimum damage.

They broke it to me afterwards that they'd found a torn

cartilage. Then came the far more worrying news: 'third degree sprains to the lateral collateral and anterior cruciate ligaments'. In other words, ruptures. The worst you can have. Neither the physio nor the surgeons had seen such a combination of injuries. It was rare. Footballers aren't medics, but those words strike fear immediately. The rest was a blur. Operations, reconstruction, rest, rehab. Suddenly nothing was certain. All bets were off. There was a chance, the surgeon explained, that it might mean the end of my playing career.

At the end of October they operated to stitch the torn ligaments and remove a loose piece of cartilage. I was told that only extraordinary dedication and sensible living would get me back where I was. Even then, it was never guaranteed.

With the medical advances nowadays, serious as my injuries were, it would mean a lay-off to let the ligaments settle, then operations to repair them and maybe six to eight months out. There is more certainty of success. Back in 1986, that sort of surgery was in its infancy. There was so much insecurity, and that's what drives you mad. By no means everyone returned from cruciate trouble in those days . . .

I was devastated. You cannot believe it can happen just like that. It's what everyone in my position says, but it's true. You really never think it will be you, so you're never prepared for it.

After the op I was in full-leg plaster for months. For as fit and active a person as I was, it was torture. To start with, I didn't realise just how difficult it would be. Other people are good with rest, but not me. I hated being immobile and it got me down. On top of that, the solid career I had assumed for myself was no longer mapped out. It was a very low time for me.

Some small compensation for my situation was that at least I was able to spend time with my children. In mid-December the plaster finally came off and I was hobbling around grumpily on crutches. Two weeks later, on Boxing Day, Maria gave birth to baby Pierre – my sixth child in seven years. They always seemed to arrive right in the middle of each serious incident in my life.

The injury meant I had to take stock of where I was in all sorts of ways. I wasn't the networking type, as Gilkesy was. Sensibly, he was always nurturing contacts in the media and different local projects, and that has stood him in good stead since he retired from the game in 2000. Although I'd done some community work around Hackney, I wasn't as diligent about it as he was. I wasn't the type to chat to a local paper journo or feature on the radio. I just wasn't the schmoozing kind. I didn't plan, I lived for the moment.

So when I was thinking the unthinkable – that my playing career was over – there wasn't a great long list of radio producers or community project leaders I could ring up for a job. I had hardly any education, and no media experience. Admittedly, I'd thought about doing something with music – another great love of mine – but that would mean a totally fresh start.

I decided that I wanted this football life so much I would move heaven and earth to make it back to the pitch. I was desperate to prove to myself I could play at the top level again. I kept going in for the check-ups and as time passed the good news was that the operations seemed to have been a complete success.

Perhaps I never showed as much determination in my life as I did to return from that horrific injury. Along with fears that I might not come back, I was going to have to push the memory of my busted knee-cap and the scaring pain at Roker Park to the back of my mind right up until the start of the 1987/88 season. There were times when I found it hard to get up and face the day but mostly I had to force myself to rest and take it easy – not to go out.

By January, the severe stiffness in the knee had eased and I was able to move it 90 degrees. I was working with the Reading physio, stretching, building the strength back into the right leg. Back then they had nothing like the medical technology and facilities they have now, so I mean it as no denigration to the club when I say that progress was entirely down to me and the medics, not rehabilitation technology. We even had to use the cycling equipment in the gym of the nearby Post House Hotel, would you believe. Mark White – another long-termer who'd suffered a double shin-bone break around the same time I was crocked – and I were slaves to those restrictive friction cycling machines. At least I never got into trouble for trying to change the handlebars!

I was hoping to get running on a treadmill again by the

end of January but it was so hard to rebuild the strength. Look at pictures of my legs in those days and you can see I had huge thigh muscles but little definition round the knee. I had to work my butt off day in, day out and it was good to have Mark's company. He was nearing the end of his career and was in his testimonial year – I was still in my mid-twenties. Still, I was amazed when I saw the results of the local newspaper's player of the season poll – I got more votes than Gilkesy!

My life was too complicated to move to Reading even though it would have made sense. The travelling to and from Berkshire didn't help my recovery, but what could I do? Yet again the muddle of my personal relations was closing in. My life, my kids, my women were in north London and my club was in Berkshire. It seemed never ending and there were definitely times when I felt I wasn't making sufficient progress and the knee was never going to heal.

A lot of goodwill and cards were sent to me at the club, which I very much appreciated. But, oddly enough, as the healing process wore on, the well wishing seemed to accentuate my own frustrations. I knew they meant well but every time someone – a fan, a friend – asked me when I was coming back or how I was getting on, another little dull ache started in my stomach. I wanted life to be like a video recorder, and to fast-forward to my comeback at Elm Park.

No one really knew how churned up I was inside because I put on a brave face and stayed outwardly positive – the family traits of secrecy and stifling emotions operating again. Mum would have been the same – don't reveal your hand in case it betrays weakness.

With a force of will to keep the life I'd built afloat, in the summer of 1987 I achieved one of the biggest things in my life. By July, I was training along with the rest of the team in preseason, big smile on my face. I was so single-minded about clinging to my career that I had forced my way back into Ian Branfoot's plans for the 1987/88 campaign. I was still receiving treatment but I wanted to declare myself available, ten months after the disaster at Sunderland.

A week or so after that, I turned out for an hour in a friendly against a team from my old stomping ground, Slough Town. The real business started a few days later. In 1987/88, the Second Division was temporarily stocked with twenty-three sides. The odd number meant that one team was without a game each weekend, and our day off came on the first Saturday, 15 August. Ian Branfoot organised a 'Probables v. Possibles' game at an open day instead and I played, but strained a thigh muscle. Branfoot kept telling me to be patient. He was very supportive.

I never truly felt right and didn't quite make the start of the season, but I got a fantastic ovation at our second home match, a 3–0 win over Oldham Athletic. While I was out, my old friend Francis Joseph joined from Brentford. He did a pretty good job that season and was alongside me that day.

We both scored, and I set up Colin Gordon for our opener, but that papered over the cracks in my game.

Technically, I'd scored in four of my last five games for the Royals. Under other circumstances that would have been a statistic worth celebrating, but those games were stretched over a year. My knee was throbbing after the Oldham match, which wasn't a great sign, and I was shattered by the effort. I'd actually signalled to the manager that I had to come off after sixty-five minutes and the reception from the fans was exceptional – like I'd scored again or something.

I don't think even Gilkesy recognised what a strain it was for me to keep it all together. No matter how much effort you put into a recovery, the setback is always waiting round the corner to mug you and take away your dream. That's the pressure I was playing with.

The next game was Stoke at home, and I lobbed the keeper from thirty yards but George Berry cleared off the line. I was back on corners, trying to feel the buzz. Against Bournemouth I had loads of chances to score but just couldn't get the ball past Gerry Peyton. It was even more frustrating because the vultures were gathering round Elm Park. The club was in financial difficulties and key players were being sold off. I was already under threat and could do with a few breaks.

I watched the draw for the League Cup on TV-AM, and had to laugh. Out of the blue, we were paired with my old club Chelsea.

I had a thigh strain and was in the stand for the first leg at Elm Park, which went down in history. Reading won 3–1 thanks mainly to two goals from Gilkesy, who was now establishing himself as a crowd favourite, and the performance of Steve Francis, my old team-mate from Chelsea who'd recently joined Reading. The whole city went mad for days after that win. A group of supporters brought the squad personalised champagne. I wasn't in the mood to celebrate, though. I was starting to wonder if I'd ever be fully fit again.

I was picked as sub for the second leg at Stamford Bridge on 7 October 1987. I was nervous as hell before the start. I remember being in two minds about being a part of the game, and not just because my knee was hurting me. I really didn't know what sort of reception I would get from the Chelsea fans. Would it be the jeers and hoots of the early days or the applause, chants and shows of affection I received towards the end there?

I steeled myself for when my name was read out over the stadium Tannoy, and to my relief the home fans clapped. Not a hint of a boo. A few among the 15,000 or so there even gave little cheers. I was surprised and touched. That's how it's supposed to be, and I've learned that the majority of Blues fans are like that.

The Chelsea–Reading game was an exciting one, proper cut and thrust. Chelsea were up for it and Durie scored a first-half hat-trick. Gordon got one back for us to make it 4–4 on aggregate at half-time but we were playing all-out defence and up against it. Mickey Hazard was brilliant for Chelsea. Early in the second half we got a lucky break when danger man Durie hobbled off, and a few minutes later I came on. Soon Gordon had scored to make it 5–4 and that's how it stayed. It was a brilliant win but I couldn't feel it like some of the boys. Still, a Second Division side taking a First Division scalp always feels great.

Fitting as it was that the Bridge should be one of my final appearances as a professional, it was no consolation a few weeks later when I had to admit that the injury was too much for me. I could no longer play at the same level.

I remember Gilkesy was one of the last beneficiaries of my generosity – I put it on a plate for him in a 3–2 home win against Huddersfield Town, and he still watches it on cine film! It was his fifth of the season. I was dropped for the game against Bradford City and was back to trying to prove myself in the reserves. Mark White started instead of me.

That was October 1987. The following month I suffered enough of a recurrence of the knee injury for me to need a serious rethink. I met with Ian Branfoot and reluctantly we agreed I couldn't carry on. My professional future stopped instantly at that moment.

When I made the decision to retire, I don't think even Gilkesy, my closest friend at the time, realised how crushing it was for me. I probably still came across as the same old carefree 'P'. Inside I felt wrenched apart and empty. He very kindly says I was a major loss to the changing room, the club and to him personally.

Unbelievably, both of my former clubs, Chelsea and Reading, were relegated at the end of that season – they obviously both missed me on the wing.

Financially, it meant I was pretty much set adrift other

than a small amount the club could claim on their insurance and forward to me. Nowadays, the players' union, the clubs and everyone ram it down your throat to get cover of your own in case of career-ending injuries. They want you to be secure. It wasn't like that in my day. You had to sort out your own affairs. As I said, I hadn't set about arranging personal insurance until the day before the injury. Far too little, far too late. I was left with nothing to show for my professional football career, the victim of my own bad planning.

CHAPTER 18

Hard Times

I would have no insurance pay out, and soon no regular salary. The offer of a testimonial benefit match to be played in August 1988, Reading v. Chelsea at Elm Park, was welcome but scant consolation for the loss of a future. Before that, the mid-eighties were pretty good for me. I had a house, money, a great social life. I was happy-go-lucky. Suzy Sabaroche, a short, dark girl from Hackney – another homely one – and Joyce King, a tall, Amazonian black woman who liked to party as much as I did, were two of the women I was seeing. The Hackney rave scene was generally my point of contact with all the women I had relationships with. At times I'd look around the room and it seemed full of girls I'd moved in with and left. Sometimes I was the only thing they had in common, and understandably that didn't go down very well – especially when I was seeing two or more of them at the same time, and both of them were carrying my child.

I was still footloose and barely considering what a difficult life I was building up for myself, even though I genuinely love every child I've ever had. As you'll realise by now, I've never done things by halves. Even at the time I had to give up my pro career, I had two more babies on the way – one with Suzy and one with Joyce.

Udine was born on 7 January 1988 while Joyce was living with me in the house in Edmonton. Suzy gave birth to Nickel on 23 February 1988, a week before my twenty-sixth birthday. I had eight children with eight different women.

As far as my relations with Mum were concerned, things were much better. It wasn't like I'd sat down and rationalised everything that happened in my childhood, but I'd made a success of my career and I think that surprised and pleased her. It wasn't like I was dragging her off to the magistrates or busting up with her boyfriends any more. I was out of her hair for a while. Maybe that's why I was happy to name one of my children after her.

Mum, too, was more comfortable in herself than at any time I remember. She had moved to her own place in Walthamstow, and June, who had stayed in Middlesex, and I were self-sufficient. I was living nearby and popped in regularly to see if she wanted anything doing – something fixing round the house, a lift somewhere. I'd never stopped trying to prove myself to her in that respect.

In 1987 she had finally returned to the nursing plan that

had originally drawn her to Britain. One catalyst was the death of her father. I think she felt guilty as he'd always wanted her to achieve her youthful ambition. It also helped that in the mid-eighties they were asking for mature people to train for the profession.

She failed her exams the first time, but passed the second time. I was so happy for her. It had been really tough for her, but she kept going, as usual. It was twenty-five-odd years later than she had hoped, but she'd finally become a nurse in England. The secretarial work had brought some financial comfort, and now she had the professional qualification she always wanted and an upstanding role in society. While she was studying, she'd come to quite a serious realisation about her past. The sociological aspects of what she was learning suddenly hit home, especially about the nurturing role of the mother. She was reading about the very basics of motherhood – love, affection, praise – and it struck her that she had never really shown any of these to her children, especially me. It wasn't like she suddenly got in a cab, rushed round and threw her arms round us both, declaring her eternal love. She just realised and felt it inside. Nothing else changed much. Yet I bet the same coldness, the brisk, no-nonsense, unemotional approach, is what made her a bloody good nurse.

Dad was back on the scene since the Sheffield Wednesday game three years earlier, and getting on much better with Mum. Both of them had grown up – they were teenagers when the break had taken place and I knew from my own painful experience how hard it is to handle powerful emotions when you're that age. He'd ceased painting the town red and she was more calm and self-confident than before. Suddenly, it seemed, against the odds, as though the loose pieces of our dysfunctional family might fall into place again. Believe it or not, he actually moved back with Mum. Dad was sleeping in the front room, Mum in the bedroom. It didn't work, though, as the same incompatibility issues arose. They were arguing cats and dogs for almost a year.

June and I were bystanders while this was going on. It wasn't our business and didn't make much difference to our lives; perhaps we never saw it lasting even as long as it did. We just wanted them both to be happy, together or apart. After a while, Dad found his own place in Downs Park Road, Hackney, but eventually switched back to Slough. Wherever he was, I still stopped by to see him regularly and had gradually got to know the father I never had.

We'd have a drink or just chat. He loves cricket and other sports, as I do. I have a key to his place in Slough and stop by there. We're relaxed – unless he overdoes the booze and gets bad tempered or morose.

Every now and then he would tell me his version of why Mum left him. In his eyes, it was because she was such an exacting person and so very hard to get on with. I think I already knew that! Dad and me, we're similar. We're more laid back. We do things at our own pace.

Sometimes he'd say, 'Boy, you know, I love your mum still, but she's so stubborn.' I'm sure he meant it, but what could I do?

'I know, Dad. Don't worry about it.'

The gift of charm remained strong in him in any company, especially ladies and children, and I always made a point of introducing him to his grandchildren. But it was clear to me that Dad is the sort of person who does what he wants to do, in his own way. You can't force him to be what he's not. I like and relate to that. And I think that casual approach to other people's needs is what Mum saw and disliked in me.

If I was still struggling with the concept of faithfulness, after retiring from professional football it should also have been obvious to me that money was going to be tighter than before, but I didn't act like it. While I was at Chelsea, even when I was teenager getting my first big wage packet, I'd been given no advice on how to invest my salary or plan for my future – that's something that the trainees had a little instruction in and I'd bypassed that system. It had been up to me to be aware and deal with my own finances properly, as well as to prepare for the worst. Apart from investing in the house, I hadn't done that. I'd been living for the day. I don't think even now players get much advice on how to deal with the end of a career. To me, it felt like bereavement and I was still mourning in August 1988.

Reading and Chelsea had kindly agreed to stage a benefit match for me on the thirteenth of that month. It was the first opportunity to have it after my retirement and formed part of the preseason schedule for both clubs. It was a Saturday afternoon and there was a great turnout.

Gilkesy played for Reading and it was sweet to see a few of the old Chelsea boys, especially Bummers and Joey McLaughlin, from my days at the Bridge. Chelsea won 3–1 with goals from Clive Wilson, their new black left-back, Bummers and Gordon Durie.

A lot of people said nice things about me in the souvenir programme. The *Chelsea Independent*, a fanzine that had taken a really strong stance against the sort of racism I had to endure, took out an ad saying: 'Thanks Paul, for some great moments. Very best wishes for the future.' And Ian Branfoot was so complimentary: 'At the time of his injury,' he wrote, 'Paul was beginning to look like an attacking player of vast potential. There are few left-sided players around who possess the qualities that Paul had. Pace in abundance, good at crossing, scored goals and defended willingly when called upon to do so. His injury was a huge blow to everyone at the club and a great personal tragedy to Paul. I'm sure everyone here today would join me in wishing Paul the very best of luck in his future career.'

Just after the testimonial match, I took delivery of a brand new BMW from Germany. A blue convertible, with blue hood, leather interior, the works – it was the Don Daddy of motors and had been on order for ages. Back then, there were hardly any of them on the road. It was mint, and gave me a boost at a bad time in my life, but it probably wasn't the best thing to be spending my money on at the time.

What a car it was to drive around in, especially with a decent Pioneer sound system in it. I took Gilkesy out in it and we went back to his flat in Winnersh, near Reading. As we left, I asked if he could drive me back to London in the Beemer as I was tired. Of course, he jumped at the chance. It was the sort of car anyone wanted to drive. It must have taken us about three hours to get back to London, which wasn't bad when you consider Gilkesy stalled it every time he pulled away. When I think back, it was typically impulsive of me to go through with splashing the cash on a car as soon as I received a large amount of money.

I've never really been materialistic but around then I also got hold of one of the first mobile phones – the brick, people called it. Not even MI5 had one as quickly as I did. I remember walking around Hackney with it. People would look at me and call out, 'What the hell is that?' It was the size of a BT telephone box. The funny thing, of course, was that it hardly ever rang because no else I knew had one. I looked cool, though! It was as if I was buying myself treats to take away thoughts of the retirement.

Nothing had replaced football in terms of career. I was like a fish taken out of water, gasping, confused, floundering. Mum says that she'd like to see a trust set up to help footballers like me who have their livelihood taken away. I'm one of hundreds who were totally unprepared for life outside the game.

The trouble for me was that I had earned proper dosh for such a short while before the injury. And the money I received from the testimonial soon disappeared.

Football did remain a part of my life in a smaller way. Once I could move again, I became a hired gun in non-league. I still had one good leg, and luckily it was my left. From 1988, over the next seven, eight years, I turned out for Enfield Town, Northwood, Burnham and Maidenhead United – all of them decent outfits.

It wasn't just the problems I'd always had holding on to money that were coming back to haunt me after my football career ended. Now handling the number of women in my life was becoming really complicated.

That summer, just before the flashy new BMW arrived, Joyce and I had this huge barney. When I ordered the BMW they gave me a Ford Granada to use until it was delivered. One Saturday morning, I needed the car quickly to go and get something – I was playing football just up the road for Enfield Town later – and Joyce wanted it to go to get provisions for the house.

'Look, here's the money for the shopping,' I said. 'Go and get yourself a cab – I've given you money for that too.' I took the car and did what I had to do.

When I came back, she hadn't gone shopping after all, and was still there. I had to head off and test the dodgy knee again, but Joyce was still after the car. In the heat of the moment I flipped. 'If you don't like it,' I said as I left, 'you know what to do.'

I regretted saying that all afternoon while I was out at the football. On the way home it was in my head that I wanted to see her to make things right again. I never mind apologising and don't beat about the bush when I do. I'll say it straight: 'Sorry, I was angry. I didn't mean it.' That's me. But when I got back to Edmonton, Joyce wasn't there.

She still wasn't there by early evening. 'Come on, Joyce,' I was thinking while I was waiting, waiting. I waited all night and nobody came in. By the morning I was worried. 'What's going on here? Where's my baby Udine? Where's my little girl?' So I made some phone calls. Joyce used to go out with our mutual friend Sharon, so I rang her.

'Sharon, where's Joyce?'

'She's not here. But Udine's by Rose.' Rose was another friend, who lived round the corner from Sharon.

'By Rose?' So Joyce was somewhere else.

And soon Rose phoned to say, 'Where's Joyce?' She wanted to return Udine. So now, where was Joyce? I collected Udine, fed her, changed her and put her in her cot. It's something I've done since I was a teenager. I never mind doing the baby stuff like that at all. I like it. What I did mind was that pretty soon it was eleven o'clock at night and still no Joyce. Now I was angry. I locked my doors. A little later Joyce came back and, of course, couldn't get in.

'Where you been?' I was leaning out of a window, still furious.

'I was out.' She loved to rave, did Joyce.

'Yeah, that's what I'm asking, where you been?'

'By Cecil.'

'What you mean, "by Cecil"?' Cecil used to be her man a long time ago. I wasn't happy with that. 'I'm waiting here and you've been staying by another man. You'd best stay down there then.'

'Oh Paul!'

'No, fuck off! Go on, get away from my house.'

I was having none of it and this carried on for a while until we were both in a bit of state. I went back inside and unbeknown to me, Joyce called the police, saying that her child was in danger!

The cops arrived and demanded to know what was going on.

'Excuse me,' I explained, irritated, 'this is a private thing, a domestic matter, mate. She's come here, she can't get in, it's my house.' I couldn't take this. I didn't need it.

I don't know how, a window maybe, or perhaps the police gave her access, but Joyce had managed to climb into the house.

'I'm going upstairs to get my child,' she announced.

'After midnight?' I said, livid with her. 'Are you that stupid? She's a child – you wanna be taking her at this time of night? Look, put her back in her bed and we'll talk about it in the morning.'

I still wanted to sort it out. Joyce and I had been good together and I wasn't going to let things go as quickly as I had with girls in the past.

And then the police came inside, saying that because of the report from Joyce they had to check on our daughter. I really objected to that. (In the cold light of day, though, they didn't know me and they had to take her complaint seriously. It showed how time and policing had moved on since the sixties, when they wouldn't take my mum's complaint about Dad's aggression at all seriously.)

'What? Got to check and see her? Look, get out of my house. I'm not messing with a gun or something stupid like that. I ain't gonna harm my own child for God's sake. I told you it's a domestic, now clear off!'

'You can't be talking to my superintendent . . .' And with that, next thing, I was surrounded. I was overpowered, thrown to the ground, and bundled off to the nick. From there the situation cooled down. After a while, I explained the situation and they dropped the case, warning me to keep the peace. Then they dropped the bombshell. I actually had to stay in the cell.

'Huh?'

'We've got a warrant for your arrest for non-payment of child maintenance.'

'Who for? How much?'

It was Christine again. Damn. This was so stupid. It was money I owed over a couple of years. It was a mistake, but we had barely spoken and Christine knew where I was if she needed me. And what with all the stress of the injury and retirement, I'd missed a few more payments, which was out of order. The trouble was I didn't have that sort of money. I had to call Mum. She had savings and was happy to draw some out and pay it so I could get out. (I paid her back eventually.)

I went back to my house in Edmonton and Joyce and Udine were there. This was a challenge. There's no way I would ever have kicked out Udine, but after I felt Joyce had let me down so badly, we couldn't sleep in the same room together. She was sleeping upstairs and I was downstairs. Even by my standards that was a mad one. How was that ever going to work? I didn't look at it like maybe I should have – Joyce had disappeared just like I always did at signs of conflict.

That was typical of Joyce. She always gave me as good as she got. She had the upper hand in our relationship a lot of the time. That wasn't the only argument we'd had. We came to blows on occasions. Big as she was, Joyce could really fight like a man. I'd never hit a woman. No matter how angry I was, I always stopped short. That was never a line I wanted to cross. But soon after the incident with the police, we had another argument, and I raised my hand to her face. That was it. As soon as I did that, I said we should go to the doctor – together.

'How did you do this?' the medic asked, suspicious.

'I hit her.' I wasn't hiding any of it. I had to face up to what I'd done.

'And do you feel proud?'

'If I felt proud, would she be here, mate?' I've never been so regretful about anything. I hated myself for doing it.

Clearly, things weren't working with Joyce and so I told her she had to find somewhere else to live. As usual when I lost a woman, half my possessions went, too. Whether I lived with them or they lived with me, I used to give them furniture and all sorts of other stuff. The sofa may have cost £2,000, but they could take it. I'm thinking of my child – what's my kid gonna sit on. Cooker, take it. I wasn't one of those people who could bargain over this and that after a break-up, not when it's my child's babymother.

CHAPTER 19

The Crack
Creeps In

Despite the way I went from woman to woman, for many years I had said that the person who had two of my children was the one I was going to marry. By that rule, the first Mrs Paul Canoville should have been Tracey.

At the time she was not the kind of person I really did check, because she was pretty and she knew it. I always tended to go for form and personality over beauty. And enough men were on her case. I didn't normally check for women who were likely to make me jealous of other fellas. I met her in dances. Tracey and her friends used to do club and warehouse promotions. They were called the Spoilt Bitches, and their gimmick was that they went round in hotpants.

Once football had ceased to be an option, music had taken more prominence in my life. Like the football, I spent so much time doing it for fun anyway, it seemed natural to try to make a career out of it. I had known lots of DJs around Hackney for a while and, a few years earlier, had hooked up with the sound system GQ, run by two guys called Vibert and Bernard. I'd been buying tunes for years and had begun to make my name as a DJ on their sound. It was a good buzz and I found I was pretty good at reading the mood of the crowd and selecting the right tune to keep the floor working.

GQ played rare groove, r&b, two-step. We'd play blues parties in the black community around Hackney and Shoreditch – clubs, winebars. We had a huge sound system, Pioneer decks, the lot. We had all the rare tunes and were very serious about it. I had a pretty good system at home, too. 'We know when you're in, Paul,' a neighbour used to joke, 'because our windows rattle.'

Our clever trick with GQ was in our marketing. Around 1988/89 we used pictures of sexy naked men on our party flyers. People thought we'd done the modelling for them, which didn't do any harm. It meant that women flocked to see if we were as tasty as the flyers made us appear. And once word got round, men came because of the number of women. So we were getting a big reputation, building up a considerable following and getting hired to play at some high-profile events.

People started calling us the 'three wise men' and we were playing all over London, not just in Hackney but south of the river too. Although I'd eventually fitted in with the football dressing-room culture, it was very 'English' – the banter was all about what the white boys were up to, what they watched on telly and what pub they were going to. I didn't mind that one bit, but it wasn't the world I was used to or lived in. When they saw me drive off in my BMW, it was like I crossed a frontier into my black world. It was the flipside to the London they knew – often less mainstream, less legal, more marginal.

I felt much more at home in this world, and black American influence was growing in the circles in which I moved. African America, as we saw it in films or magazines such as *Ebony*, was more ambitious, confident, slicker. And I found I could be successful in this world too. It was a new beginning for me.

Spoilt Bitches were active at the same events. Tracey and me, we'd see a lot of each other, and I suppose we grew on each other through familiarity. Eventually, one time at a dance we were watching her operate and I just said to my mate next to me, 'You know what, I'm gonna knock it. Watch.'

We chatted and I took her to my place. I went straight in for the move, holding no bars.

'What you doing?' She was half-smiling, like she thought I'd wanted us to be just friends.

I said, 'It's like you don't want me to.'

'All right.' Her face broke into a smile.

'Then come here.' Bam! I gave it to her sweet. So sweet, that girl did not stop ringing. She was one of those who would just chase you down. I mean, I thought, 'Oh, she got hers, just keep her there, keep a distance.' That's how I liked to be with women. Bam, and move on.

But no, she was on my case, phoning up and asking, 'Where are you?' Coming up to my place, too. So we got together again. The problem was we were a fiery cocktail. Like two chemicals that are safe when separate, but explosive when combined. I remember when I found out how much balls she had. GQ had a dance that we had organised coming up. We had to buy the drinks to sell to people on the night, and that took upfront cash. You would recoup easily twice, three times what you paid when you sold it in the dance. I asked Tracey to lend me £100 and said I'd pay her straight back. I borrowed some money from Joyce too – even though we'd broken up. I gave the money back to Joyce straight away, but I didn't have enough to give to Tracey and she wasn't the kind to wait when a man's word had been broken.

'Look,' I explained, 'wait for a couple of days and I'm gonna get your money.'

'No!' she shouted, firmly. 'I want my money now!' She was little but boy she was excitable.

'Don't be silly, I'll give you your money. Take it easy.'

My charm wasn't working but I wasn't prepared for what happened next. I came home and my TV was gone, along with a few other things. Tracey had spare keys for my flat and I guessed she'd taken her money's worth in consumables. I was straight on the phone to her.

'You been round my flat?'

'Yeah,' she said, feistily. 'I took your telly for my £100.'

I was doing my nut. I went up to her house and banged on the door but she was hiding round a friend's place. I rang that number and her friend answered. She could hear how annoyed I still was and tried to act as a go-between.

'Paul, she said she's sorry,' said this friend, 'she didn't mean anything, but she's heard that you couldn't give her no money.'

'Damn this, I don't want anything to do with her.'

'But Paul, she's so sweet on you. She really checks for you.' That's her friend, and I knew she had warned Tracey about me: 'He ain't no good, you know, he's got too much woman.' She knew me as a womaniser, a 'gyallist' man. Still Tracey had fallen for my fatal charm and gentle humour. Tracey had evidently told her, 'I don't care.' I must have some sweetness where it matters. We were soon back together. That television episode gives an indication of how Tracey was, and how we were together – a volatile combination. Despite my womanising, we were together on and off for several years. Whether we were good for each other is another matter.

The London rave scene was incredible back then. I'd been into hip-hop and that was huge. The Acid House thing had gone cool and people were listening to something a bit more soulful, less electronic, more organic. I didn't really check for bands with a rock element, such as the Happy Mondays for instance, but for Ultra Naté and bands produced by Todd Terry. And I was still into the whole rare groove scene – especially if the tune was imported and only a few copies had come in from the US and cost a fortune.

I tried crack for the first time in 1991, completely by

accident. The music scene was buzzing and ecstasy was going round like nobody's business. Other drugs were doing the rounds as well. It was just like that at the time. Everybody was trying them out and when we went to gigs in winebars there was cocaine – 'charlie' – and crack. Personally, I preferred to make do with a little weed, smoke a likkle herb.

Then one night we were playing at a winebar down in Vauxhall. In the toilets, a geezer I know says, 'Want some?' and offers me a spliff. I take it off him and draw deep a couple of times. After a few more, I get suspicious. It doesn't taste like marijuana.

'Fuck! What the hell's in this?' I say.

'Crack.'

I go absolutely mental. 'Oh my God, what are you trying to do to me?'

He's holding his hands up, excusing himself. I don't know whether he knew what he was doing or not. All that was going through my head was what I'd seen and heard crack does to you. Meteoric high, then straight back down, and after that all you want is more, more, more. I'd known friends whose lives had been ruined by getting hooked on that evil freebase. I'd never wanted to touch it. Ever. And now I'd tried it without even knowing.

I went back into the main room to play some music, sweating on what was going to happen. I was waiting for the peak they all talk about, scared how it would affect me. I was horrified.

But the big hit never came. Instead, it was just a kind of

mellow sensation for me. It made me feel confident, lively, on top of everything; I was still able to DJ as before. Maybe I was even a little sharper picking the tunes and working the dancefloor.

Of course, in retrospect, that was even worse than what I'd feared before I first tried it. It lulled me in and made sure I went back for more.

CHAPTER 20

From Bad
To Worse

In the early nineties I was still earning money (not a lot, but very useful) playing non-league football for Maidenhead United. The heavily strapped right knee was no good but at least the left still had something in it. Even with just one good leg, my commitment and technique were an advantage, and I could always hit a ball. I could barely run with ease, but as long as I could jink and sell a dummy I was motoring. I'd take free kicks and corners, too.

I remember a game against Epsom and Ewell in January 1991 when I grabbed my second goal in successive games. I cut in from the right, beat two defenders and unleashed a drive that rocketed into the bottom left-hand corner of the net at the Bell Street end.

A few months later, against Horsham, I hit one in the corner from the edge of the box with minimal backlift.

Around the same time we beat Cove, a side from Farnborough in Hampshire, 5–1. It was our tenth win on the spin and at the end of 1990/91 we had set a league record of thirteen victories.

The local paper was generous about my display in that Cove game: 'With a comfortable win already sewn up, the Magpies confidence was sky high and they treated the crowd to some outstanding play. It had virtually become an exhibition match and the crowd gave their loud approval, particularly after Canoville tricked one would-be marker with an audacious dummy that was reminiscent of his Chelsea days.'

I was only twenty-nine years old. By rights I should have been enjoying the life of a full-time professional. That realisation kept visiting me like a recurring nightmare. I still felt I'd been robbed.

The crack helped me suppress such painful thoughts and all the conflicts in my life. I could wrap myself up in a joint and forget all my problems for a while. I don't think there's any way I would have got into it if I'd still been a pro footballer. And boy did I go for more. For a time I'd just take the odd bit from friends who were users. There was always somebody who'd give it to you. But after a while I wanted to be more in control of when I had it. I started to buy my own.

It came in 'rocks', formed when cocaine powder is mixed with a base, such as baking soda, and water. I think it was £20 for a quarter gram of rocks then, and I'd bring it home and do it every now and then. Eventually, that became every weekend. I'd smoke it until it had gone and then wait till the next Friday.

Later, I started doing it during the week too. At £20 a pop, it was expensive. When I didn't have the money, I didn't do crack.

Being of a naturally secretive nature, I didn't tell anyone about my habit, and it wasn't a lot at first. I was trying to keep things together and make a new life – with Tracey and my daughter, Paris, born on 13 September 1992. Paris is a lovely girl, my ninth child. Tracey and I lived together for a few years but it didn't stop me seeing other women, or my other children. The number of birthdays to remember with a call or a present was increasing, but I tried my best to remember them and see them when I could.

Crack and being civilised don't go together very well, though. Once it gets a psychological hold, it's like a ratchet. Time passes, there's another click and it has a tighter grip without you feeling you've done anything different. After a few years of using it more and more, as 1994 became 1995, I came to a point where I felt like I was on it every minute. Rather than leave the crack alone when I was skint as I had done previously, I ended up looking for money to feed the habit. And that's when the problems really started.

Despite the drug dependence, I was playing for Egham Town, near Twickenham in Surrey, who were another decent team. I was thirty-two, thirty-three by now and finding it harder to get around the pitch with my bad right leg. I remember one amazing game in the FA Vase when we were 0–2 down to Brockenhurst, an unfancied side from the New Forest in Hampshire, after twenty minutes or so. We came roaring back, grabbing six goals without reply. I scored the last one, chipping over their goalie from thirty-two yards out. I still had it. Occasionally.

Amid all of this, somehow I was about to bring two more children into my world with two different women. A new lady, Sonia Watson, was tall, big-framed and the most hardcore female raver I had ever met. She could outlast me partying, and her dress sense was definitely out of the ordinary. A talented woman, she made nearly all her own clothes. She had her own strong mind and took no nonsense from anyone. As a result, I was always in trouble, but we stayed close, up and down, for years. She was expecting my baby in November 1995 and Tracey was pregnant at the same time. It wasn't even as simple as that – my life never is. They'd known each other for years, each knew I was seeing the other and, to add a further complication to the knots I got myself into, they didn't get along one little bit.

As I mentioned, I had a serious reason to think about the situation of Tracey being pregnant. I'd always said I'd marry the woman who bore me two children, but I was in no state to think straight. I was a mess.

Tracey loved me and wanted me. But the two of us living together, we were so volatile – like a house on fire. We were arguing constantly, especially when I was high. If I'd held true to that promise to settle down with the first woman who bore me two children, it would have been with Tracey. Paris's brother or sister was due to arrive in late 1995, early 1996. Maybe it would have forced me to change how I was acting, but there didn't appear to be much chance of that, the way I was.

At first when I was doing a lot of crack, I wasn't really showing that I was drawn into it. Tracey didn't think I was too bad on it. I was convincing her I was the master of it. Later on, mood swings started and we were arguing like mad, about anything, most of it pure stupidity. I didn't realise what it was at the time. I was just fractious. 'What you doing?' 'Who you talking to?' Anything anyone said I would blow up.

Looking back, I can see that my nature had changed. I was bad. Even when my mum said something innocuous I blew up. We had been getting on much better for the last six or seven years and I was a loving son. This was a throwback to the Rendvill days. She must have known something was going on I was so aggressive, and that's not me.

When I was off the stuff, I was right as rain, the nicest geezer going. Then my head would fill with problems and I couldn't stand it. Crack abuse makes you anxious, irritable, then depressed and feeling worthless. You get such a rush, try to sustain it and eventually feel so, so tired.

At first, the craving was there when I had money. It was the first thing I bought when I had dosh. I'm not a person to think, 'God man, I need some more, I need to rob.' I hadn't robbed since I was a teenager and, bad as I was, I wasn't going to start that again. That's the worst and I knew people who did it. I couldn't because I didn't have that in me. That was something frightening.

I wasn't about to start mugging old ladies but I took from my babymothers and my mum – the same old lifting of a few quid here and there, as always. Like grandmother Sylvanie and Mum, I didn't see that as stealing. With my girlfriends, I was always giving them money for various things, a treat or something they needed to buy. But I'm not going to disguise the fact that, if I'd known where they had money, I'd have gone in that bag and taken it. That's what I did. To start with I knew I could hand the money over again in the next few days but I couldn't wait. When you need crack, you want it now. You think you're in charge of it, but it keeps pushing back your boundaries.

In the end, crack makes you do bad things and tell lies, lies, lies to obtain it. People will tell you I'm always dropping by, paying visits to say hello, see how you are, pay my respects and chat. Now when I was seeing my children's mothers, I had a different agenda.

'I need some money because I've got to pay someone. Can you lend me £50?'

'All right, Paul, £50.'

'I'll pay you next day.' You never saw me. And I did it with everybody. I did it with my baby's mothers. Even though I treated them with disrespect at times, I had been loving and helpful a lot of the time too. I had helped them out with money, support, lifts and tried to be there for them. So now, when I needed something, I would turn on the charm so they trusted me as usual, but I was taking their money and not coming back. And they were the women who were raising my children . . .

They needed all the money they could get, and I was just taking it. I was cheating, but I was in denial. Totally.

Taking money like that was absolutely shameful. I can't believe now that I would stoop so low as to take money from the mothers raising my children. But I'd rather thieve from them than go out and mug – some last remnant of decency stopped me doing that. Problem is, by this time my habit had become so serious that every penny I was giving to them I was taking straight back. That's the change it made in me. This was money that could have been used on my children's clothes or a new sofa.

The crack was eating up any cash I had until we divided up the profit from the next rave. In the meantime, I would borrow on credit cards and didn't think of the consequences. As a DJ I had been used to spending a lot of money on a single hot tune. A US import could cost £50. And when I had lost control of the crack and needed some money to score, it suddenly clicked with me that I could sell my treasured tunes, even though it would ruin my livelihood in music. That's the way you think when you need that hit. It's like a hungry dog eating itself, tail first. I'd often made dumb decisions in my life, but now the hunger for crack removed all reason. It was like an inferno I didn't want to put out, even though it was consuming everything I had of value.

People heard I was considering letting my tunes go and someone from a different sound system approached me about selling my collection. When he asked how much for the lot I had no idea and was so desperate I said £1,000. Boy, that was a giveaway. It was worth two or three times that.

I went ahead anyway. As usual when I got the money I just spent it on the crack and short-term thrills. I hired a nice car, bought a nice telly. And I'd sold the collection I'd worked so hard to put together. Unbelievable.

The other GQ guys said, 'But Paul, why didn't you come to us first?' The state I was in I didn't think of it. It was the money. A grand of it. It was right there.

Back then around Hackney's rave scene, from being one of the 'three wise men' I suddenly became the village idiot. Club promoters knew I'd sold my records, and when people were looking for DJs for big events, they would laugh and say, 'Why don't you ask Paul to play?' and then add, sarcastically, 'Oh no – he's sold all his records!'

Even now when I go out to a bar or a club I'll hear a song and think, 'God. What a tune – I used to own that . . .' My status was lowering by the week, and my self-esteem, built up over five good years, was plummeting.

I went through proper jobs during this period as well. I worked at a hardware company and started lifting tool sets on the side to sell for drugs.

When things got really bad, that's when I kept low. Didn't see anybody. I didn't want to know. I was in my own world. I didn't want to distress anybody, but didn't realise that by hiding away I was hurting people anyway. I was hurting a *lot* of people.

When I wanted to take crack, it was just to forget things – forget this argument, forget worries, forget bills, forget everything. I'd always run away from relationship issues. Crack became my bolt-hole. I just wanted to get out of uncomfortable situations, and at the time the rocks were the only thing there for me.

The thing with the drugs was that it was so nice to forget your troubles and get that high, until, bam! You came down, reality kicked in again and the phone started ringing.

'Mr Canoville, is that you?' It could be a credit agency. 'We just wanted to ask about the money outstanding . . .'

'Oh. No, he's not here, sorry!' I'd pretend I was someone else and put the phone down. Of course, you're deluded if you think you can put these things off. Everything started closing in on me, getting on top of me. I just wanted to get away. I swear, after two years of that turmoil, cheating, lying, hiding, the ups ever lower and the downs deeper, I just wanted to die.

Still I didn't want people to know how bad things were. I was so embarrassed that I was smoking this hateful, irresistible drug. I couldn't shame myself any further by confiding in anyone, least of all Mum or June. I was terrified that I'd be 'outed' by someone, although the signs must have been there for anyone to see.

A big thing for me was the one great achievement in my life apart from my kids – playing professional football for Chelsea. I didn't want anything to damage that proud attainment. I became petrified I'd bump into an old team-mate and they'd recognise me when I was really bad, or that I would be exposed in the Sunday papers: 'Ex-Chelsea Star Canoville's Crack Shame'. I could just see it on the terraces at the Bridge.

'Paul Canoville, what's he up to now?'

'Didn't you see? Crack head.'

'Jesus.'

I couldn't have taken that.

Crack eats up your life so quickly I don't remember a lot of what I was doing day to day, month by month. I dropped off the social scene. I was dishevelled, looked a mess and was embarrassed. But I couldn't stop. In 1994 I even pawned the promotion medal I'd earned with Chelsea ten years earlier. My mum proudly kept it in a cabinet next to the match ball I was given after my only hat-trick, against Swansea.

I got £70 from the pawnshop for that medal and spent it all on crack. A memento of my proudest achievement in football handed over that cheaply. I promised myself I would return to buy it back, but I was fooling myself. It was gone for ever, just like that. I hated myself for that afterwards: 'Paul, you said you'd buy it back. But did you try? Did you really want it? Did you hell.'

What I made Tracey, Sonia and all the women I was leaning on put up with on a daily basis was disgraceful. But no matter what I did to other people, no one could have loathed me more than I loathed myself. Few people realised how bad I was. I'd often gone off-radar after a

break-up, so it wasn't like my crack-related disappear-
ances were out of the ordinary.

Not even June or Mum knew how my life had disinte-
grated. Once when the fire for crack was raging in me, I
slipped into Mum's when she was out and went through
the bedroom looking for valuables. I found some of her
jewellery – items she really cherished but didn't often have
occasion to wear. I pocketed them without conscience,
convinced myself I would get the money to buy them back
before she had even noticed they were gone. Of course, she
was aware of what I'd done straight away and was
furious. After that she changed the door locks to restrict
my access to her home. She'd had enough. This wasn't a
few quid lying around on a sideboard, this was her prized
possessions. They weren't top of the range, but they were
her 'crown jewels'.

At the time I wasn't able to accept how devastated Mum
was when she discovered what I'd done. I think something
snapped inside her. It was the neighbours' television all
over again. It would take me years to win back her trust,
and I completely understand why.

When I bought the gems back from the pawnshop, I had
to post them through Mum's door. That's how isolated I
had made myself, even from the people who cared for me.
I could only sneak a view of my old life through a
letterbox, shut out from the safest place for me.

All my life I'd given away money and borrowed it; it
was how I had always been. Now it was all one-way traffic
and friends suspected the secret truth.

'Paul, you're not taking that stuff?'

'What you talking about? I'm not taking that rubbish.'

None of my raving friends, close ones who knew, were saying anything to stop me. One or two of them were doing it too, but I suppose the rest didn't know where to start – would I have listened anyway? I learned that one of them was talking behind my back – 'Paul's a druggie, he's a crack head. Don't be talking to him.' I had been a professional in the clubbing world and that had carried a certain status. I had been on the ball, organising events, taking responsibility. Now I'd sold off my tunes for drugs and lost control, I was a shadow of a man. A song by Gil Scott-Heron, 'Home Is Where The Hatred Is', articulates what junkies feel. It goes: 'Stand as far away from me as you can and ask me why, hang on to your rosary beads, close your eyes to watch me die. You keep saying, kick it, quit it, kick it, quit it. God, but did you ever try, to turn your sick soul inside out, so that the world can watch you die.'

I suppose people feel appalled and scared at the same time. It's easier to leave damaged souls alone. Thank God some people feel they have to intervene.

Once you're branded a junkie, people can never see you in the same old light again. You're a constant reminder of badness. You stand alone. But it's your responsibility, your choice to do that shit.

CHAPTER 21

Lifeline From An Old Friend

In autumn 1995 my friend from Chelsea days, Simon Chandler, had moved to Victoria Park. He happened to be jogging near Kingsland Road when he saw someone he thought he recognised, but dishevelled, hunched, in a right state.

He called out, 'P!' I looked up and he ran closer. For most of the time when I was caning it, you would not have imagined I was a crack head. I had a wardrobe full of clothes and still looked sharp. But now I'd run out of money. I wasn't working. I wasn't buying clothes. I was barely going out because I didn't want anyone to see me. Simon hadn't seen me for a long time and had to look twice. He was absolutely shocked. I looked smaller, shorter, much thinner. My head looked shrunk and my hair was shapeless. I was wearing track pants and Reeboks (yes, I know).

He asked me for my phone number and rang me up soon afterwards. He sounded anxious. We met up at a Mauritian restaurant in Finsbury Park, Chez Liline. He told me after that he couldn't believe what he was seeing across the table. I was dried up, unshaven, rough. I'd been a kind of idol to him at Chelsea and he was devastated at how far downhill I'd slipped.

He contacted Tracey – I was living with her in Finsbury Park – and asked, 'What's up with Paul?' She didn't hold back, and what she told him was hardcore. I'd been taking money from her purse and from other babymothers', flogging the kids' presents, selling anything I could.

'It's crack,' she said.

Simon got back in touch with me. Now he was desperate to help. 'Whatever it is, I can sort it out, Paul, no matter what,' he told me. He was as good as his word. It was fate he'd bumped into me while he was out jogging.

He encouraged me to put the relationship with Tracey on hold while I sorted myself out. We were too volatile together. That would have pleased Mum. She and Tracey never got along. Then again, Mum was disparaging about most of my women. She always thought I picked the wrong type, or the wrong sort got their hooks into me. She blamed them for a lot of my problems.

'You and Tracey are bad for each other,' Si insisted. But Tracey had our child, Paris, who was just three, and she was pregnant again. The thing I'd always said about settling down with a woman who had two of my children was going to be tested if I let her alone to sort myself out.

Maybe a family commitment would also be the spur I needed to kick the crack. I was confused about what was for the best.

Then Simon suddenly stepped in and took charge of my life. If I couldn't help myself, he was going to make up my mind for me. At his insistence I moved in with him in a place in Victoria Park. It was like a black version of the film 'The Odd Couple', with me being bossed around, sorted out and resenting it like mad.

He reined me in and tried to pick my life out of the chaos it was in. There were no half measures because he could see my life was in danger. He made enormous personal sacrifices. His relationships were complicated, too. He had a wife and child he'd broken up with living outside London and had responsibilities towards them. But he stopped work and put himself on the line for me. I owe him so much.

I needed routine back. Every day at 11 a.m. he would drag me out running to get back to fitness. I've always loved exercising, keeping fit, but I'd wasted away.

Simon was very professional and serious about it. He cut off my money supplies so I couldn't buy crack. He told all the girls who used to give me money to give it to him to mind instead.

We had big arguments over me getting cash to buy some clothes, and especially about women. He told me they were a distraction. I had to focus. I needed to get serious about saving myself. He said he wanted to cut down my juggling of women. There were only two of my babymothers he ever wanted to see coming round. It's his big thing that, even at the height of the drugs, women were the most important thing in my world. I found it easier to kick the crack than the women.

When I was out, he'd look all around the house – under the bed, in the bathroom, among the towels – to see if I'd hidden a stash there.

With Simon's help, after a while I was OK enough to get a little job delivering for a plumbing firm in Dalston. Simon wasn't conned, though. He could see that I still needed proper help.

Fair dos to him, he researched how to help crack addicts through books and pamphlets, social workers he knew. He would go through the various options open to me and explained the two processes I needed to go through to earn back my life – detoxification and rehabilitation.

These involve going into a residential home, cut off from the drugs, and the people who provide them, and talking things through with health professionals while the poison works its way through your system. Once the body is clean, they start on preparing your mind for society again with rehabilitation. Inside one of these places, you are educated about the drugs you were taking, and exposed to the detail of what it does to you and the effect it has on your life and on the people you care for. You're taught how to deal with moments of weakness and how to rebuild your life without the dependency. Gradually, you are exposed to more of the outside world. There are 'halfway houses' where you start to reintegrate but still have support. The whole process can take months. And it's not as if you can just turn up at one like it's a doctor's surgery and say, 'Hello, I'm a junkie, can I have a prescription for a new life please?' The hostels are heavily used and they don't take on just any old client. They cost a lot to run and don't want to waste money on no-hopers.

The amount of time Si spent on me! He got on the phone and rang everyone to see if I could get a place in a hostel. He drove me to assessment meetings and back for months.

I didn't return his hard work in the way I should have. I probably took him a bit for granted. Drugs make you selfish but that's no excuse. I was still in denial and didn't take my plight seriously enough. I went into survivor mode. It was a mechanism I'd developed, where I'd just go quiet and uncooperative.

If he found a spare hostel place in Tooting, I would point out that all my babymothers lived miles away, north of the river. If he found a place closer to hand, I'd say I didn't like the vibe from it. I always had an excuse. When I listen to that Amy Winehouse song, 'Rehab', with the line, 'They're tryin' to make me go to rehab, I say no, no, no', it reminds me. I was sad to see that eventually she ended up in there, just like I did. There's only so much denial a life can sustain.

I never did crack in front of Simon, but I did lapse. He was so committed; he kept working to get me straight anyway. Thank God he did.

CHAPTER 22

The Tragedy Of Tye

During all this, while I was still manic on the drugs, one of the most traumatic events in my life knocked me for six. Five days before Christmas 1995, Tracey went into labour and the little boy we called Tye Paul Canoville was born. Of all the many children I had with all the different mothers, he was the one who looked the most like me. June said he was the spitting image of his father.

But as soon as he came into the world we were made aware he had a serious defect. His tiny heart didn't have enough valves to feed it and he needed intensive care in the maternity hospital – the Whittington in Archway, north London, about five-to-ten minutes' drive from Tracey's in Finsbury Park. There's nothing so sad as seeing your new-born baby fighting for his life, tubes coming in and going out his little body, isolated from you in a protective box.

The doctors explained in detail where the problem lay, not that you can ever take it in all in one go, even when it's so serious. They described how it was possible to operate on the heart and make it function more successfully. But at the same time, they made it clear that it was an extremely risky procedure, especially as he was so young and weak.

The bad news didn't end there. The medics went on to tell us that even if the surgery was 100 per cent successful, he would need constant attention, twenty-four hours a day, probably for as long as he lived.

The alternative was unthinkable. If they didn't operate, there was little chance of him surviving at all. Tracey and I talked it over and both agreed that they should operate and we'd dedicate ourselves to looking after him, whatever happened. It was going to need total commitment but, looking at his tiny frame struggling for life, the two of us were unshakable. We wanted this for him more than anything. This was the kid I'd always been waiting for. The 'second child' rule I'd laid down for myself, and the commitment I'd promised, were going to be tested in a way I couldn't possibly have foreseen. Lifting the veil of my crack habit, I was determined to prove I could abide by that promise.

True to our words, Tracey and I did shifts to stay close to him in the hospital unit, taking it in turns to hold a bedside vigil, night and day, while awaiting the operation. Mum and June came to visit. Nothing else in my life mattered. I remember hardly being able to sleep. I'd just stare at that tiny little body, fighting for its start in the world. At least the prospect of the surgery gave us some faith that the situation would change soon. We were utterly powerless to do anything for Tye ourselves, except be there for him. It was down to the medics and the operation. Emotionally, I felt like I was in chains.

That petrifying stalemate continued for about a week. Then the doctors called us into a room. They looked more nervous than usual. They said that after the most careful consideration they had concluded that they couldn't do anything about his condition after all. It wasn't worth operating because he would have no quality of life afterwards. It was a bombshell that neither Tracey nor I had expected.

'What do you mean?' I screamed, distraught. 'What the fucking hell are you trying to say? You said it was all right to operate before, now it's not! What's going on? Why can't you just try it?'

I was wasting my time. There would be no lifesaving operation. Tye's only hope had been extinguished.

That really tore me apart. To see the state he was in, to have that chance put before you, then snatched away, was the most agonising thing I've ever been through. Our baby would fight a hopeless battle for survival all on his own, with just his mum and dad keeping vigil by his side. Useless. Powerless. Hoping for a miracle. Christmas is supposed to be the time for that sort of thing. But in 1995 the miracle never happened.

We wanted him out of the hospital straight away. If he was going to die, he'd be with us at home for as long as we could have him. No tubes going through his nose to feed him, no injection in his throat so that he can breathe.

We brought him home to Tracey's in Finsbury Park. She was upstairs, I was downstairs with him. I couldn't sleep. Every time I heard a noise I was up. We had nine days of that.

Tracey and I had his name registered as Tye Paul and that same day he started to look really poorly and we had to rush him back to hospital. The doctors looked sympathetic but just said again that they couldn't do anything for him.

It was clear Tye was close to death and was going to stay in care.

Mum was at the hospital with us. Tracey was in a dreadful state and, although she and Mum had never much cared for each other, we were all drawn together by Tye's condition. Mum was trying to comfort me. 'Don't worry, Paul, it's one of those things, you can't do anything about it.' Surrender talk like that, however well meant, wasn't what I wanted to hear, quite honestly. Like I should lie back and accept what was coming. A lot of the time that had been my way of dealing with my troubles, but not now. Not like this.

Then one afternoon I just picked up little Tye in my arms and held him. I looked up, to heaven I suppose, knowing I wasn't leading a virtuous life, and pleaded, 'Don't take him! Take me instead! I'm the one that's fucking useless right now!' I broke down. I was sobbing out of control with nurses standing around, not knowing where to look.

I never cried in public but now I couldn't stop. My body was shaking with sorrow. Boy, when you see these things on TV you don't think it's like real life.

Tye was there in my arms, I held him, heard the last breath come out of his mouth – *sigh* – and he was gone.

I couldn't cope. I left him lying there in the hospital. I took £80 out of Tracey's purse, went off to buy some crack and got totally wasted.

CHAPTER 23

Checking In Before I Checked Out

When Tye died and I went straight off to get hammered, nobody could stop me. Simon knew what I was doing and tried to get in touch but I was out of my head for hours. I simply had to escape from real life.

When my head cleared, I took stock. After what we'd been through with Tye, I couldn't face Tracey straight away. There would be too much raw emotion involved.

Instead, I thought about another child I'd had the month before. As expected, Sonia had given birth to Caysey in November. Of course, they had a just claim on my time, and I'd been spending all my days and nights with Tye and Tracey. That wasn't the reason I went by Sonia's house, though. After holding Tye in his final moments, I just needed to be close to my other baby. I couldn't let anything happen to her. I stayed with her all night.

Obviously, Tracey heard I went down there. I don't know what she must have thought. There was always animosity between Sonia and her. Tracey was grieving just as much as I was, or more. She needed me to be there for her but I wasn't.

I was in chaos. Confused, angry, guilty, tormented. I couldn't deal with it. My grieving made me introverted. The emotional impact was massive. It provoked me into thinking again about how I was leading my life generally.

Simon tried to channel it as a way to make a change. 'This is not you, Paul. You need to get away. Do it for Tye,' he said. I was hiding. I felt worthless. I was embarrassed. I had no morals. I wanted to change but I wasn't strong enough to do it. I needed the decision to be taken out of my hands. I needed to put myself in a position where that could happen.

As days passed I went back to the driving job at the plumbers in Dalston. But now I had a non-caring attitude. I didn't give a damn. This was the end-game for the crack head. I wanted to stop this life and get back to the old, clean, caring Paul.

I had decided what was required. I needed to be caught and punished by the police. That would make the decision for me. I still wasn't prepared to take the responsibility for myself. I had always looked for excuses and I wasn't even capable of facing up to the duty of care I had to my own body. No one else should have been made to do it, only me; I simply didn't have it in me at the time. I needed someone else, or the authorities, to wrest control of my life.

I'd steal from the plumbers, get caught and let the cops intervene. They'd find out my drugs problem, I'd get a sentence and treatment. It would force the issue.

The day I chose I knew that security at the plumbers had been stepped up because people were apparently stealing stock from the warehouse. They had CCTV and were checking every van leaving to make sure drivers only took the stock they were supposed to deliver.

I put some extra radiators that weren't on my schedule into the van in full view of the cameras. I was going to let them watch me steal them. As I was driving off, a security guy asked me to pull over and asked me if I knew what was in the back of my van. Straight away I confessed.

'I ain't gonna lie to you, I've got radiators.'

I was taken to a manager, expecting the whole healing process to kick in. Instead, she just said, 'OK. We're going to have to let you go but we won't contact the police.'

They even gave me two weeks' wages! I had desperately wanted them to get the police involved. It would all have come out then, they'd put me somewhere and I would get some help. But the plumbers weren't going to press charges. Nightmare.

So I stayed by Simon. I drank camomile tea, had acupuncture, anything he thought would help. I gave him so much trouble, but he stood by me. He was so dedicated to getting his mate well that he was turning me round, but it was taking an age.

Out of the blue, a detox place Simon had previously contacted on City Road called. It was a crisis intervention unit in Angel, Islington, not far away in north London, with a twenty-four-hour crack cocaine helpline, the works. I went in to see about the first stage of getting clean. It's called self-referral, when you approach them yourself rather than come in via their community drugs teams. I had to show them how much I was doing. I had to lie more or less as well.

That was the weird thing. You had to say you were doing a bit more than you were doing; otherwise you weren't really in trouble. So I exaggerated. I was doing this amount and that amount and this drug and that one. The next thing I knew, they were saying, 'Oh, you're a serious case.' That's the only way I could get into the planned detoxification process.

I was accepted on their scheme, and that was the start. I was glad to be there. It's a place for people who, like me, had lost control of their lives through drugs. A three-week 'course' included examination by medics who looked into your health issues – one-to-one sessions where you could talk about your problems and plan gradually how to get out of the hell you were in, provided, of course, you were committed to getting clean again. It reminded me a little of the depressing homeless hostels I'd stayed in when Mum first moved to Slough. People's problems were much more obvious here than among the strays of Southall, though. I still found the whole 'opening up' process a problem. It wasn't how I'd been brought up and I wasn't ready to accept there was any value in it.

Simon would pick me up to take me out for a break.

June and Mum visited, too. That commitment element was the problem. I wasn't altogether ready for the intensity – counselling, complementary therapies and all that. It was so alien to me, this social worker world. I'd been used to hard knocks and getting on with it. I suppose part of me still thought I deserved what was coming my way and should take it.

There was something else, too. You're meeting complete strangers in the hostel, and the last thing I wanted was for any one of them to know or find out who I was and where I was from. In these places, people are called clients, not patients. It's to do with the fact that the word 'patient' is historically linked with 'suffering' and that's too negative for rehab. So it's 'client' because that makes it sound like you have more power in the relationship with the staff and social workers.

I was hearing these other clients' stories and I was thinking, 'God, I thought I was bad, but these stories are truly terrible.' Some of them had no parents and some of them had been raped – men as well as women. It was a different world, even by my standards.

It amazed me. Like that remand home when I was a leary teenaged tea-leaf awaiting trial, I thought I was big time, but I was an amateur. Some of these boys were seriously screwed up, way ahead of me.

A while into the course, I felt clean and saw the light. My head had been just so far up my own arse, my life had been so dominated by drugs. But after two weeks' detox, a clear head, no substances, no drink, I was on my way back to being normal. I looked in the mirror and for the first time in a long while I saw 'me'. I was telling my friends, 'This is clean time!' It was great to be back.

Now I wasn't on crack, I was appalled with myself. 'What the hell were you doing? God, man, why did you do that then? What made you?' It's not normally in me. I'm not greedy or addictive. Affection is all I crave.

I think of myself as a loving person. But when crack door-stepped my life, I hadn't had the strength to kick it out. It left no place in my life for love. The trouble is there is nothing so intensely enjoyable as the euphoria crack-cocaine gives you. There will be moments that remind you of the high – just like the tobacco smoker who always craves a draw after sex or a meal. You never forget that; you just have to resist it. The only way to avoid it is never to try it. Ever.

Now I was OK again, my thoughts were to take life day by day. But I couldn't help thinking about what options may open up – ideas, plans about what to do with my life. 'God, this is what I could do now . . . and this.'

Straight, I was reflecting on the things I didn't do before – travel, work ideas – and thinking, 'Why didn't I do it?' It was important to get that optimistic vibe during the recovery. It was a positive difference.

Crack is like a cuckoo, kicking everything else out of your nest – family, interests, friends, work. It makes you so lethargic you just don't want to do anything. You could sleep for a whole day after a session. It's like a warning to you but you're blind to the one important thing – those drugs are gonna hurt you and the people around you.

When I was on crack I was just so incredibly selfish. I would stay with any one of my girlfriends, and come and go like it was a hotel. I could come in from a session at six o'clock in the morning. When she got up to go to work, I was comatose. And when she came home, I was gone again. Terrible behaviour.

How the hell was I getting away with it? How the hell do you have a relationship – if you can call it that – under those circumstances?

Mum and June hadn't realised at first how badly the drugs were affecting my life. Usual thing with me – I didn't tell them how it was and they didn't see me as much when I was out of it. At first, when I was working and not doing too much, it was easy to conceal. But even when I had to sell my house in Tottenham, after struggling so hard to keep up the payments, even when I was left with nothing, I kept what I could from my closest family. I'd learned how to keep secrets from an expert after all – my mum. But when I was doing crack, you couldn't get through to me anyway. I wasn't listening to anybody, Mum, June, Simon, any of my girlfriends.

I would demand some things that didn't belong to me – money, things to sell – and it couldn't have been nice because I would say, 'I want it, I need it!' I was given it regardless, despite everything. No it wasn't nice. I wasn't nice.

After the detox at City Road I had to get a place in a

rehabilitation unit immediately. It was really good to be clean again and I was back living with Simon while trying to get on the next stage, which is intended to set you up for a future without dependency. It wasn't easy keeping straight. A hell of a long battle loomed ahead.

CHAPTER 24

Tryin' To Make Me Go To Rehab

That year, 1996, has to be the worst year of my life. After Tye passed away and I had gone through the detox, I was in and out of rehab places throughout the year, still living with Simon in between.

The rehabilitation can only happen after you have been detoxified from the drug you use and you're staying off it. With the primary care, you're lodged in a 'sober living' centre along with helpers (normally former users) and other recovering junkies. It provides routine and communal living and you try to help each other while you're coming to terms with a new approach to your old life. It takes as long as it takes. There's group therapy or one-to-one sessions and you're regularly tested for various health issues.

The secondary stage, when you're prepared and equipped for a return to independent living, comes about only when the assessments show you're definitely ready. How long it takes obviously depends on the individual and his or her devotion to getting right.

Although I had now been through the detox OK, my return to normality had hardly even started, and I was doing my best to make it hard for myself. I'm not about to pretend I was an angel. I went through a few primary care centres.

Although Si kept on at me, ferrying me about, I was a poor patient. You were supposed to be largely isolated from the outside, but I'd sneak women into a rehab hostel at any opportunity. I'd just go missing every now and then. I didn't like being cooped up and I missed female company.

Other than that I was fairly well behaved in rehab. It was ironic that when I first went in after detox, people kept saying to me, 'Why are you here? There's nothing wrong with you.' I appeared normal, just getting on with chores. Like I was eight years old again!

But over a few days things nagged away at me. It was supposed to be about sharing responsibility, but all I could see was that no one else was pulling their weight. I was cleaning, cooking, filling and emptying the dishwasher. Nobody else lifted a finger. One afternoon I felt I'd had enough. I stood in front of everyone and really let off at them. I went absolutely berserk.

'Well,' someone said, 'all this time we thought there was nothing wrong with you. Now we know you have your own troubles.'

After losing my temper like that it was obvious I had lots of problems and they began the counselling with me. The first counsellor was a white guy. I didn't like his way of asking me questions and didn't feel comfortable enough with him to open up. I'm not a racist but the state I was in, I couldn't connect with him. I asked if I could have a black counsellor.

So this black geezer took over. He had picked up on my issue with women and asked me about it. He kept bringing it up again and again and I got fed up. 'Was I unable to say "no" to any woman?' was one question he asked. He was spot on, but at first I wasn't ready to talk about it and gave him a hard time. I had so much anger in me.

But as I was mulling things over in my mind, he was really starting to get through to me. It was just in the way he approached things and how he seemed to understand my mindset. He wasn't judgmental and had wise things to say. Soon I couldn't wait for these regular sessions. They meant I was getting a lot out of my stay. Some seeds were sown in that place that would help me later – I realised I had to open up to grow up emotionally.

He moved on, though, and a black woman took over. I've always found women easy to talk to and don't have a problem with respecting them in positions of authority. But she told the staff that women were sneaking in to see me and lost my trust. It wasn't the same. The sessions stopped being useful to me and I felt frustrated. Once I felt like that, I was losing faith in the place.

I moved around to a few other centres as my treatment

progressed. At some of the hostels I'd been to I'd feared the worst about being recognised – once, a West Ham supporter had known straight away who I was. Another woman remembered me from the dances in Hackney. I was worried, but it never really got out. There's a rule in rehab: what goes on in there, stays in there.

Towards the end of my rehab, while I was in a semi-independent hostel, a halfway house in Victoria, I was recognised again. A bloke who was measuring up the place for new carpets happened to be a Chelsea fan. He approached me, cagily.

'Excuse me,' he said, 'aren't you Paul Canoville?'

This was all I needed. I said no. 'Hold on, you are Canners, aren't you – I'd know you anywhere.' I had to come clean. We talked. He told me how exciting I was as a player, and how he'd never forget my performance in that Sheffield Wednesday 4–4. And he apologised for the Chelsea fans who'd made my life a misery in the early days. He'd been a regular supporter and had seen it first hand. He was disgusted by them.

'Abused by your own fans,' he said. 'How did you ever get over it?' It brought me up short. I'd not thought about that for a while.

'Tell the truth, it's affected my confidence ever since,' I told him. 'I reckon I never really recovered from it.'

I lived with Simon for a year in total. Then he found out a close friend had cancer. He'd done all he could for me, beyond the call of duty as a friend. I needed him, but I was fighting him. Someone else needed him more.

It must have been a relief for him in the end. He used to get so frustrated with my ways when I was living with him. One time he was back in Reading, where his ex-partner and kid lived, and I was at his place. I was going to see a woman but couldn't find a key to his house, so I just left the door on the latch and went out. That was unbelievably selfish when I think back now. A neighbour, very kindly, shut it. But when I came back and couldn't get in, I had to ring him up and call him back to Hackney with a key.

Another time I asked Simon to take me to pick up a debt from someone over in north London. He thought the act of calling in what was owed to me was a positive thing and drove me there. I asked him to stop, walked to a phone box and made a call. I hung around for ages waiting, but the geezer didn't come. Simon got agitated. He wasn't the kind to hang around for forty-five minutes by a telephone box. Eventually, he decided I was taking the mick and was trying to score some crack. He shouted, 'Let's go!' and drove us off. It may have looked bad to Si but it was totally innocent, nothing to do with drugs.

After a bust-up with one of my girlfriends, I went AWOL and he was really upset. He actually drove all round the West End searching for me and eventually tracked me down to another woman's house.

Simon used to get so mad at me because I was still preoccupied with women even when I was out of his care in rehab. The sneaking out, smuggling in, did his head in. He'd tell me I lacked focus, I was putting women ahead of getting straight. He was right. He was making a big personal commitment to helping me, and I still wasn't taking it as seriously as he wanted.

He saw women as a distraction. I saw them as my passion. I just wanted to be loved, but people always say I just had low self-worth. I can never say my relations with women or men have been like most other people's.

Simon always points out that I've never had the kind of friendships where you pop round with a bottle of wine for dinner as a couple, or go out for a family picnic, the normal things couples or friends do all the time. He's right. I've always been in the shadows, and flitted around between women. I've had friends in social or work situations, at times in my life, or in particular places. They are in separate compartments. In some cases I've kept a relationship going with just enough oxygen to survive, dropping by out of the blue after years away, or ringing and texting. But mostly, I've had too many new girlfriends keeping me preoccupied.

I never really told Simon till now how much I appreciated what he did for me. When June found out what he was doing he told her I owed him nothing, that it's what anyone would have done. But it was way more than that.

The last and best of the rehab places I found myself in was Milton House in Holloway, north London. It was the final stage of my drug treatment – preparation for a life without dependency outside. Not everyone was residential, as I was; some were community based already. I was there for four months and completed the course from start to finish without a lapse.

The process is well worked out to smooth the transition back to normality. It started with the focus on settling-in and formulating your own care plan, what you need to achieve before you can go back on the street.

Next they start to get you looking at trying out work options, maybe voluntary work or college placements, based on your needs.

Then, finally, the emphasis shifts on to more practical things, such as helping sort out housing, learning, training or employment – you won't believe the number of good people who, without making a song and dance, offer places for recovering drug addicts on their workforce.

At the same time there are opportunities to get fit, play sport and enjoy communal living.

By the end of the course, you're ready again for independent living. It was a challenging but supportive environment at Milton House.

Perhaps the lack of belief in myself was why I liked order and discipline imposed on me, and responded to it for the most part, especially there. Maybe it reminded me of the rigours of my childhood with Mum. Things started to improve. I was put on a computer course. I got my head straight and my morale back. I was enjoying picking up my fitness regime. I felt like the old Canners again.

Everything was going well for me and I was confident I could make a fresh start in all sorts of ways. Then one day, shortly before I was due to leave Milton House, I suddenly felt a terrible abdominal pain. I was doing some trampolining, would you believe.

On a trampoline you have to use the right technique, otherwise you land with a jolt, your guts and your diaphragm go south and it wrenches your innards like mad. Well, that's what happened this time. I landed badly and pulled a groin. Although it hurt like mad, it was the sort of injury I would have played through as a footballer.

I didn't think much of it and just took some Nurofen. But every day for two weeks I was in agony with this groin pain. I was waking up at two in the morning in hot and cold sweats, thinking it was because of the trampoline business.

When I mentioned it to June and one or two friends, they all warned me I should see a doctor. Typically, I wouldn't listen. I'm stubborn. I didn't say anything to the staff. It had gone so well at Milton House but I didn't want to have to stay around any longer than I needed to, so I didn't seek medical advice.

The thing was, Mum was a qualified agency nurse by now and when I told her about the pain, she kept telling me to get it checked. Then when she came to visit me at Milton House and saw how much weight I'd lost, she suspected something was seriously wrong. Now she was insistent. 'You have to go to your doctor,' she said. Eventually, I couldn't take the agony any more. I made an appointment with my GP and after an examination I was referred straight away to hospital with no delay.

They gave me some scans and then broke the news that I needed an operation. The trampoline injury had been masking my real problem.

'What d'you mean?'

'You've got lymphoma, inflamed lymph glands in your abdomen, and we have to take them out straight away.' They didn't use the 'C' word, but 'lymphoma' is a cancer. It attacks the glands and tubes that take white blood cells and lymph fluid around your body. What they were aiming to carry out was 'de-bulking', an ugly term for removing the cancerous tumours in my groin.

'We will operate as soon as there's an available bed and you have to be ready for whenever that is.' I was taken aback and bemused by suddenly being thrown at the mercy of surgeons. I felt I had gone through enough as it was with the rehab. I had no idea how much worse things would get.

It was a matter of waiting for a bed to come up at the hospital.

Just ten days later I was called in and had the operation to remove the tumours. It was pretty standard. I was under general anaesthetic for a short while and woke up with an intravenous drip in place and a pipe down below to drain the wound. The doctors were happy that they had cleaned up the growth. But then they broke it to me that I had non-Hogdkin lymphoma (NHL), Grade 1. Excluding skin cancer, NHL is the sixth most common form affecting adults in the UK. There are about 9–10,000 cases a year. It was attacking the lymph nodes in my abdomen. The 'Grade1' part meant that it was localised to one area of my body, and hadn't spread. In some cases NHL can affect the spleen and other organs. The survival rate for NHL sufferers in Britain aged 15–44 is around 65 per cent. That's skewed, though – more women are still around five years after diagnosis than men.

Whatever name they have for it, it's still cancer, and cancer is a killer. I couldn't believe it, of course.

'From where?' I said, as if you 'catch' cancer. Fit man like me, full of life. 'I've been a professional footballer.' That counted for nothing now.

'It normally affects men between the age of thirty and forty,' they said.

The thing with NHL is that it strikes at the cells in your body's own defences, especially when your immune system is low. They don't know exactly what causes it but there are 'known risks'. One of those is recreational drug use. I have to face the fact that my drug taking may have contributed to my fate. Crack affects your immune system. You don't have the vitamins your body needs and your white blood cells can be damaged. I contracted cancer after I'd been caning the crack.

I was in hospital for about ten, eleven days. I didn't broadcast the fact that I was ill. Mum and June knew, of course, and I knew they would be there for me. My kids and their mums knew, and one or two very close friends, such as Simon. I didn't want anyone else to know about it, or want to discuss it. I didn't want any fuss.

After the operation came the real punishment – chemotherapy. Naïve as I am, I thought it would solve everything just like that, as straightforward as Night Nurse or something. I didn't know anything about it and I've never thought too deeply about such things, I just take it as it comes. It was 'the cure' and that was enough for me. The day before I was about to take it, the medical staff tried to prepare me for what I was about to receive.

'Paul,' they said, earnestly, 'this will make you very weak.'

'What you talking about?'

I'd been kicked all over a football pitch by 14-stone defenders out to kill me in the past. I'd had to play through the pain barrier again and again when I was injured. I'd be fine.

What a shock! I soon got out of that complacency! I tell you, what this chemotherapy stuff does to you really is something else. The fitter you are, the more likely they are to give you a stronger dose. Imagine what they thought a former professional footballer in good physical shape could stand! I am not gonna lie to you – chemo is a torture that can make you pray for death.

When I first went in, I noticed that the treatment chair was a luxurious armchair. It's a drawn-out process. The fluid is slowly induced into you through a needle. I'm no good with needles, anyway, like most men, and my skin was so tough they couldn't get through it, which didn't help.

'Lovely veins,' they said.

'Just get on with it.'

They say chemo is a poison and I can vouch for that. I thought they would inject it and I'd be out in a few minutes but this stuff has to drip in slowly and take its time to go round your body. I took their treatment every two weeks, for several months.

And I found out why there was a comfy chair. When that 'medicine' goes round your veins, you feel eighty-five years old. It's like they've swapped your blood for lead, and heavy metal is coursing through every vein and artery. You cannot go through a chemo session on your own. And when I was out, it was straight home to bed. That was back at Mum's house for the time being. I could not move.

I was coming to realise how fortunate I was that Mum had convinced me to get that pain checked when she did. It was because the cancer was caught so early and the treatment did its job that I was in remission for so many years.

While all this was going on, my love life was catching up with me again. No two of my babymothers – of whom there were ten – could come to visit me at the same time because they didn't see eye to eye. One didn't want the other visiting me.

One time I got back to my mum's and one of my ex-girlfriends was there. While we were chatting, there was a knock at the door and another one of my babymothers came in. It was like one of those farces at the theatre when a man's life starts to rebound on him.

'What's she doing here?'

'I got more right to be here than you!'

I don't know what they based their claims to me on. This was the sort of conflict my flitting around from woman to woman was causing all the time.

There I was, comatose from the chemo, and they were hollering and cussing at each other over me! It was a mad situation. If they carried on much more, there might not have been much of me left to fight over.

That's the mess I laid myself in. Mum had to look after me. Every time I went in for the treatment, I was out for three, four days. My arms were so weak I couldn't lift a pot to boil water.

The treatment took its inevitable toll in other ways. I always loved my hair styling – slick side parting, tidy cut – and of course I was about to lose all my hair. After the doctor warned me, I was waiting for it. It doesn't happen straight away and a part of you likes to think you're the one who's going to escape that side effect.

Then, when I was shampooing one day, this whole load of hair appeared in my hands. I looked in the mirror and there were patches missing all over. Aaaagh! Whatever you've imagined, the stark reality is a shock. I tried to wash it again to get the rest out but it wouldn't come off.

Hat on. Straight on the phone to my barber, asking, 'Can I come down now?' Because I hadn't told anybody about my condition, when I took the hat off, he was shocked.

'I'm having treatment for cancer,' I explained.

'You're joking! Why you never say nuttin?'

He cut off all the rest of my hair for me but I felt weird. I've always had hair and couldn't get used to it. I didn't like going out after that and stayed inside pretty much for two weeks. I kept shaving my head to allow hair to grow back evenly all over.

At last I decided to let on to Vibert and Bernard, my mates from the GQ sound system, because I knew word was going round.

'Look,' I said, 'before you hear any rumours, I've had cancer.'

I had to clarify the point because the story had circulated that I'd got AIDS. That's how the Hackney scene was – like a goldfish bowl. And I had been putting myself about a lot, as everyone knew, so there was the risk.

People who saw me then were shocked. They'd always seen me as bubbly, joking. The looks on their faces made me feel worse – 'Oh Paul . . .' I didn't want their sympathy. I wanted to be over this punishment.

Straight after the chemo I was lined up for radiotherapy in the hospital. They do this to increase the success rate where there's a larger concentration of tumours, as I had had. It's a way of killing cancer cells in a specific area using high-energy rays. Basically, you lie on a bed and they bombard the affected part with radiation. It lasts a few minutes and you can talk to the doctor over an intercom.

The weirdest thing was that, although the affected glands were in my abdomen, I had to wear a metal box, like a silver codpiece, to protect my private parts during the treatment. I looked like Larry Blackmon from Cameo! But it wasn't funny.

Radiotherapy doesn't hurt when it's taking place but it can leave you with sore patches of skin, and like the chemo it makes you dog-tired. I went back day after day and rested at weekends. That lasted a couple of weeks.

One side effect of the radiotherapy was that I could not have any more children, although I did put some sperm in storage. Finally, the whole treatment was finished but I never felt less like celebrating. I was shattered and felt like sleeping for a year.

Then I thought about the word they kept using – 'remission'. It doesn't mean 'healed'. The cancer's gone but it can come back. What kind of cure is that?

And there were still other concerns. A side effect of chemo is that your immune system is virtually non-existent. The doctors told me that even if I caught a slight cold I had to tell them as a matter of urgency. 'If it goes so long we can't do anything, you'll die.'

After staying at Mum's during the treatment, I had got out of her hair and was now staying with Maria, who was raising our son Pierre. He was around ten at the time. While I was there, I had this little cold, just a sniffle really, and despite the doctors' clear warning, I thought it was nothing to worry about. I guessed I could control it. But after three or four days it was obvious I couldn't. What a mistake! It went so quickly from bad to worse you would not believe it.

It's difficult to explain, but it went from a sniffle to my entire body seizing up over the course of a day. I was petrified. I called out, 'Maria, get an ambulance!'

Once they knew my case history I was rushed in for treatment. I couldn't move any part of my body now except my head. I was literally scared stiff. It was horrifying.

I arrived at the hospital in a right state. Straight away they gave me an emergency dose of antibiotics and put an oxygen mask on me. It stabilised my condition and the threat to my life was over. I'd had the treatment just in time. While I was recuperating in hospital, the doc spelt out to me in no uncertain terms how close I had been to death. She was furious. I hadn't had a telling off like it since I was a teenager. The doctor happened to be a Chelsea fan.

I was in a brand new wing for cancer patients at the Royal Free Hospital in Hampstead, north London, a leading cancer specialist centre just a few minutes from Hampstead Heath. I had my own room, telly, everything. That was May 1997. I know that because while I was in there, I remember Mum coming in to see me, and we both sat and watched Ruud Gullit lead the Chelsea team out at Wembley, and my boys beat Middlesbrough 2–0 to win the FA Cup. That was great, cheering away for Zola and the Blues – the doctor, too. You couldn't fault my timing this time! Mum even managed to cheer the right side.

So it was 'Yeeah!' when they lifted that FA Cup in 1997. It lifted me too for a while and set me back on the long road to recovery.

It still took a year, two years before I was really back on the ball. I wasn't able to work at first and was on incapacity benefit, getting my life back together. Eventually I started working again and had just about enough to buy a small flat in Hornsey, near Finsbury Park. I kept totally clean of the drugs and had to take things slowly.

Friends started coming back to me. I'd known Stefan for quite a few years. He was one of the many mates I had made on the Hackney rave circuit. He was, and still is, a nice, genuine guy. He was the only one of my friends to say to me, 'Paul, I apologise, because I was cursing you and saying you were a crack head. But I was wrong and I should have been your friend, just been there trying to support you.' Maybe he's right, and I appreciate the sentiment, but it was up to me to win back people's faith.

I was only in remission, though. I'd gone through all that pain maybe to be given just a stay of execution. I desperately needed to make a positive change. I didn't know what, but my life had to be different from before. I decided to go back to the West Indies. I talked it over with Mum, got the brochures, made the arrangements.

I was going to see my relatives and chill in Saint-Martin, home of my ancestors.

CHAPTER 25

Island In The Sun

I flew to Saint-Martin in late 1998 to see if I could heal my broken body and soul. It was my third visit to the Caribbean and I've always been proud of my West Indian roots.

I had been a city kid, used to grey streets and small parks, and it never failed to amaze me the variety of fruits and vegetables the local people produced from their tiny smallholdings. Fresh produce on the market stalls formed a rainbow of colours – pink and white grapefruit, hot red peppers, green bananas and limes, Valencia oranges, and deep purple eggplants. There were sweet potatoes, coconuts, watermelons, water nuts, cinnamon, ginger. Back home in London I was more used to corned beef from a can.

Each Caribbean island I'd been to had its distinctive feel. Dominica, where Dad was from, was raw, naturally beautiful and very friendly, but it didn't feel like home. Anguilla, where Mum had grown up, was like Little Slough. Loads of the generation who had left the island and come over to England to find work in the fifties had settled between Heathrow Airport and London, in Slough and Southall. They experienced prejudice and limited access to jobs and homes, but stuck at it, worked hard and squirreled away enough money to make retirement comfortable to say the least. Go to Anguilla now and they're back, all set up in the Hollywood 'A' list-style beach homes and living the life of Riley. It's their children who slave away in Slough now.

I was staying with one of Mum's sisters, my aunt Gladys, on Saint-Martin. It was a good time for me. I was clean, recovering and the island was like paradise.

Although it's only eleven miles from coast to coast, the island is actually split in two. Saint-Martin is the French side and the other, Dutch, side is Sint-Maarten. There are 71,000 people living on it, and it must be the smallest inhabited island to be divided in such a way. On the French side you have calypso and its French Caribbean version, zouk music. The Dutch is more international and developed, so you get more American r&b and hip-hop.

My family live in Grand Case, on the north coast of the French part, and I stayed with them for a couple of months.

Saint-Martin's a beautiful island like you won't believe. The weather is just wonderful – very hot, which I like. If you're living near the sea, the breeze is ideal. There are so many great beaches, even a few for the naturists, and fresh exotic fruits. Watching the sunrise . . .

What I loved about it was that everything was so natural.

'What d'you want to do today?'

'Let's go to the beach.'

And it's on your doorstep. We'd season up chicken the night before, carry it along to the beach with some kit, and make a fire to cook it over. There were no restrictions, no licences, no one saying you can't do it. Drinks were in an ice bucket. And everybody hung out, soaking up the rays, playing dominoes.

Every morning I would get up, go into the sea for a swim, come back and have a shower. And every morning I'd have bacon and eggs with fresh bread on the veranda at half six, seven o'clock. I couldn't believe myself. You would not see me get up at that time for anything in England.

In Saint-Martin I was woken at six whether I liked it or not. It wasn't the crowing of the cockerels everyone keeps there. It was the heat. The average temperature throughout the year is 27°C. At six o'clock I just felt the intense warmth and that was it. So I was up and about, getting well again.

The French side is known for its restaurants and Grand Case is no exception – French Caribbean, Chinese, Italian, Portuguese, every style going. It was the first time I ever tasted lobster and I couldn't believe such a sweet meat.

I did feel a bit awkward staying with family. A phrase

you hear a lot whenever West Indian people talk about visiting relatives in the Caribbean is: 'To see me and come live with me are two different things.' In other words, it's one thing to sit down and chat with your relatives after a long time apart, but it's another to have them camped out in your house for months on end.

Mum's brothers and sisters were welcoming and friendly, yes, but even though West Indians appear laid back, they all have their set ways and they expect certain things of you. You can easily offend them without meaning to, just by disrupting their daily routine.

I found Gladys and her husband Sammy, who owned a local garage, surprisingly accommodating, though. One of the odd things that happened was when another uncle came to take me out. Unlike me, his wife knew where we were going and put a Durex in his top pocket.

Our destination was called the White House. When we got there it was rammed with eye-popping women in bikinis – Puerto Rican, Spanish. It was a brothel. I was shocked. While we were there he told me he had wanted me to stay with him previously. He thought I'd be in trouble at my aunt's because they were quite pernickety.

I was looking around at all these fine girls and my uncle simply said with a smile, 'Pick one.' I didn't know what he was on about at first. 'What's the matter – you gay?!' He was teasing me, but I didn't catch on at first that it was a knocking shop. Once the penny dropped I made my choice. She was a South American girl. When we got down to it, all I remember she kept saying was, 'You finished yet?' I kept telling her, 'Not yet.' I made sure I got my money's worth. Or rather my uncle's money's worth – he was paying for it!

A woman introduced to me by another relative, my cousin Josianne, had a far longer-lasting impact. Her name was Veronica, she was around my age, and I liked her a lot. She was my usual type and good fun.

All too soon it was time to go and I arrived back in London in November 1998. As luck would have it, pretty soon I was handed an excuse to go back for a few days, all paid for, and renew my acquaintance with Veronica.

It was January 1999 and one of Mum's cousins, our aunt Roselyn, had died in England. Mum asked me to represent the family and help out with the burial, which the family wanted to be at 'home' in Anguilla, but Saint-Martin is close to enough to pop over by boat.

So while I was there, I sailed over to stop by Veronica's. As I was visiting the island I wanted to show respect, so I told my family I was there, just not staying with them.

I really got on brilliantly with Veronica. I was open with her, except about the drugs. I told her about my kids, and we spent a few sweet days together before I had to return to London. It was enough of a taste to make me want to come back, and quickly.

The best part of a year after the chemo and the radio-therapy, I was still recuperating, and it was wonderful to feel the healing warmth of the Caribbean sun. It was exactly what I needed and it made me think seriously about moving there for a while, possibly on a permanent basis, and that's what I decided to do. What was best for my children was a priority and I felt I was more use to my kids properly clean and healthy than thrown back into temptation in London. Veronica wanted to pay for the flight for me and I would be back in Saint-Martin a few months later.

We had a big leaving party at Mum's with everyone there. The tears flowed but it just wasn't happening for me in London. I had to get away from there. Now I'd met someone I liked, loved the island, and the weather . . . c'mon man, it can't go wrong.

The morning I left for Saint-Martin for good, I hugged Mum and cried. It sounds crazy, but that was the first time ever. 'Don't worry, Mum, I'll be all right.' She was finally showing some affection towards me.

But this time when I returned to Saint-Martin, my old ghosts were packed in the suitcases right alongside my hopes.

CHAPTER 26

Paradise Postponed

By now it was April 1999. I was staying at Veronica's place in Sandy Ground, which is a small village on a strip of land that juts out from the west side of the French capital, Marigot.

At first, it was wonderful. My uncle Sammy found me a little job at his garage, so I was earning some money. And because I wasn't staying with family, just Veronica and friends, there was less pressure. I felt I could live on my own terms and join in as I saw fit. I was on the mend. I paid for my children Caysey and Paris to come out with June to see the island and meet the family. I dreamed of having all my children visit in the future.

They're big on special community projects in Saint-Martin and I mucked in with everyone else. One Sunday morning the whole of Sandy Ground joined together to clean a road and pick up rubbish. It was like that scene from 'Witness' when all the Amish cooperate to build the barns. People brought out food and drink for everyone who was helping.

News of a project is put around by word of mouth and the local media.

Somehow word got around that an English footballer was helping out and the human interest angle caught the ear of the local radio station on the Dutch side. I was approached by the station and an American guy interviewed me live on his show. It was the first time in about a decade that I'd been interviewed – and that was back when I was with Reading – so I was a little out of practice to say the least. The presenter did this big build-up: 'Here on the show we got over from England Paul Canoville, former professional footballer with Chelsea! How you all doing Paul, you having a good time on our little island?'

'Er. Yuh.' I was so nervous it was pathetic. At that precise moment I couldn't possibly have imagined doing what I do nowadays, holding court to a room of a hundred schoolkids.

Then, just as things were going so well, Veronica didn't know it, but she did just about the worst thing she could possibly do. She would barely remember it, but I will never forget.

She was driving me round the island, showing me the grand tour, when she pointed to a sleazy street on the outskirts of Marigot, and said, 'See that spot down there – you don't ever want to go down there.'

'Why?'

'That's where all the drug-pushers hang out.'

'Oh no! . . .' I wanted to sound shocked but I was really etching it in my memory. Just in case. Unknowingly, she'd switched on a light.

A big reason I'd decided to head back to Saint-Martin was that I thought on a small island like that I could get my body healed and my head right. Get away from the big-city drug culture.

In truth, I'd already started doing a little crack again in London, but I was clean at first in Saint-Martin. It was one of the reasons I wanted to get back there. What I still didn't realise is that the main part of keeping off drugs is the desire that has to come from within.

I'd done the rehab. I'd battled the cancer. Now I felt more in control. After a break of a few years, I convinced myself that I would be able to do a little crack and then leave it alone. I could surely stop again when I fancied. I wouldn't let it get on top of me. I just needed to get it out of my system one last time. You are kidding yourself if you think that, as I began to realise soon enough.

Once I knew where I could get crack if I wanted it, a timebomb started ticking away inside me. I was wary of checking out that dark alley and aware of what it would mean to my life. Deep down I knew how this story would end.

When I approached the alley I didn't really know what to expect. You won't find this place reviewed in the *Rough Guide* to Saint-Martin. You can't say to your family, 'Would you mind dropping me off at the crack house and waiting for me in case there's a spot of bother?' It's something you have to do by yourself. And face the consequences. So do you or don't you? Unfortunately, I did.

I found the place again easily enough – my innate sense of direction put to less positive use. It was so pitch black, anything could have happened in there. I couldn't see anybody at first. Then suddenly there was a voice, urgent, aggressive:

'Wha' you wan'?' Jesus. I nearly jumped out of my skin.

'Yeah, erm, you got any . . . shit?'

'Wha' shit?! Wha' you mean shit?' Clearly he didn't share my street slang.

'Crack, cocaine . . . ' I explained.

'Yeah yeah. How much you wan'?'

'I dunno, four pieces?' I'm thinking $50, $100 for that, around thirty quid.

'Twenty dollars.' Oh my God, that was so cheap! When I saw the stuff I thought I'd struck gold. These were big rocks like nothing you got in a Hackney crack house.

I left my uncle Sammy's garage after a while when I landed a job as a security guard. My aunt knew the head of a firm guarding buildings at night. It was funny. They gave me a gun filled with rubber bullets to carry. I received no training. My boss just said to me, 'You won' get no trouble, but from when they see that they won' mess about.'

If anything went off, he told me just to aim for the body

where it might wind someone, not the head where it might split like a melon. The uniform was black T-shirt, black trousers and a cap. As well as the gun, I had a truncheon, handcuffs, the lot. It was ironic, really. Mum always wanted me to be a policeman.

I was guarding a tourist advice building. It was nothing much really. I was there from when it shut in the evening and worked a twelve-hour shift, 7 p.m. to 7 a.m., every other day. They had a lot of break-ins unless the buildings were guarded, because of computers and other electrical equipment. I had a chair in the doorway.

The place was situated right near a popular nightclub in the capital. You weren't supposed to park there, so you'd get a procession of rich white French geezers pulling up in their cars to go to the club. 'Can I park here?' they'd ask, and they'd slip you $20.

It was so boring and so hot. At two o'clock in the morning it was sweltering. You felt like going to the club for a break in the air-conditioning, then coming back to your post. But I didn't take the mick. My aunt had stuck her neck out to get me the job and I didn't want to let the family down. I admit I had double standards – I was putting my job on the line by smoking dope on duty, of course.

Anyway, the boss would come round every now and then to check on me. Once, I was smoking some weed round the back of the building and I'd just put it out when he turned up unannounced.

'You arright, Paul?' he queried. 'What you doing?'

'Just patrolling!'

I was that close to being caught out, and my family don't even do weed as far as I could tell. It wasn't like Jamaica here. Dope was around of course, but you didn't see marijuana fields in the hills. Even though Sint-Maarten was Dutch, cannabis was still very much illegal if you were caught. All hell would have broken out if I'd been done for smoking dope. I didn't want to be a scapegoat.

I bent the rules in other ways. Obviously, you're supposed to stay awake in a job like that, but did I hell. I'd walk around looking important every now and then to give the right impression. Then about three, four o'clock I'd drop off to sleep. But I'm a light sleeper and would wake up at disturbances. I'd wake up anyway before six. Seven o'clock was time to go home. That's how I was running it.

I was gradually increasing my use of the crack when I wasn't at work but somehow managed to keep it from Veronica and she was none the wiser. She knew about marijuana, so when she asked what I was smoking I told her it was skunk, 'another sort of weed'.

'Oh, right. It's just . . . the way you're doing it, you're smoking it so rapid. I've seen people smoke weed, but as soon as you're done, you want more.'

'Well, er, that's how I like it.' She was naïve, but I felt a fraud for not telling her the truth.

I had kidded myself I could control the beast this time, but I was dependent again. One night about one o'clock in the morning, I'd finished my stash and just had to go out and get more, the craving was so deep. Veronica was suspicious.

'Why you going out?'

'I've just got to meet someone.'

'Meet who?' I don't remember if I replied. She thought something was going on, another woman perhaps.

My uncle Sammy had given me a little car to run around in. I'd fixed up the battery and got it working, although I didn't have any insurance or anything. I went off in it to score some crack. Veronica had her own car and she followed me. I pulled over and she stopped behind me.

'Where you going?' She was anxious.

'Why you following me?' I couldn't believe it. 'Just wait for me at home. I'm coming back.'

I got the stuff and returned home. She was puzzled. 'Paul, I can't understand why you like the skunk so much.'

That's the way it continued. After buying food, drink and stuff for us, all the money I earned, everything else, went on the crack.

I ain't gonna lie. I'd finish at seven o'clock in the morning, head off to pick up my money from the Western Union where it was transferred at nine o'clock on a Thursday, go buy my crack, and come back in the house.

I'd get in, lock the bedroom door – bang – and put towels round it. No fan on, in case it blew the smoke out and the smell escaped.

This is a private form of hell. I was burning hot. My senses were so hyper I could hear everything. When I was preparing the crack any little pops or fizzes from heating it up sounded like fireworks to me. My heart was pounding with anticipation and fear.

'Paul? Y'awake?' I was awake. I was anxious. But I was silent.

'He must be sleeping.' They thought I was resting after the night shift. Then I would draw. Deep. For the quick hit.

I'd smoke till it was gone and I was wasted. I could do hundreds of dollars' worth just like that. Every single week. After the euphoria of the hit, I'd be laid out for hours; listless, useless to be with. However wrecked I got, I didn't have to go to work until seven. So I could always sleep it off.

It was terrible. Truly fucking diabolical. I don't forget that. That's what they always say in rehab, and they're right – when you reminisce, go back to the worst times, not the buzz. Remember the bad version.

Eventually, I recognised that I couldn't go on like that again. It was just getting nastier. I thought I'd shake off my demons in paradise, but it was even easier to get possessed here with the simple lifestyle and a cheap supply. I had to get back to England to get sorted out again. I made an excuse that I had to return for a check-up about my illness.

Veronica wasn't going to let go that easily. She didn't want to leave me. She followed me to England. And I treated her disrespectfully, by not coming clean and by trying to do things on the sly. She must have thought she was doing something wrong for me to act like I did, but she didn't do anything wrong. It was all me.

Back in London I still had my Hornsey flat but I stayed

at my mum's in Walthamstow. I used to leave Veronica there, go out and score crack, stay out all night. I'd only come back in the morning. When she asked where I'd been I'd say I'd been with friends. But there was only one thing I'd been with, and it was no friend.

Veronica was on my turf now and, pumped up as I was, I wasn't going to answer to her. With me acting like that all the time, Veronica had soon had enough, quite rightly. She was so distressed she left for Heathrow without even booking her flight, just couldn't wait to go.

My sister June, who still lived over that way and liked Veronica, found out and picked her up and took her back to her place. June was furious with me. How could I do such a thing to a sweet girl like Veronica? But that's what the stuff does to you. You don't give a damn. It's like a big open fire that burns up everything in your life. And you keep on feeding it.

Of course, when you're straight you hate yourself. You're ashamed. You're sorry. You make excuses.

June told Veronica what I was on and she came and asked me why I hadn't told her.

'I couldn't tell you that,' I tried to explain. Now she didn't want to leave. She wanted to help me. That was typical of her; she was such a kind person. I told her no, it was something I had to do myself.

Chaos was reigning again. I had a huge argument with Mum, picked up my belongings and moved out to my Hornsey flat.

Veronica came too. It must have been awful. I had

dragged this poor girl into a terrible situation. It wasn't fair on her. All the time in England she had been giving me money, I was scoring crack with it, and now the money for her flight home had been eaten up. So who did I have to ask for help? Mum. And she willingly bailed me out with the money for the flight. That was the thing with her. She really was always there for me in the end.

Veronica flew out. I told her I'd join her soon, but I knew I wouldn't. I was no good for her – the last vestige of my humanity told me that. I'd grown up enough to feel that I didn't want to drag her down any more. The further she was away from me, the better.

When she was back in Saint-Martin I had to come clean about joining her. It was one of the worst phone calls of my life. Pleasantries over, I whispered that I wanted her to get on with her life. She didn't understand at first. I repeated it.

'How can you do this to me?' She broke down and there were heavy tears at both ends of the line. I had to be strong. I knew how I treated people when I was on crack and couldn't bear subjecting her to that. It wouldn't be fair to Veronica, who had no real idea about any of this. In the past I may not have been so resolute, but it would have been pure selfishness to cave in now, and I knew it.

'I just don't want to waste your life right now.' I was determined she would move on from me and my troubles.

'I'll wait.' This was tempting, but I couldn't trust myself. I still had to be firm.

'Wait for what? It could be years.' It was horrible but I

know I did the right thing. I didn't want to cast a long shadow over her life as I had others in the past.

She was a really nice, laid-back Afro-Caribbean girl. Her previous relationships had been with black guys, and every one of us had let her down for various reasons. Maybe she just attracted the type of Caribbean man who wants to be mothered, then takes her for granted and looks elsewhere. Maybe we're just like that because of island culture. I said to her that, after me, she wouldn't be dealing with black guys any more.

We've kept in touch on the phone since then. True enough, she fell for a white guy, became pregnant, settled down, and now she has a lovely daughter. I'm genuinely pleased for her.

I miss Saint-Martin and have fond memories. It's so beautiful but I made that beauty flawed. It can never be the same for me.

CHAPTER 27

Back On The Street

Of course, I knew by now that my problem with the crack was spinning out of control again. It followed the same pattern as before. I never turned to burglary or mugging but I regularly took valuables from my mum and my babymothers. I'd become a teenager again. I was unreliable to everyone, even my children. I couldn't be trusted.

When she'd returned home, Veronica had phoned up June and said she thought I needed to go into rehab. June and Mum had already said the same thing. Everything came to a head when June talked Mum into saying to me that I desperately needed help again and someone had to push me into getting it.

I didn't want to know at first. The first part of beating a problem is appreciating that you have one. The next is accepting that you need to deal with it. I wasn't making that giant step.

It didn't matter how much you talked to me. I was in denial – the move back to England hadn't changed anything. Money was flowing out of my hands. My whole life revolved around drugs, drugs, drugs.

It was worse than before. I used a pipe to smoke now, not a spliff. I started mixing a little street heroin with the crack for a bigger hit. I'd get an even more intense rush, followed by a heaviness in my limbs. After smoking that crap I'd be drowsy for hours, out of it, suspended from real life.

A lot of users fool themselves that smoking the brown gives you fewer problems – no HIV from shared needles, not so susceptible to addiction – but most medical people will tell you that when you start messing with 'street heroin' in any way, it's the end game in your drug-taking career. It doesn't get much lower. No change and it's goodnight Vienna. I needed help. I knew it. But I didn't care. My life was complicated because of the way I'd lived it, what had happened to me and how I'd dealt with it. I took the badness because it kept me away from all the problems. When I was straight, the dilemmas came back.

No matter how bad a state you're in, and how much you need to make a change, the idea of enduring the treatment and losing that kick can be worse than the horror of the life you've made for yourself. You flip from wanting nothing more than to kick the stinking habit to having your whole body ache for another hit.

Like a recurring nightmare you have moments of straight-thinking, then the madness takes over again.

Imagine you have a toothache that is agony every now and then, but you're scared of dentists. When it hurts you're heading straight for the surgery door, and you'll knock the door down if you have to, but if the pain goes, suddenly you kid yourself it won't come back. Now multiply that by a hundred.

In my time I've had near misses from being caught in crack den raids. One time I managed to walk innocently out of the house at the last minute, just as the police were coming in. Against the odds I've never had a conviction for drugs. As far as the public was concerned I was still Paul Canoville the former footballer, not the decrepit crack head. It was only a matter of time before push came to shove, though.

It happened closer to home than I imagined it would. One day Mum and June simply told me they were going back to spend some time in the West Indies. 'But,' they both added, 'you're not coming with us.' They didn't want me there in the state I was in, and I hadn't responded to their increasingly urgent demands about getting straight again. It was all too much for them both, just too much heartache for them to bear. That was the first time they'd ever united against me. I swear to Lourdes, tough love felt very bad that day. Now I really felt set adrift, out of reach from everything. I was in the wilderness.

It was shortly after that, in 2004, when John, a very good friend of mine, gave me his support and encouragement to go back into rehab. I'm lucky that at my most desperate times people have seen the last thread of goodness in me and thought it was worth saving, like Simon had a decade earlier. He showed he cared and was prepared to put up with the usual nonsense on the road to getting me healed. Enough was enough.

Still, it's easier said than done. You don't just sign up and hand over a credit card the way the celebrities check into The Priory. You are referred or apply for help, and then a series of assessments, which can seem interminable, determines whether you're a suitable case for treatment. The sponsors of the treatment pay thousands of pounds. It's only right that they don't waste it on a hopeless case.

You also know you're not going to be pampered when you get there. I wasn't going to be hanging out with Robbie Williams and Gazza. But just like them I was going to need strength, will-power and commitment.

With John's help I approached the Hungerford Drug Project in Holloway, saying I urgently needed help to get on their programme. Not in six months' time. Now. Life is a horror show. I'm letting everyone down. I can't fight the beast on my own. And I need to get away from my situation in Hackney.

The option came up for me to go for detox and rehab in Norwich and then Bexhill-on-Sea and I agreed. The point about rehabilitation is that it is designed to save you from the personal, social and legal consequences that lie in wait for you if you don't give up. It's there to save you from yourself.

The system was as before. The detox removes any physical dependency, cleanses the drug from your system, and takes two weeks, depending on how you respond. You're intentionally cut off from friends and narcotic supply lines. The second part, the rehab, is about removing the psychological craving for the drug, and is twenty-eight days minimum for a basic process, but more like six months if you include the halfway house element when you're ready to return to society. This is when you're given counselling, assessment, re-education in what drugs do to you, and where, with your help, they try to modify your behaviour – permanently.

Once I'd committed to this path, a part of me was relieved. The moment couldn't come soon enough. I was counting down the days.

It's funny how it works, though. You want it, you want it, you want it! And when the day actually comes, you have two thoughts. One is feeling good that you can cleanse yourself. But the second – and this is what drugs do to you – is reminding you of the incredible buzz you're giving up. When you're still getting that kick regularly, it's so hard.

I was booked to travel to Norfolk on a Thursday. I'll never forget. Wednesday night I did the last of the crack all in one go – even more than usual. If anybody tells you they don't go for a last binge, they lie.

Man this was a *binge*. I was in a hotel in Stamford Hill doing that shit till six o'clock in the morning. Nine o'clock was the time for the train to Norwich. I rushed back the few miles across north London to Mum's in Walthamstow to collect the cases full of clothes for a few weeks. A few weeks . . . Then it hit me where I was headed. I just sat in the house alone between seven and eight like a zombie, bleary-eyed, voices in my head screaming, 'Make an excuse . . . "Train was late . . . Train derailed . . . Train *something*!" ' Then: 'Come on Paul, get yourself together, this is what you've been counting on . . . you need this. Think of Mum and June.' I was literally slapping myself, slapping the sense in.

I made it to Liverpool Street station through huge crowds of people on normal journeys – work, day trips – and made my way on to the train. I stowed my cases, settled down and saw a paper sign next to me on the window. It said, 'Norwich' but it might as well have said 'Hell'. My spine suddenly chilled. Oh no, fucking hell – detox. It would have been so easy just to get off the train there and then. My God I wanted to. But I stayed on.

That had to be the strongest day for me, in my entire life, staying on that train by myself all the way to Norfolk, watching fields pass and stations flash by, images of green Saint-Martin flitting through my mind, thinking of the people I needed to do this for, Mum, June, Veronica, my other girlfriends – my children – knowing what unpleasantness inevitably lay in wait. Easy was no longer an option. It showed me I'd grown as a man, even though the other side of me had binged all night. I was forty-two. I arrived determined and ready to grit out the healing.

I was met at the station by someone from the hostel.

'Paul Canoville?'

'Yes.' I was searched for drugs. 'No, man, I ain't got

nothing.' Damn, I felt like a prisoner. It was humiliating but necessary if I wanted to avoid becoming a convict for real.

At the centre I kept myself to myself for the first few days. These places seem pretty much alike. You're encouraged to be sociable and welcoming, and here people came in and introduced themselves to newcomers, like anywhere else. They were all users trying to get clean, some for the second time, like me. By definition the ones who approached me were friendly and amenable. They'd say hello, ask your first name. No one in detox or rehab needs a surname.

But the secretive side of me was suddenly strong. I was more concerned with anonymity than amity, and I was nervous in case anyone knew who I used to be. Although people were there to get themselves straight, they were not well people, and certainly not above phoning a tabloid to say, 'Guess who's just checked in with a crack problem?'

And I had voices in my head again. 'Paul, who are these characters?' the voices were saying. 'They're not your mates. You know you're not supposed to be here.' The voices were telling me to check out, go home, I would be all right. Why go through all of this again?

But went through it I did. They fed me, looked after me, had me do housekeeping chores along with everyone else, and kept me off the stuff. Some people go through torture in this phase, but I was lucky. I was in detox twice and didn't have physical withdrawal symptoms either time. No cold turkey, just that sullenness. With me and crack cocaine, it was the rehab stage that was the real test, taming the psychological craving and my weakness for it – the temptation, remembering what you were giving up, the high it gave you that you'd never have again, the narcotic refuge where problems don't matter, the sensation that was gone for ever. The need is so easy to recall. It was exactly the same this time as it was before, when I made Simon's life a misery. It's not the pain, it's the pleasure that kills you.

CHAPTER 28

Getting To Grips With Myself

After that cagey, paranoid start I settled in to the regime in Norwich and it was there that my life changed for ever. It wasn't just the cleansing of my body. It was the opening of my mind.

With the detox my head started getting straight again and everything was improving. The wit was coming back. I was giving straight answers, not being evasive. I felt confident to say what I did and didn't like. I was never someone who just accepted what was said to me. They had to explain because I wanted to understand exactly. That's how I knew I was back – that's me. When I was doing the crack, I just took in whatever anyone told me as gospel – not much mattered to me. I hadn't been myself. Now my head was right again, I was starting to crawl from the wreckage of my life.

The things I'd been doing while I was on crack, the level

to which I'd stooped had gradually killed my self-esteem. Now that I was getting some of my old confidence back, I started to react to the way the staff treated us. I noticed little things, such as the words people used. Even the ex-users among the helpers would make generalisations about 'drug addicts' and I would object to that. Every one of us is different and was in this state for a different reason.

When I complained and asked them to clarify what they were presenting to us in meetings or discussions, they didn't like that. I can understand why, but I was enjoying getting my faculties back. I was probably extra prickly because I was drying out. It was like a workout for my soul.

I was the only one who spoke out for the rest about some of the decisions they made around the hostel. They called me into the office and asked if I had a problem. I said they were making like I had issues simply because I was disagreeing with them. I explained that's how I am normally. Now the drugs were coming out, I was getting back to being the real me. One of the women was appointed my personal mentor and she unlocked something inside me. She assessed me and talked things over, any concerns I had. More than that she just listened. She connected with me in such a way that I started talking about my private self, visiting my past, probably for the first time.

They must have felt I was ready for it. I've never discussed my inner feelings with anyone. Not June. Definitely not Mum. I've always hated intense discussions like that, resolving personal conflicts. Ask any of my girlfriends. In relationships I was always affectionate, loving, but only so far in. At the first feeling of tension I was outta there. I couldn't discuss things that were deep inside me. I had 'issues'. That word.

But this woman would really make me talk and help me express myself. Perhaps it was that I had sunk so low, perhaps she had a special gift in communication or empathy, but we connected. For the first time I felt I could talk about myself and unbolt my feelings. What a relief! Once I opened up you couldn't stop me. I looked forward to our sessions just so I could say more, and as I said it, it was like thinking and reasoning aloud. She told me she thought it would be helpful if I could write about myself, my life, my relationships, and read it out to the other clients. It's part of the treatment that you share here.

The idea is that people become dependent on drugs for a reason. If you don't address the root cause, you'll be back on them soon after you've got clean. Talking about your inner self helps bring up some of the likely causes.

So Norwich is where I finally learned it's all right to share private things. It's therapy. Over the next few days, I sat down and wrote about my life. She asked me to be completely honest and dig deep. It just came tumbling out and I wrote page after page. I still read it every now and then. There's a lot of resentment in there. I resented how other kids seemed to have an easier life. I resented my Mum's strictness and lack of affection. I resented some of the male friends in her life. I resented my dad not being around. I resented how I was treated by my first proper girlfriend, Christine. I resented losing the one thing I aimed for in life – being a professional footballer. And I resented myself for getting into the state I had.

I signed off: '2002 and 2003 became a nightmare as I started on the pipe for that extra and stronger buzz. I also started to mix the brown [street heroin] with my crack addiction. I was constantly letting down my mum, sister and kids, which made me truly realise I couldn't continue like this. I started seeking help through a drug clinic. I knew I needed another chance at a rehab centre and went and sought a drug worker. She was supportive and she could see I was desperate to change. She put me through to my funders, which was not easy as there was a waiting list of six months! I'm very lucky to be here with my peers sharing this with you as I'm on my last legs and looking to fight and conquer this ADDICTION. Thank you for your patience.'

It was a blessing to get these private things out of my head after years of bottling it up, all that anguish. I was like a champagne bottle. When the cork popped, everything came flowing out and I didn't want to stop.

I read it out in front of everybody. It was incredibly difficult but it had to be done.

The other clients were asked to respond, verbally and especially in writing. That's a discipline they might not have had to tackle for years, and it requires more thought and consideration than talking. I kept all their letters to me and I still cherish them. They had a lot of insight into my personality and problems.

One wrote: 'You are obviously very needy as you have had a lot of women. I think this comes from craving a love and affection from your mother that you never got. I think this played a huge part in your behaviour and with the end result being your addiction. I think you really need to sit down and talk to your mother to try and find some of the answers that you are looking for and move on to the next part of your life.' Lots of people talked about my need to sort things out with my mother because I so obviously craved affection she wouldn't give, but I let her down too.

'I strongly relate because for twelve years crack has been an everyday thing for me as well,' another client wrote, 'either selling it or smoking it. It is evil, it ruins our lives, but we love it.' That last line is spot on.

The responses that really touched me made me look at myself as if I was someone else. 'It couldn't have been an easy ride for you, having to deal with all this racism from the [football] stands and from other players,' one man wrote, 'but I think your love of the game and inner strength carried you on. I don't think you found it easy to accept your injury and feel cheated and robbed because your career was ended suddenly. Not having anything to fall back on made it all the more difficult. And lastly, the loss of your son devastated you. I had my daughter taken away at three weeks old and can relate strongly to your feelings around this. I think you know this sent you over the edge like it did for me. I think you're a very strong and determined person and I admire you for this, so tap into your inner strength and face the pain and hurt. You've come a long way and through a lot already. Keep going. Your friend in recovery.'

You always feel you're the only one, but so many people are going through almost exactly the same thing.

Some thought I should dig deeper. 'Why have you not talked about your relationships?' I told them I'd never stayed in one long enough to describe the experience. There's the barrier again. The mood I was in, though, that barrier soon broke. I thought about my attitude to women over time and, again, picked up the pen. I wrote that I've struggled with personal relationships all my life. Truth to say, the least complicated relationship I ever had was with crack.

I could safely say then that the relations I had with women were never totally sincere – which was down to me. Some people are probably thinking, 'eleven children from ten different women – you don't say!' but it took something for me to admit it.

Too often with me and women it was a purely physical thing – a conquest, and a need to satisfy, to be wanted.

Friends who know me well will tell you. I was the same when I was raving – hiding in the shadows of a club or a dance, checking out the ladies, taking my time. You could stand next to me and spot exactly the type of woman I would go for almost every time – big, full-figured, powerful black women. I wanted someone who would give and take. The shape, the curves of the body, excited me and I'd just want to go and get intimate. It was never top of my agenda to look upon a woman as a long-term partner.

Don't get me wrong – at the same time, as soon as any woman showed interest in me, no matter what she was like, that was it. I had to go with her. June always used to say I would go with *anything*. Indiscriminate. Low self-esteem. I'd be nice and polite to get what I needed. Once I got it I'd become bored and leave. For me, when the word 'love' came out of a woman's mouth, it was easily said but not to be taken seriously. Maybe that will change. Perhaps it already has.

I think the root of all this is partly tied up with me trying so hard to please Mum, and not getting the love I needed from her. But it's more to do with that first experience with Christine when I was eighteen and came out of Borstal to see my new baby and ended splitting up so horribly from Christine. It was so hard for me to commit myself wholly again after that early shock.

Other young men would have reacted differently, but I got into a repeat pattern of treating women like props that I could pick up and leave. Caribbean people are like that. We say we have faith but really we're very fatalistic. And if you leave things to God, as the saying goes, you end up not making the effort to change when you have the chance. In 2004, I hoped it was not too late for me.

I was a resident in Norwich for two weeks and then moved on to the Phoenix House in Bexhill-on-Sea for the tougher process of rehabilitation. A woman from the Hungerford in London had to come all the way up to check how I was and to escort me to the Sussex coast. Mentally, this was a totally different journey from the torture I went through on the way there.

Bexhill was beautiful, a nice little Victorian resort town full of retired folks. The residential home was a large, three-floor, red-brick house with a small drive, part hidden from prying eyes by a tall privet hedge. It had lots of rooms, some in the loft with windows topped by small gabled roofs. It was near the seafront too, where there was a nice beach and pavilion. It was very small and very English, which I like.

It was like a set from an old-fashioned Hitchcock film. I don't know whether it's my age – or what it says about me – but those are often my favourite types of movie. I enjoy black and white way more than colour. And there's something about stepping back to a different time, maybe a more innocent one.

Bexhill is two hours from London, a million miles from Marigot, and a whole world apart from what I'd known for the last few years. Like the other clients, I was committed to a six-month stay, followed by the halfway house period, after which you were ready for a fresh start. The place was renowned for having a high success rate. So there I was, feeling much better and encountering some different types among the thirty or so people in there. You had DTTOs (criminals under Drug Testing and Treatment Orders restraints) as well as voluntary clients. Naturally, a few of the DTTOs were there only because they had to be and fought the regime, which was quite strict. Your urine was tested regularly for signs of narcotics and you were not allowed out unescorted at any time.

The year I was there, a DTTO conned the staff by passing off someone else's urine as his own. He was trusted to go out but instead absconded and committed seventeen crimes in west London while he was out, nicking electrical equipment to sell for gear and stabbing a couple in one raid. One of his victims needed forty stitches in a stomach wound. That's the sort of geezer you might have to deal with while you were trying to get your head right.

For most of us the rules were less challenging. The idea was to get some routine into your life, and adhere to the small disciplines that get your life back on track – be up and dressed by a certain time, eat breakfast, lunch, do chores around the house, and hit the sack by a reasonable hour – which was all very well, but after my emotional outpouring at Norwich I wanted more from rehab now. I understood I had to leave Norwich as part of my programme but when I arrived at Bexhill, I expected to get a similar experience.

This was a life-changing moment. Now I needed to talk to someone. Now I knew I had a load on my chest that I needed to get off it. Unlike the first time I did rehab when I was my usual secretive self, I had a lot of things to say. I wanted to continue the counselling because it felt so good for me.

But rehab doesn't work like you want it to. It's not demand and you will get. The reason you're there is that your judgement has been bad in some way and you've been making wrong decisions. Part of conditioning is that you 'earn' the things that are good for you, which, in my case, was counselling. It was so frustrating.

With the DTTOs in the place, things used to happen that didn't sit well with me at all. You're not so out of it as an addict that you don't pick up the vibes from locals as you pass by or visit shops, no matter how polite and well behaved you are. No one wants a load of junkies playing up in their manor. You never went out on your own. One time I had to go to the opticians and two pretty rough-looking characters came with me. And let's face it, it's not as if that little group didn't stand out in ultra-white, over-sixties Bexhill.

While I was being seen in the opticians, I knew something funny was going on because the other two kept whispering to each other and then disappeared for a while. I have no idea what they were up to, but it was suspicious. Still, they came back when I was finished with the optician.

'Oh, Paul,' they said, 'we just need to pop into the supermarket on the way back.' Good idea, I thought. I needed some toiletries anyway.

I was paying when the other two walked out round the back of the tills and through the door, setting off the alarm, then bolted. Shoplifting. Great. I found them round the corner and laid into them for such an act of stupidity.

'You don't think they'll know where we're from in a tiny place like this? Jeezus!' I was furious.

'Sorry, Paul. Please don't say anything or we'll get thrown out.'

I agonised over my decision, but kept quiet, although I made it clear I wouldn't keep shtoom a second time. They got away with it, somehow.

There were other conflicts at Bexhill. You're always going to get that in places filled with damaged people. One woman seemed to have a real problem with me. She kept butting in rudely or disturbing me when I was writing, just as if we were halfway through a conversation. Personal space is considered highly important in rehab. You're not supposed to infringe it. What with my frustration at the lack of counselling, this woman was doing my head in.

Problems like that are channelled into 'circle time', when you can air your grievances. You all sit around and talk openly, but no cussing is allowed, no finger pointing or accusations. At one session I said straight out that I thought she had an issue with me personally. A more established client recalled that she'd been awkward with another black man before me.

Well, then it came out, big time. It turned out that this poor woman had been kidnapped by a group of men who had raped her and kept her locked up for a whole week. All the assailants happened to be black. I felt so bad about bringing it up. I was being open and honest and had no idea she'd experienced such a horrific nightmare. I leant towards her and said, 'I'm not here to harm you.' It was all I could do. It cleared the air. It just shows that for every problem you think you have, someone else has one at least as big, but different. However much I saw myself as a victim of events, other people were having to deal with things that were much worse than anything that had been thrown at me.

CHAPTER 29

The Curse Returns

In late summer 2004 I was two months into my six-month spell at Bexhill. I was settled in there on the coast, feeling better within and about myself, and more positive about my future and life in general than I had for many years.

I also started reading a bit for the first time. I'm a big fan of E. Lynn Harris, a young African-American, especially his books *And This Too Shall Pass* and the autobiographical *What Becomes of the Broken-Hearted?* He writes a lot about relationships between black people – gay as well as straight – and the tangled web woven by life in the city. People may think it strange that a serial womaniser from Britain could relate to a gay scribe from Arkansas, but I've never had a problem with homosexuals and try to treat everyone the same regardless of race, religion or anything else. It's about basic respect for me.

I empathised with his character Zurich Robinson in *Pass*. He's a young black kid wanting to become a quarterback in the USA – a rare sight ten years ago when American football seemed to consider it too much of a 'technical' position for an African-American. Far better, the coaches thought, to hire a white guy there and keep the blacks for muscular positions. It had echoes of the time I was breaking through at Chelsea and put a wider perspective on things for me.

Since the eighties I'd really come to appreciate African-American culture. It had a self-confidence born of success. In America, there were many more black lawyers, stockbrokers, film stars – anything they wanted to be – than in England. I read *Ebony* magazine and loved US music. There were some good role models for me to aspire to. Now that I'd taken up reading books, I felt I was expanding my mind.

I was even working my way back to physical fitness, which was always a sign that I felt at my best. Every morning I would go for a run around the boating lake in Egerton Park, along the promenade, taking in the sea breeze, which was wonderfully therapeutic by itself.

One day I was out jogging as usual along the seafront. Not for the first time it made me smile to think of dear old Johnny Neal on the dunes at Aberystwyth, inhaling the ozone, shouting into the bracing wind to the Chelsea lads, 'Get that in your lungs!'

But this time I suddenly felt a familiar, searing pain in my groin. I've learned to my cost that when I've waved goodbye to the crack, its ugly sister usually knocks on your door. I knew straight away that the cancer had returned. My heart sank but I knew what I had to do.

I needed to get things sorted out quickly and I soon found out that the procedure down in Sussex wasn't right for me. They were talking two months to see a specialist. So I rang my specialist, Dr Whittaker at St Thomas's in London, and was sorted with an appointment in a week. I went back and then had a biopsy in Hastings. The whole process of dealing with that sickness kicked in again, just like a recurring nightmare.

I transferred from Bexhill to Featherstone Lodge Rehabilitation Centre in Peckham, south London, closer to St Thomas's, where I knew I could get the best treatment. (Two years later I could not believe that Phoenix House had closed the Bexhill centre down because of costs. Very sad.)

I was still supposed to be in the second stage of rehab, not the halfway house. I was nowhere 'cleared' of my addiction, and I felt under pressure to resist the temptations of London. The new place would have been great for some people but was too laid back for me. I wanted more discipline, but I had the cancer to focus my mind.

Featherstone Lodge is the rehab centre Prince Charles made Prince Harry pay a visit to after he'd admitted smoking a bit of weed and getting drunk down the pub when he was seventeen. That was two years before I arrived and he was only in there for the day. If he becomes king, I'll remind him.

I was trying to stay positive and it seemed a good idea to start thinking about a new career and life beyond rehab, even though any plans would be put on hold for the time being. I had to go through a long spell of the hated chemo again first.

Over time, tumours become more resistant to chemotherapy, so this time I was given an even stronger dose than before. That meant even more sickness, even more feeling like death warmed up, as well as the shaved head routine again.

June had to be so strong alongside me. After standing up to me when I wouldn't listen to her and Mum, she was backing me with a vengeance now I'd come round. She helped me make it to the treatment, stayed strong and kept me going. She was ringing, cajoling me, coming to see me and nursing me through the chemotherapy.

There were extra complications now too. When the lymph problem arose, a skin cancer called mycosis fungoides came with it. It spread in big patches under my skin and itched like hell. I needed cream to ease the discomfort but it wasn't very effective. Sometimes I'd feel like every nerve needed scratching. That was very depressing and hard to deal with. In another treatment for it, PUVA, ultraviolet light was shone on to the affected parts. I had that twice a week, Tuesdays and Thursdays, but it irritated my skin as much as the mycosis and I wasn't keen to continue.

My medical problems didn't end there, either. On top of the lymph and skin cancer, scans showed that I had lumps in my abdomen. I felt battered by wave after wave of bad news.

The lumps turned out to be gallstones the size of golf balls. I had an operation to remove them because they represented a risk of more cancer in a new area. I was in and out of the revolving doors at Guy's or St Thomas's, in and out of rehab meetings. But my periods on the wards became longer, the chemo was worse than ever and I was so, so exhausted. Something just had to give.

On the back of the horrendous chemo I needed something positive to give me a lift. I was determined to alter the course of my life drastically. The counselling in Norwich and the working through I had done in rehab had convinced me I had to make some permanent changes.

With a fresh spirit, I started to think about the future. Immediately, working with kids came back to me. After the things I'd put myself through, I was in a great position to warn young people how not to live their lives. 'You think you got issues? I got the set.' I hoped I could bring that to bear with youngsters and help them make better choices than I had.

So in November 2004, I wrote a letter of application to do voluntary work with youngsters. It turned into more of a statement on the effect of drugs on young people's lives. This is what I wrote:

I am an individual who is at this point in a drug rehabilitation centre, with no convictions. I'm 42 years old, and turning my life around. I want to put something back into society. I was brought up in a multicultural society and believe that my calling is working with youth. There are many youths today who have no goals in life. Many believe education is a waste of time. They resort to hanging out on the streets, having no positive people in their lives to keep them on the straight and narrow. If they've been raised in homes, some get lost in the system. There is no safety net for them, having little or no role models in their lives. Too many of our youths get lost believing nobody cares. Becoming lost sheep, they resort to associating with bad company, ending up as mules, muggers, drug abusers and generally a menace to society.

I was a professional footballer between the age of 19 to 24 playing for Chelsea FC. I had to retire due to injuries.

With my history I feel I can have a positive impact on some, if not all youths, encouraging them to keep on the straight and narrow.

Thanking you in advance,

Yours sincerely,
Paul K. Canoville

When I read it now, it's like I was applying not for a job, but to get the rest of my life back. It was very hard for me just to be honest and come out about the fact that I was a drug addict, but I reasoned, 'You know what, Paul, you've come through being a professional footballer and had that taken away, being in denial, being involved with drugs, fighting cancer . . . you've come through the lot – what more could you have done?'

I got an interview, along with around a dozen other applicants, to do youth work in Finsbury Park. I answered all their questions honestly and they said, 'OK, would you like to mingle with the children for a while?' I walked outside and these kids are fifteen, sixteen years of age. The boys are playing football, the girls netball. I was straight in there with the banter.

'Call that a shot?'

'Who are you?'

'Pass the ball and I'll show you.'

Right away we hit it off and I got the job. It was very fulfilling. Some kids had disabilities. One was a girl of seventeen with learning problems who wouldn't talk to anyone. For some reason, though, she latched on to me, went for walks and started communicating with me straight away. I didn't do anything special, I was just myself. Maybe it's something to do with having been through what I have. I treat everyone absolutely the same, without judgement.

Unfortunately, the illness and the job together became too tiring so I had to give it up. I was lucky that I found another one, ferrying disabled people for social services in Camden. They were understanding about my situation and were flexible with my hours, but I realised that there's nothing I like more than kids, and that understanding stayed with me.

At Christmas I decided not to stay in hospital or in Featherstone Lodge. I desperately wanted to go back to Mum's in Walthamstow. Both times I was ill with the cancer I went home to my mum's. We were getting along better again and, anyway, your mother's home is always your home. She said she couldn't bear it any other way. Then as soon as I was better she would sling me out again – mostly because of my loud music. And she still wouldn't give me a key, just in case.

I split my time between hospital and Mum's. With the heavier treatment of chemo now, I had even less energy than before. It was doing my head in. I was so poorly and I couldn't eat the food in Guy's when I was there after chemo sessions.

I remember my lowest ebb came in Guy's that January 2005. The ward was so boiling hot, I was so low. I wouldn't say I was giving up, but I'd had enough. No more.

I looked outside and there was snow on the ground. It looked beautiful. I took my big hooded coat, put it over my pyjamas and sneaked outside for a cigarette. I never smoked cigarettes a lot. It was just tobacco, something to help me break out of what was happening to me. The air was fresh, cool, crisp, nipping at my nose. Amazing. Just what I needed. It was the cold fresh air that convinced me. I'd had enough of heat, treatment, schedules, routines, do this, do that. I needed to take control of my life again.

I wanted to get out of there for a break. In fact, I begged

the doctors to be allowed to go home. They refused. The only way I could go, they said, was if I signed myself out. I said I would. I couldn't take more than a month of the chemotherapy. It wasn't the full recommended period but that was it for me.

They ran some tests and said my vital signs were OK enough for me to leave. I felt as though I'd taken back the management of my life there and then. From now on, the only scheduled visits would be for an annual check-up – the date that every cancer patient hates.

There were so many tablets to take anyway – eight, twelve every day – and a district nurse came round to give me injections for three weeks. It wasn't like I unplugged the tubes from my body, walked out through the gates and went back to leading a normal life. I was still knocked out all day at Mum's. My stomach was wrecked. I felt constantly cold then hot. I could barely walk and had no immunity to bugs. Mum was making me fish soup just to keep me going. I lost two stones in weight in January and February.

I was supposed to work on one of my kid's bikes – something I've been good at all my life, well, after that first problem with the handlebars when I was twelve. I couldn't do it. I didn't even feel like a man who could provide for his children.

The ordeal didn't end there. My system was so messed up. One day I climbed the stairs to the toilet, stood before the porcelain and the next thing I knew I was in the most horrific pain. I had blacked out – it felt like for ages. I'd fallen in such a way that my knee was underneath me with my weight on it. It was torture when I came to. Within a couple of hours my knee was the size of a beach ball. God knows how long I'd been lying on it. I was rushed to hospital again and more tests were carried out but it was nothing specific. It was simply a reminder of how bad I really was, a warning that I'd overdone it – too much, too soon. I was given a walking stick at the hospital. The last thing a footballer wants is to be seen with one of them! Not for the first time, I didn't want anyone to see me.

Next to give up completely in this soul-destroying sequence was my digestive system. I was constipated for ages. I had this cramped, unbearable pain that I thought was wind. I had to go back into hospital and they told me my bowel was blocked. I needed yet another operation to remove the blockage and I had to have a catheter fitted – God, I hate those things.

I was on the edge again, stuck in the ward going mad. I rang a friend and asked him to bring me a spliff at the hospital, just some weed to cool me down. My head was spinning so bad. I smoked it, hoping it would calm me, but when I got back to the ward I vomited all over my own bed.

They ran some blood tests to see whether there was a reason for my sickness and for obvious reasons I was apprehensive when a doctor returned with the results. He said they were inconclusive and told me not to worry because he 'wouldn't say anything'. I was relieved but played it cool.

'What about?' I queried.

'The amphetamines we found in your blood.'

'What? I just had a weed spliff!'

Of course, word soon got round the medical profession. As a nurse doing agency work, Mum knew some people in the hospital and so she was humiliated by me all over again. She rang me up and had a go.

At the same time, one of my daughters was going away and needed me to sign an authorisation form. I also wanted to give her some money. So I left the hospital for a short while but when I came back half an hour later, it was to find they had given my bed away. It was outrageous, but I hadn't been a model patient. So there I was, standing in the ward, desperate, arguing, drip still hanging from me, until the specialist sorted it out. I left hospital for the last time in March 2005 and I've been clear since. Clear of the cancer, clear of the crack.

Anyone who's had the big C will tell you. The most daunting thing is the regular check-ups and tests. It's like your life is on hold till you hear the result. It takes so much out of you. Each year when the time comes around, it seems like it was only yesterday you had the last tests.

I dread it so much that I'm in a terrible state in the weeks before, in case the outcome is bad news. The doctor asks me how I've been, how I'm feeling, looking for any changes in the last twelve months. They take a blood sample and test it for red and white blood cell count, and an indication of how the liver and kidneys are doing. The big fear, though, comes in the reading for LDH – lactate dehydrogenase, a substance in the blood that is generally higher in people with active cancer growth than in others. So far I've been fine.

I'm often asked what I would do the next time, should there be one. I tell them I didn't want the chemotherapy last time, and it was only June and my babymother Sonia who convinced me to go through it again. It puts you in such a despairing state you wonder why you bother. But Sonia and June were so strong. 'It's not just for you,' they said. 'Think of your kids. People who love and care about you.' They gave me the strength to carry on. The truth is you never know how you'll deal with it until you face the consequences. I hope I'll never have to.

I found it very difficult sometimes to go in for the treatment. But I knew people had put themselves out for me, and several more rely on me being around.

Everything around cancer just makes life tough in general. A bad case of indigestion, a skin rash, some fatigue, and you think the worst – I never mess about and go straight to be checked. It has to be the priority and I have to drop everything when it happens. How can you hold down a full-time job when you need so much time off? You need understanding. I was lucky with my driving job running disabled people about for the council because my boss had had some experience of what I'd been through. When I asked for time off he was always cool, and I'm really grateful to him. It helped to ease me back to normality.

As I write, it's been three years of remission so far. I take things day by day. I don't think big. I don't want great responsibility apart from helping bring up my children. I want to do right by the people who depend on me.

I know there might be a link between my dependency on the drugs, a low immune system and the cancer. I've learned so much in the last few years. I know I can't take risks any more.

CHAPTER 30

Facing My Demons

People judged him as he stepped on the green
All of them hated him, even the fans of his team
United together they tortured and abused him
Lifeless in his heart, feeling he was a sin

Cold was his mind, his soul and body
As all the abuse left him alone with nobody
'Nigger' and 'Negro' is what they would say
Other people would just look away
Very very brave, Paul was to go on
In time the fans of Chelsea changed their song
Little by little, he grew to fame
Little by little, of his colour, he had no shame
Eventually the racist taunts, he began to tame

'Paul Canoville' by Jack Delaney
Year 9 student, St Paul's Academy, Greenwich

My life has been like a car crash – some might say a mass pile-up. I'm still crawling from the wreckage – injured, a bit bewildered, grateful I'm still here. I'm learning every day, a piece at a time, making fewer mistakes (I hope).

One thing I've never been able to do is take control of my destiny – it seems as though I've always been tossed about by other things. From a strict childhood, prejudice, to the drugs and the cancer, something else has ruled me. Now I know myself better, I'm a better judge, and I can make decisions about what I think will be good for me. It's me now controlling my life, on my terms.

In November 2004 I read a piece of prose by an unknown hand called 'Character of an Addict'. It reminds me of where I don't want to be.

He or she may believe that the world owes them, and nothing they do is wrong.

An addict has many mood swings. They also suffer paranoia.

An addict also develops low self-esteem and they also lack respect for themselves and others.

Personal hygiene is not the first thing for them. Everything else becomes unimportant to them.

They are confounded liars, although sometimes they say things they do mean. However, when encountering drugs that meaning becomes meaningless.

Sometimes drugs can lead an addict to steal from loved ones. Personal possessions have no sentimental value.

As well, addicts can sell themselves for drugs, i.e. prostitution.

Their sleeping patterns are disrupted, mind always ticking over to see how they can find the means of obtaining the drug.

They have no regard for other people's feelings and they do not like for people to tell them how they are.

You have so much ground to make up as a recovering addict. It's daunting. When I think what I put people through – June, Mum, Simon, my children, my baby-mothers – it feels like I was a different person. I try never to let myself get depressed, although some days I don't want to talk because I'm struggling to cope. Maybe I should still talk more.

When I was young I used to pray, and maybe I had some help walking with me. Believe me, there have been times when it was really difficult to go on. The worst thing of all in my life, worse than the chemo, worse than the crack, was not having any maternal affection.

An incident a few years ago showed me how much ground I still had to make up. Mum kept her jewellery in a small bag that she'd put in the zip pocket of her handbag. When she went to look, it wasn't there. She thought straight away that I'd taken her precious things, pawned them, as I had so often in the past. She thought I was up to my old tricks. Without waiting to think it through, she rang up very angry and accused me of stealing it. She ripped into me, and this time it really hurt. I began to cry.

It was the first time I'd done that for a long time.

'Mum,' I sobbed, 'I'm not doing that any more.'

A little later she went to her car for something and suddenly remembered – she'd left her valuables in the boot. And that's where she found them. I hadn't reverted to my old ways and pawned them, only to post them through the letterbox later.

She phoned me straight away, and sent a text: 'A thousand apologies. I just find it so hard.' I kept that message for ages. I realised she was more worried about me relapsing into crack than she was about her gems. It was her way of showing that she cared. That's still how it comes from her – in glimpses.

When I was small she never really used to sit and talk to me, guide me. I found it hard to relate to her. She was never someone I could confide in. Even at a very early age I had to cope with all my problems myself in the best way I could. It wasn't enough.

Now when I look back I realise it must have been really tough for Mum, bringing us up alone. At the time I was too resentful to notice.

Mum and I have never sat down and had the heart to heart the Norwich residents wrote about. Both of us are still too cagey, probably. I'm resigned to the fact that she will never open up now; it's not her nature. I'm just grateful that my rehab counselling permanently changed me from being the same way. But we get on much better now and would do anything for each other.

I remember a time she was having trouble breathing but

she refused to think it was serious. 'I'm taking you to A and E,' I insisted. Good job, too. They found her lungs were congested, gave her a stack dose of steroids and used the nebuliser on her to help her breathe. She could have ended up with pneumonia.

We're very much alike, but I don't see her as a good role model when it comes to children. I'm far more loving and gentle with mine than she ever was with me. But we both have a very good heart. We're very short-tempered, short-fused, and we get taken for a ride easily because we believe in people.

To tell you the truth, Mum still can't actually say she loves me. She was never wrapped in affection by her grandmother, who brought her up. She knew that Granny loved her, but she wasn't told. So she found it very hard to be demonstrative in that sense, and still does, even though she knows how important it is to me. I suppose she was too old to change by the time she knew.

I'm totally different now. Hear me on the mobile to my kids and the word 'love' comes straight out within the first minute every time. I know how important it is to feel special. Mum thinks June and I should know that anyway, and we've come to accept it.

She's always been proud that I achieved my life's ambition. It was all I ever wanted to do. She's glad I got there because I wanted it so badly. She knew it meant a hell of a lot for me.

Now I think she just thanks God I'm alive, and will support me whatever I do next. When I got very ill the first time, she was devastated. Despite all we've been through, she depends on me a lot. I'll do anything for her. Anywhere she wants to go, I'll take her, no matter where. She knows that. I'm still that little boy, eager to please. I don't know how she'd cope without me, to be honest.

And then there's Dad. Yes, I would have loved him to be there as I was growing up because I needed a man. He's regretted it, too. But maybe I would have picked up some bad habits from him. You never know, you really don't. During the bad times, he couldn't be as supportive as Mum and June were because I didn't involve him in it as much. He's my dad but he didn't go through what I did as a kid – he caused a lot of the trouble. I didn't feel I needed him as much as I did them. But that's passed. I can't live on that any more. I'm old enough to have moved on. I'm just glad I know him and he's there. That's what counts the most. At least I understand him more now and why he wasn't there for me when I was young – the hole in my life that was there till I was in my twenties has been filled a little, or I can accommodate it better.

He's still got charm. I had a birthday party recently and he came over. Some of my kids were there – Pierre, Caysey, Udine, Nickel and Paris. He lives close by June now. She's doing well in her career, working as a project and planning coordinator, helping some of the country's biggest corporations to bring their goods to market. Her experience in helping her big brother through some of the logistics of his life must have been useful! I'm very proud of her and her three boys.

All the grandchildren enjoy being with Dad. Pierre knew him from day one really, but the others less so. He spends a lot of time with them when he can. He'll play with them, get up and dance with them, joke with them. He's left a mark on them. They've been phoning me and asking, 'How is Granddad?' It's nice to hear that.

It's funny. I had issues with Mum because she was always there but never gave us the attention we needed. And I had issues with Dad because he just wasn't there at all. But I don't go in hard on him like I have with her.

I suppose I wasn't reminded every day of his disappearance like I was with Mum's rod of correction, and by the time we met again I had moved on. I think we all know each other now, and we're all settled with that. I understand that they did what they did simply because it's in their nature. I don't begrudge either of them being how they are any more.

CHAPTER 31

Back In The Chelsea Family

Chelsea were celebrating their centenary in 2005/ 06 and they put out a call for former players to come to a special event. Someone alerted June to this and she decided it would be a travesty if they went ahead without their first-ever black debutant. She had a harder job convincing me about going. I was still wary because of the times I'd had in the early 1980s. As far as I was concerned, Chelsea had forgotten about me. Reading kept in touch with me more than they did, especially as Gilkesy and Simon were still in and around the club.

Despite the awful time I had with some fans, Chelsea will always be my team, no matter what. I've lived mostly in Gooner territory, and if anyone ever ran down Chelsea I was straight on their case. I watched them play on the telly whenever I could, and shared the delight of other supporters witnessing the skills of Gianfranco Zola and

Ruud Gullit. It's been wonderful seeing the club turned into a force again over the last few years.

Talking football in a north London bar, a hairdresser's, or anywhere, people knew me as a fan, but they didn't know me as an ex-player. I never mentioned it. I'm sure they'd be shocked if they knew what I went through for my club.

The last time I'd really had any contact with ex-players was in March 1995. I'd actually taken the field at Stamford Bridge one last time. It was Kerry Dixon's testimonial and I was a second half sub. What I most remember is meeting Frank Sinclair and Eddie Newton. Here were two black boys who'd come through the Chelsea ranks after me and who went on to play in that 1997 FA Cup win I watched with Mum on my sick bed.

Both of them made a point of coming over to me at the testimonial. Frank shook my hand and said, 'Respect for what you did.' That meant so much to me. I'd never thought of myself as much of a pioneer, but it showed me that others really did. In my adversity, I paved the way for them, and for Ruud Gullit to be the first black manager to lift the famous old trophy at Wembley, and become an icon at the Bridge.

In Chelsea's centenary season I didn't really want to know, but June eventually talked me into it and contacted the club. It was all worked out. A cab would take me to the ground to meet the other old boys, from where a coach was laid on to take us to Old Billingsgate Market where the event was being held. Afterwards, the coach would take us back to the Chelsea Village hotel at Stamford Bridge to spend the rest of the evening talking over old times.

That was the plan. Unfortunately, the taxi turned up very late and although I phoned ahead to warn them, by the time I got to the Bridge the coach had already gone. What I should have done was get the driver to take me to the dinner. Instead, I just sat in the hotel for hours trying to phone the woman who was organising the event. She was obviously busy and I just could not get through to her.

At ten o'clock I was so hacked off I went home in disgust. Same old Chelsea! I was fuming and wanted to give them a rocket, but June saw that wasn't the best way to deal with it. She sent them an email toning down my anger and explaining my point of view.

The woman at Chelsea wrote a very apologetic reply, and invited me to another of their centenary events at the Hilton, which I did get to. It was nice to be acknowledged for my Chelsea connection and great to see a lot of the old spars from the eighties, including Patesy, Pat and Kerry. Brilliant.

Gary Chivers was involved in the Chelsea Old Boys team and I was invited to play for them. I found the ancient, battered legs – not used since my non-league days half a decade earlier – still worked and we had a right laugh after the game. We had a few beers, remembering the scrapes we'd got into twenty years back. Of course, no one discussed the abuse I'd got from the fans, especially not the fans who came up and shook my hand. Some of them might have been there at Selhurst Park in 1982 for all I knew.

Pat Nevin sent a mix-tape down to me. This time, though, it wasn't a music compilation but a collection of video clips, including the legendary Sheffield Wednesday 4 Chelsea 4 match.

A supporter, Rodney George, compiled a wicked DVD of clips of me playing for Chelsea. I really appreciated him doing that because I didn't keep any mementoes like that myself. It set me back, to be honest, when I watched it all through the first time. I was amazed and quite proud – I hadn't remembered a lot of the games I was involved in that he included. You play so many games you forget the detail. Some footballers (especially goalscorers) have a photographic memory, but like most of my team-mates, I remember bits and pieces.

The compilation included Arsenal at home in 1984, the season I'd made my First Division debut. I'd totally forgotten about it. I was reminded of Everton the same year as well – they were champions in May and won 1–0 at the Bridge. Had to laugh when I saw myself having a ding-dong with defender John Bailey as we walked off at half-time. I could dish it out, right enough. Their right-back was Gary Stevens – for a white boy he could run! I was flying and he was staying with me. That's the match when I realised how different the teams were from those in the Second Division. All good memories of my Chelsea career.

The Old Boys' game reconnected me with a football

network I had virtually lost touch with. If I'd been smarter, I could have used some of those connections when I'd had to quit playing twenty years earlier. Now the network might prove quite useful for work opportunities, or just socially. On the back of meeting some of the eighties boys, I was offered some after-dinner sessions in pubs. They were question-and-answer occasions really, sitting among Chelsea fans with Ron 'Chopper' Harris and other people. I made jokes about being a black man in front of such a white audience. Twenty-five years ago I wouldn't have felt safe. It was cool now, and good fun.

I was invited on to Chelsea's in-house TV station, and did a show for them about my career in a series called 'Legends'. Supporters were able to ring in and many of them mentioned the abuse and how impressed they were that I'd kept going and eventually won over the lunatics by not conceding an inch and always playing with pride and determination. They talked about me as the man who had enabled the club to benefit from the black players who came later and served the club well – Eddie Newton, Frank Sinclair, Ruud Gullit, Marcel Desailly, Jimmy Floyd Hasselbaink, Michael Essien, Didier Drogba ... I began to realise that people valued my place in that history.

Eddie Newton was on the same show, saying that as a youth-team player he would be up in the stands hearing abuse towards black Chelsea stars coming from the fans, and he just couldn't believe it. He said, 'It's a fact, you know, we owe a lot to Paul Canoville because he was the pioneer for all of us, so that when we came into the team, it was nothing like that any more and it had all been swept away a bit.' It was nice to hear that respect.

A mate of mine looked at the Chelsea webchat page after I was on and the supporters online were all buzzing about me being back after so long. Of course, a lot of them mentioned Selhurst Park. What was especially interesting was that one of the people posting on there actually admitted to chanting racist abuse at me. He said he knew what he was doing wasn't right, but that loads of people seemed to be doing it so he just joined in. He'd felt guilty about it since and was glad I seemed OK.

It must have made him feel better to see me talking affectionately about the Blues. But it doesn't change what I went through, and how it affected the rest of my life. What's that line? 'The only thing necessary for the triumph of evil is for good men to do nothing.'

I don't know why those racist people continued to come to games just to hoot their heads off. I know fans let off steam in all sorts of ways at games, but this seemed more personal and orchestrated. And when the honest fans finally started to shout them down, did they continue to come and watch, keeping their views quiet, did they change their way of thinking, or did they disappear from football altogether? I think they are still probably the same deep down. It's the world that has changed.

I've been to watch Chelsea games a few times in the last few years and was there at the Bridge for the Charlton game in September 2006. I witnessed the reception given to the great ex-Blue Jimmy Floyd Hasselbaink by Chelsea fans. There was loud applause and they were singing his song – 'Oh Jimmy Jimmy, Jimmy Jimmy Jimmy Floyd Hasselbaink!' – when his name was read out. This is for a Charlton striker. Then Jimmy scored against Chelsea. He actually looked apologetic, arms raised, no celebration. And in the stands? The whole Chelsea end stood and cheered him, and chanted this *opposition* black footballer's name again. That's how it should be, but it shows how different the game is now from my day.

Once I was back on the scene, things started to snowball. I began to work a lot with the Kick It Out campaign to drive racism from football. You only have to see the abuse Chelsea's black players get now in Spain or when they're on England duty to see there's still a job to be done. In October 2006 I was with Marlon Harewood and Paul Elliott at the House of Lords, meeting and talking with the media and individuals. I felt proud and honoured and it is always enjoyable to do. Lord Herman Ouseley made a speech about the abuse I'd suffered at Chelsea and I made a presentation to a Chelsea club member for their contribution to Kick It Out's work. It turned out that the head of the Commission for Equality and Human Rights is a big Blues fan. While I was ducking the insults on the terraces, Trevor Phillips was one of the black faces doing likewise in the stands. We both stuck it out and came out on top.

I now have a network of contacts offering me work that I didn't have back in 1987 when my career ended. I even got a call from my old friends the Metropolitan Police to do a day with them on race awareness!

It was a surprise to discover I hadn't been forgotten after all, once I was back in the Chelsea fold. Amazingly, I soon found out Paul Canoville was actually on the curriculum in some London schools. I had become the best – or worst – example of racism in football. They had researched my story and had the basic facts spot on.

I found out in 2004 that while I was 'missing' from the football fold, Peter Daniel, another Chelsea fan, had been using my background as an example of bigotry in football and society in his work with kids through City of Westminster Library Services. Like quite a few people, he'd been trying to track me down, without success. But he'd built up education resources around what he could find out about my time at Chelsea anyway, and was taking it into schools.

Peter would go into classrooms, looking at the Caribbean experience in Britain centred around my career. He'd got a brilliant poet, Crispin Thomas, to help the children make up rhymes about me, and they'd create stories and pictures based on what they knew of my life and the prejudice I faced. It helped them think about their own lives.

I was completely oblivious to all of this until I met Peter and saw the work the children produced. It was very moving and humbling to think that generations of kids were growing up having learned my story.

Crispin's work with them is amazing. He printed out

some of the poems and artwork the kids had done from his website, and it truly blew me away. He'd given them a format, such as an acrostic, where you a write a line for each letter in a name, and they'd talked through the emotions I would have felt when I had bananas thrown at me on my debut, and things like that. Children are so open and direct in how they express themselves. It was really uplifting for me. I would never have imagined this was going on.

An eight-year-old, Elljay, had written a poem called 'Black and Blue':

Some called him king, some only wanted a win
Some racially abused him
Because of the colour of his skin.
Playing left on the wing
Some threw bananas at him
Every time he touched the ball there was monkey chanting
His name was Paul Canoville
He was the first black in blue
A villain to many a hero to few
The first black player to wear Chelsea's blue
Even when he scored his own fans would boo
No cut no scratches not even a bruise
But Paul Canoville will always be black and blue

Now that I was back on the scene with Chelsea, I was invited to contribute in person to the work the schoolkids were doing. I went to meetings with Peter at Westminster

Libraries, and with Suzi Raymond and Wendy Buddin from Chelsea Football Club's education department.

That was in 2005 and I was working as a driver again, ferrying disabled people around for social services. It was rewarding work, out and about, and I enjoyed it. But all of a sudden, my life was taking a new, different and exciting direction. There were schedules and plans and work with kids again.

Although I was just talking about my own life, it was a little daunting at first. I hadn't been in a classroom for over twenty-five years and I'd always been quite shy in crowds. But it was well organised and managed and even though I was facing thirty or so kids from different schools, I found it surprisingly easy to stand up and talk in front of them. Peter and the others went through it with me and helped me to understand roughly what to expect. That got me comfortable. Mostly they wanted me just to be myself, and I found that people quite liked me, especially when I opened up. I thought about some of my own school experiences beforehand, trying to remember useful lessons I'd learned, but the kids were so smart and enthusiastic they made it very easy for me. The amazing questions children ask you. They don't hold back, they just say what's on their mind. I was never like that when I was their age. Some pupils helped make a DVD animation of my life story, with ska music on it. It was wicked.

Since then, the whole thing's mushroomed so that now I'm regularly addressing a whole school year. It's the most rewarding thing I've done. My life has significance to these kids. They're learning lessons from it that took me half a lifetime to understand.

It would not have been the case before my last rehab in Norwich, but now I go into these situations thinking, what have I to fear? I can be honest and tell things as they were, or still are. I can be myself. This is not fiction or fakery, this is my life. It feels good to talk.

I also have a mission to try to stop people falling away like I did. All I knew from fourteen was sport and girls. My only ambition was to make the grade on a football pitch. When that ended abruptly, I had nothing to fall back on, work-wise or emotionally. Life had come to a full stop.

So my message now is: 'What I did, don't follow.' I've been given the opportunity to pass on this message and I hope they take it in.

I was talking to one kid on the school stairs, and I could recognise that easy way about him. He just didn't want to be in school. I saw myself in him. Kids were going past, heading off to their lessons, 'Excuse me', 'excuse me' – I'm blocking the staircase, but I sat next to him and talked.

'You don't like school, do you?'

'Not really.'

'What you wanna do?'

'I wanna be a footballer.'

'Let me tell you something, man, it's not all about football. I'm gonna be honest now. If it doesn't happen for you, what is it you're gonna do?'

'Dunno, never thought.'

'That's what I'm saying to you. I was like you. I didn't

like school. I played football, got through – late – but was injured out of it. I was twenty-five and it was all over.'

'What, really?'

'And when that happened, because I didn't go to school, I didn't know what to do next. Don't get me wrong, I like being a driver, but if I'd learned something I could have bettered myself. Is there anything else you enjoy and can take up? A hobby? Computers? Find something you like and learn about it. The teachers are here to give you something for your future life. If you don't wanna learn, they don't have to worry about you because there's other kids that do. It's in your hands.'

And he was listening. He said thanks. I got through to him.

In my day, it was, 'Who'd want to be a goody-goody prefect?' But at one school, I arrived and was greeted with the words, 'Good morning Mr Canoville, here is your itinerary for today. We hope you have a good day.' This was a child of ten from the school council acting like the PA to a top executive. I asked him to say it again, I was so impressed. Maybe schools just produce more confident people now.

It's been a long time coming, but working with young people had been on the cards for me for years. As far back as 1985 the mayor of Hackney had invited me and other local sports professionals to do a day in the parks to try to inspire the youngsters. What I'm doing in schools now reminds me of it, but in a wider aspect.

Again, when I came out of rehab in 1996 I knew what I

wanted to do – youth work in some way. For a man who had eleven children from ten different women, you might think it took me long enough to work out I like kids. I'm glad I've got time left still to make a contribution.

So the work I do now is a blessing. Going around these schools, being something like a figurehead, it's a really good feeling for me. I get paid for remembering who I was and helping ensure others don't go through some of what I did. Knowing myself as I do, I don't see myself yet as a mentor, even though others do. But back in 1982 if someone had told me, 'Paul, you'll be addressing a hundred schoolkids about bigotry, society, life and achievement,' I would have laughed in their face. The old Paul Canoville could never have faced up to that. I would have been too nervous. But I know more about myself now, I'm more confident about what I am capable of and it's a real good sensation to stand up in front of a hundred youngsters and feel that they're taking in even a little of what I have to say.

I'm just talking as I see it, and they're listening. It's as though I'm talking about myself and my experiences for the first time. I'm so enthusiastic, so it's all fresh. I'm living, breathing proof that whatever it is you're going through, you're not the only one.

I talk about being bullied and abused, and how I would approach things differently now. I tell them, 'Yes, some of you want to become professional footballers and that's a wonderful dream to have. But don't just think about football. Listen to teachers and learn skills in case that doesn't happen.' I see myself in some boys, and I think I can talk to them, use my professional football background if needs be, and relate in a personal way to get through to them. 'Don't put all your eggs in one basket. I was lucky enough to live my dream. But when it collapsed, I had nothing to fall back on, and I lost myself.' I try to instil in them not to fall down that same trap.

In the dinner hall I like to sit down among the kids, see how it is. And they all want to sit next to me, get my autograph, chat. In one playground, they formed queues for me to sign things. One young teacher laughed, 'Excuse me, this morning you'd never even heard of Paul Canoville, now you're all over him!' It's an amazing feeling to be wanted like that after what I went through as a player.

I remember when I was at school, not being able to wait for the end of classes at three. It took so long. Now when I go into schools, the time flies by. It's start, break, lunch, break, over. Where did the day go?

Paddington Green school developed a kind of game for me. It's a version of 'Subbuteo' based on what decisions you would make in certain situations in life. For instance, if you saw someone being bullied, what would you do? There are a lot of different scenarios, and we talk everything through. I learn as much as they do.

I do really wish I had paid more attention at school. I had no interest or attention span. I was blinkered and mucked about. I took nothing in. Homework was something I did on the way to the bus stop.

Parents of my age know much more about school than

our parents did. Mum didn't have the time to check up on us.

When I'm with the kids, I must come across like a forty-five-year-old who's only just left school. Even the head and other teachers are taking in what I'm saying, the way I put it, street level. They can't believe what I've had to deal with. To have someone in authority actually listen to what I have to say . . . Well, that made me realise that I wasn't talking rubbish and I really did have something of value to contribute – a completely new experience for me. I love every minute of the day I spend in schools – so different from my early years!

And maybe there's the point. I spent so much of my youth fighting the people trying to control me – Mum, police, teachers. It's nice to be comfortable with them now.

On the back of that, the big news for me came in November 2007 when I applied for and got a job as a classroom assistant and mentor at a school in Westminster that I've worked at in the past. I left the interview room absolutely buzzing, and rang round everyone to tell them the good news. It felt like the culmination of everything I'd been doing since cleaning up my act in 2004.

Soon, though, I was fretting about what might come up about my troubled background. I've got no problem with the police record but the crack addiction was never mentioned when they offered me the post. That troubled me. Gradually I realised that once this book came out the drugs might become an issue. Even though my addiction is in the past, some parents could be concerned, and the school would be put in a difficult position if I didn't make them aware.

I didn't want to let them down, so the day after the job offer I contacted the head and told her straight out about everything. I have to say that was a fundamental shift for me – taking responsibility. In the past I would have kept shtoom until the shit hit the fan, and then probably walked away. I wouldn't have faced up to it and dealt with it head-on like I did now. I'm changing.

The principal was grateful that I'd come clean and I was relieved when she said they still wanted me. A large part of my value to them is that I've come through so many of the difficult challenges facing some kids in the school. I'm a warning what pitfalls to avoid, as well as living proof you can eventually overcome them. It's a fantastic opportunity for me as well as a big challenge. It gives a new meaning to all the things I've been through and helps me make the changes I still need to make in my life.

Obviously, the new role also means I'm spending more time with all sorts of youngsters. I realise I've had more children than most myself – Natalie with Christine in summer 1979, Derry with Maureen in May 1982, then Dwayne, in Hackney, Lorreen with Marsha in April 1985, Jermell with Valerie a month later in Lewisham, Pierre with Maria on Boxing Day 1986, Udine with Joyce in January 1988, Nickel with Suzy, 23 February 1988, Paris on 13 September 1992 and Tye Paul (God rest him) on 20 December 1995 with Tracey, and Caysey with Sonia on 3 November 1995.

Mainly I'm in contact with them, although with some, sadly, I'm not. A life of ups and downs has made contact difficult. I wish things had been a lot different. In some cases I wish I'd been different. I ring them, and try to remember their birthdays. I buy what's needed when I can and go to parents' evenings. I take responsibility and talk over choice of school and things like that, as normal parents do. I want to be remembered as a father who cared, even if, like mine, I wasn't there all the time.

Seeing how confident and on the ball these kids are in the schools I visit, I'd love to have felt like that. It makes me realise I just wasn't equipped to handle a lot of what life threw at me. I needed inner strength just to survive what I was doing at times.

When I was twelve, thirteen years old at Brentside, there was no black teacher I could empathise with. It might have made a difference to me if there had been. Someone who could have got through to me in the way I try to do with the kids now. Maybe I wouldn't have rebelled so much and gone off the rails.

June is as close as ever. I see Dad regularly and things are good with Mum. In many ways I'm more settled than I've ever been.

I still have my rehab notes. I don't get them out much, very rarely actually. 'I was like a timebomb,' I wrote about my first time on crack, 'I was stealing from all my children's mothers, also my own mother.'

Reading the notes now, I can't really remember how I felt. I was not exactly another person, but my mind had gone through so much it had reached another place, and I never want to go back there. I realise that after two drug dependencies and two bouts of cancer, I'm in the last chance saloon. But I'm confident that, with the support of people who love me, I can face up to whatever I'll find in there.

Canners you can
Canners you can rise above the odds.
You can, cos you did and you will
You paved the way for many today
who like you, only lived to play ball.
Raw talent and skill shot you into the limelight
and courage and pride got you through
as you armoured your soul and kept scoring goals
against a backdrop of racist abuse.
Banana-filled pitches and razor blade fan mail
could not distract you from your dream
Instead you held your head high whilst crying inside
and played out your heart for your team.
Life was a party and you embraced it wholeheartedly
The football, the women, the raves
Your mum used to say, 'put your pennies away',
but it was too much fun spending today.
A household name, at the peak of your game,
the first ever black player for Chelsea.
But who could foresee the knee injury
that was to end your career so abruptly.

All of a sudden the world seemed much bigger
and friendships began to dissolve.
When you looked around there was no football ground
Just Canners, out there in the cold.
Stooped with the pain of your battle with cancer
and the loss of a dream snatched away.
You searched for release in the vice of the streets
in a bid to escape from reality.
A sharp downward spiral to a long lonely road
that was miles away from football.
When you're inches from death you suddenly get
all that you do have to live for.
But Canners you can rise above the odds.
You can and you did and you will.
Did they really expect you to curl up and die
Just cos they said you were ill?

Canners – this ain't your time for the bench.
There's so much you still have to do.
A true blue and blue all the way through.
The game owes a great deal to you.

Football was your game. Canners is your name.

'Canners You Can', Bella Daniels

I never said I was an angel.
I'm just human but please try
not to let this happen to you.

Paul 'King' Canoville aka Canners

Vital Statistics

Name: Paul Kenneth Canoville
Born: Southall, 4 March 1962
Career: Hillingdon Borough, transferred to Chelsea
(December 1981). Debut 12 April 1982 v Crystal Palace.
Transferred to Reading (August 1986) for £50,000.
To Enfield 1988.

Season	League		FA Cup		League Cup		Other Cups	
	Apps	Goals	Apps	Goals	Apps	Goals	Apps	Goals
CHELSEA								
1981–82	3	–	–	–	–	–	–	–
1982–83	19	3	–	–	2	–	–	–
1983–84	20	6	1	–	4	1	–	–
1984–85	24	1	2	1	9	2	–	–
1985–86	13	1	2	–	3	–	1	–

PAUL CANOVILLE

Season	League		FA Cup		League Cup		Other Cups	
	Apps	Goals	Apps	Goals	Apps	Goals	Apps	Goals
READING								
1986–87	9	3	–	–	4	–	–	–
1987–88	7	1	–	–	1	–	–	–
TOTAL	95	15	5	1	23	3	1	–